HISTORY AS THEY LIVED IT

 Shawnee Books

17 16 15 14   4 3 2 1

Library of Congress Cataloging-in-Publication Data
Brown, Margaret Kimball.
History as they lived it : a social history of Prairie du
Rocher, Illinois / Margaret Kimball Brown. — Southern
Illinois University Press edition.
    pages   cm. — (Shawnee Books)
Includes bibliographical references and index.
ISBN-13: 978-0-8093-3340-0 (pbk. : alk. paper)
ISBN-10: 0-8093-3340-6 (pbk. : alk. paper)
ISBN-13: 978-0-8093-3341-7 (ebook)
ISBN-10: 0-8093-3341-4 (ebook)
1. Prairie du Rocher (Ill.)—History. 2. Prairie du Rocher
(Ill.)—Social conditions. I. Title. II. Title: Social history
of Prairie du Rocher, Illinois.
F549.P87B76 2014   2013044770
977.3'92—dc23

HISTORY AS THEY LIVED IT
A Social History of
Prairie du Rocher, Illinois

Margaret Kimball Brown

Southern Illinois University
Carbondale

To the late Percy Clerc

CONTENTS

TABLES

FIGURES

MAPS

FOREWORD

The history of history writing about the Illinois Country is becoming almost as rich a subject as the Illinois Country itself. *History As They Lived It* deserves to be placed within the rich context of Illinois Country historiography going back more than a century.

During the colonial era, and this volume is largely devoted to that period, everyone understood that the Illinois Country encompassed both sides of the Middle Mississippi River Valley; Missouri was an appellation confined to the river and the Indian tribe of that name. When Lewis and Clark headed westward up the Missouri River in the spring of 1804, Lewis opined that they were departing "the Illenois" for remote and unknown parts of the North American continent. The Illinois Country was the end of civilization as one proceeded west from the Atlantic seaboard.

Illinois Country history writing began as history from the top down. Francis Parkman was—in his classic, *La Salle and the Discovery of the Great West*—concerned with the exploits of great, white men. The exploits of these men—explorers, traders, and priests—as recounted in Parkman's incomparable prose were, make no mistake about it, fascinating, important, and often heroic. Only occasionally did Parkman condescend to write about the "lesser folks," as when he opined that by mid-nineteenth century nothing remained of the former French empire in the Mississippi Valley but "the accents of France on the lips of some straggling boatman or vagabond half-breed." Boston Brahmin that he was, and writing in the midst of an increasingly racist Zeitgeist, Parkman could hardly avoid expressing such opinions. Ms. Brown's volume, on the other hand, is emphatically about the ordinary folks, not a few of whom were "halfbreeds," who inhabited the villages of the Illinois Country, most especially in her case Prairie du Rocher, of which she is today a leading citizen.

Scholarly interest in the Illinois Country waxed and waned during the twentieth century. Clarence W. Alvord initiated an interest in colonial Illinois at the University of Illinois that flourished on into the 1940s, slowly faded after 1950, and is now, inexplicably, altogether extinguished. One of the several ironies in Alvord's career is that he continues to be best known for his top-down (political and military history) volume, *The Illinois Country, 1763-1818*, while he was also the discoverer of the mass of source documents upon which bottom-up history (social and economic) of the region is now based.

The thousands of documents that Alvord discovered stuffed in burlap sacks in the old Randolph County Courthouse in Chester, Illinois, now compose the Kaskaskia Manuscripts (local civil records drafted by royal notaries), and no one has ever known them better than the author of this volume, not even the eighteenth-century folks who produced them. Ms. Brown (along with Lawrie C. Dean) was responsible for the monumental task of sorting, collating, indexing, and filming these manuscripts, which are now indispensable for Illinois Country scholars. Ms. Brown and Ms. Dean also extracted documents from the Kaskaskia Manuscripts pertaining to the Village of Chartres and Prairie du Rocher, translated them, and published them in the thick, essential volume, *The Village of Chartres in Colonial Colonial Illinois: 1720-1765*. Readers of *History As They Lived It* will notice the numerous references to this rich volume.

In mid-twentieth century, an extraordinary, and extraordinarily diverse, group of scholars gave rise to an efflorescence in Illinois Country scholarship. From the University of Illinois came Natalia M. Belting, whose classic *Kaskaskia Under the French Regime* (1948, reprinted 2003) is in many ways the model for *History As They Lived It*. From California came Abraham P. Nasatir, student of the great Herbert Bolton at Berkeley, and editor of the seminal volumes *Before Lewis and Clark*, published in 1952 by the St. Louis Historical Documents Foundation (reprint, University Press of Nebraska, 1990). These two volumes, with Nasatir's remarkable introduction, document the early history of the Missouri River Valley, revealing how well known it was before the Virginians ascended it. From Washington University in St. Louis came John Francis McDermott, a direct descendent of Pierre Laclède, founder of St. Louis. Although a member of the English Department, McDermott's first love was the history of the Mississippi Valley, and a bibliography of his works, including *Old Cahokia* and (ed.) *Frenchmen and French Ways in the Mississippi River Valley*, would consume pages. And from the National Park Service came Charles Peterson, the brilliant and charismatic Swede from Minnesota, who "discovered" the French Colonial buildings of Ste. Genevieve, founded the Historical American Buildings Survey, and wrote the petit classic, *Colonial St. Louis: Building a Creole Capital* (new edition by Patrice Press in 2001).

A fallow period in Illinois Country scholarship had set in by the early 1970s. Gregory M. Franzwa published his guide to the historic houses in Ste. Genevieve (which has sold more copies than any other book on the Illinois Country), and Anton J. Pregaldin was plugging away at this monumental geneaological study,[1] but no academics were working in the field. Margaret Brown's work broke this drought of scholarly work on the Illinois Country, and those of us who have followed in her footsteps are indebted to her for it.

Like many scholars who have made major contributions to the history of the Illinois Country, Ms. Brown came to the field late and by a circuitous route. Born and bred a New Englander, she took an honors degree in English Literature at the University of Minnesota before going on to do a Ph.D in anthropology at Michigan State University. Drawn to the site of the former Kaskaskia Indian village on the Upper Illinois River (across the river from Starved Rock), Ms. Brown began her scholarly work on the French presence in the Illinois Country by examining the cultural contact between Frenchmen and Illinois Indians at that seminal location. Great scholars, beginning with Francis Parkman in the mid-nineteenth century, have all recognized the importance of that site and the historical significance of that initial cultural interchange.

The focus of Ms. Brown's scholarly interests gravitated southward, following roughly the same course over which the Kaskaskia Indians had migrated nearly three hundred years earlier. Employed by the cultural resources division of the State of Illinois, Ms. Brown quickly recognized the extraordinary importance of the Kaskaskia Manuscripts, becoming the first person since Natalia M. Belting, nearly a half-century earlier, to immerse herself in these documents. Ms. Brown has always demonstrated a keen fiduciary sense (that Puritan background!), a passionate feeling about the importance of preserving cultural resources for generations to come. It was this sense of mission that impelled her and Lawrie C. Dean to devote themselves to the Kaskaskia Manuscripts project.

Ms. Brown is unique among scholars of the Illinois Country in the breadth of her capacities. Moving with ease across the traditional lines of anthropology, archaeology, and history, she also demonstrated, as superintendant of the Cahokia Mounds State Historic Site, unusual administrative and political abilities. This array of talents within one person in the scholarly world is exceedingly rare, indeed, virtually unheard of. Ms. Brown deserves more credit than any other person for the transformation of the Cahokia Mounds Museum from a motley collection of run-down buildings (anchored by an abandonned Exxon station on Collinsville Road) into the resplendent structure we now have, one of the finest Indian museums in North America. Indeed, at this point in time, the Cahokia museum is incomparably better than the new National Museum of American Indians on the Mall in Washington, D.C.

I've now known Ms. Brown for a quarter century. I excavated with her (amateurishly on my part) at the original site of Fort de Chartres, helped her found (modest help from me) the Center for French Colonial Studies, which is now flourishing under the guidance of Pierre Lebeau, and had many enlightening (i.e., enlightening for me) conversations with her over drinks at the B. K. Schram residence (Jean-Baptiste Vallé House) in Ste. Genevieve. She has been the leader in this generation of Illinois Country scholars, whose numbers, with the recent untimely death of Anton J. Pregaldin, are unfortunately dwindling. The appearance of *History As They Lived It* at this particular time is therefore most welcome, for it brings together the fully ripened thoughts of a mature scholar at the very moment that students of the Illinois Country need such a book.

—Carl J. Ekberg
Thrasher Knob Farm
Purgitsville, West Virginia

Carl J. Ekberg, who has written several pieces about the Illinois Country, now spends most of his time at his farm. He has threatened to write more about the Illinois Country, but his wife and friends (and enemies) know that these are likely to be empty threats.

[1] Tony Pregaldin died unexpectedly in 2004 before his work could be published. Most of his papers, which would be invaluable to scholars, remain inaccessible in the Mercantile Library at the University of Missouri, St. Louis campus.

ACKNOWLEDGMENTS

My thanks to Fieldstead & Co. for the grant that enabled me to complete the research necessary for this book. Lawrie Dean provided so much information through her work of calendering and translation of the Kaskaskia manuscripts. My gratitude to Pierre Le Beau without whose assistance in editing this never could have been completed.

Many people have given advice, information, and encouragement over the years: Judge Morris S. Arnold; C. Ray Brassieur; Winston DeVille; Carl Ekberg; Fr. William Flaherty and Nancy Merz of the Midwest Jesuit Archives, St. Louis University; Ruth Gilster; Dennis Hermann; Glen Holt, Director Emeritus, St. Louis Public Libraries; John Hoover, Director, Mercantile Library, University of Missouri–St. Louis; from the staff of the Illinois State Archives: John Daly, Charles Cali, Wayne Temple, Cody Wright, Ray Hammes; Fr. Michael Maher; Collette Manac'h Royalle; Ruth Menard; Terry Norris; Irving Peithmann; Anton Pregaldin; in the Rudolph County Clerk's Office: Charles Bernasek, Nell Wright, and Joyce Hermes; and all the villagers of Prairie du Rocher.

INTRODUCTION

Prairie du Rocher on New Year's Eve. A chilly winter night. Christmas lights reflect on a thin covering of snow outside houses in the village. A bus pulls up to one decorated house and a crowd of costumed people emerges from it—men in cloth knee britches, wool coats, vests with many buttons, and wool toques. Women with deep-cut bodices ruffled with lace, long colorful skirts and hooded woolen capes. Some men have fiddles or guitars and most people are clutching song sheets. The group chatters as it gathers on the porch and front walk of the house. The fiddlers strike up the tune, the leader thumps his wooden cane in time with them, and the singers in unison sing:

> *Bon soir, le maitre et la maitresse et tout le monde du logis.*
> *Pour le dernier jour de l'année la Guiannée vous nous devez.*
> *La Guiannée vous nous devez, dites-nous-le.*
> *Si vous voulez nous rien donner dites-nous-le.*

The door of the house opens and the group traipses in, filling the living room and dining room to overflowing; watching from every corner and doorway are the inhabitants and their guests. The fiddles and guitar begin again. *"Bon soir le maitre et la maitresse.."* with the lead singer singing each line first and then the whole group responding with a repetition of the line. (Translation):

Good evening, master and mistress of the house, and all who dwell herein.

For the last day of the year the Guiannée is due us.

If you don't want to give us anything, tell us.

All we're asking is a back bone of pork.

A back bone of pork is no great prize, it's only ten feet long.

And we'll make of it a fricassee ninety feet long.

If you don't want to give us anything, tell us.

All we're asking for is your eldest daughter.

We'll show her good cheer and warm her feet.

When we were in the midst of the woods, in the shade

I listened to a cuckoo sing and a turtledove.

And the nightingale from bower green, the messenger of lovers.

Go, tell my lady love always to have a joyous heart,

Always to have a joyous heart, not sadness.

All the girls who have no lover, what do they do?

It is love that keeps them awake and won't let them sleep.

At the end the leader sings an apology including, "If we are guilty of any folly, it was to try to cheer you,"and a nonsense verse follows. The song ends with all singing again, *"Bon soir la maitre et la maitresse et tout le monde du logis,"* and saying loudly, *"Bonne Année!"*—Happy New Year.

Food and drink are laid out on the table for the group. While sampling these treats the group engages in lively conversation, perhaps sings another song or two, and then goes on to the next stop.

La Guiannée is the traditional New Year's Eve celebration in Prairie du Rocher, still going strong after 280 years of unbroken observance, one of only a handful of places to preserve this tradition. How did this happen? Why is it still here? This book tries to answer these questions.

Prairie du Rocher was settled in 1722, part of the old French colony that developed in the Mississippi Valley in the late seventeenth and early eighteenth centuries. The Mississippi River was a channel for French exploration and colonization. The region between Lake Michigan and the present state of Arkansas was called *Le Pays des Illinois*, the country of the Illinois Indians, named for the tribe who inhabited much of the area. In the eighteenth century in what is now Illinois and Missouri, a French colony grew and prospered. Villages developed in Illinois—Cahokia, Kaskaskia, Fort de Chartres, Prairie du Rocher, St. Philippe, and in Missouri—Ste. Genevieve, St. Louis, and a dispersed settlement, Old Mines. Prairie du Rocher lies at the center of the old French colony in the broad, open, alluvial valley near hundred-foot-high limestone bluffs—hence its name, prairie of the rock.

Today, sprawling modern communities have destroyed eighteenth century St. Louis, overlie Cahokia, and surround the architectural gem of eighteenth century, Ste. Genevieve. The villages of Kaskaskia and St. Philippe were wiped out by the powerful meandering Mississippi River. Fort de Chartres, the governmental seat for the extensive Illinois colony, has been partially restored, but its supporting village vanished into the river. Prairie du Rocher remains in the farmlands along the Mississippi River, the only one of the seven French colonial villages that still exists as a small compact community.

The French regime ended in 1765 with acquisition of the area by the British, who held it for only a few years until the American Revolution. The Illinois villages then were taken by Virginia and, in 1790, finally were governed by the new United States. After this the American way of life impinged more and more on the old French culture.

Prairie du Rocher's suitability for study lies in its continuity, its stability of size as a small community, and the availability of records for the entire period of its existence. The continuity of the community from the eighteenth century to the present presents the opportunity to consider the reasons for the persistence of a viable rural village amid an increasingly urbanized society. Unlike several of the other French communities—Ste. Genevieve, Cahokia, and particularly St. Louis—that developed large modern areas of housing and business, Prairie du Rocher has remained a village. The relative size of the community throughout the years is given in the summary of census data in the Appendix.

      Documentary resources are available from the end of the seventeenth century to the present. Although the early archives are not complete, an impressive quantity remains. Eighteenth-century legal documents—portions of the French royal notaries' archives—are preserved in the county courthouse in Chester, Illinois. Later civil records are available there also. In addition, parish registers exist from 1695 to the present with some gaps. The village office has town records. Archives in France and Louisiana have preserved portions of the official eighteenth-century government correspondence.

      Unfortunately, what is lacking in these records are the diaries and private letters that would give personal details. Most correspondence extant is from government officials and mainly concerned administrative matters. The majority of the *habitants* appear only through their legal actions recorded by the notaries. These transactions show what people did, what they sold, bought, or leased—their overt behavior—but give little information about what they thought or felt.[1] These limitations affect our ability to discern clearly the impacts on the inhabitants as the society underwent the changes from the French regime to British, to Virginian, and then to American. Nevertheless there are materials from the period that give vivid images of the life. Quotations from contemporary documents—the words of the people living at the time—are used extensively in this study in an attempt to move closer to an understanding of the populace. Through these quotes, the thoughts and feelings of the inhabitants can span the temporal and cultural distance.

      More activities took place in the community than appear in the records, however. Guesses can be made about some. Dances are a simple example of this. Later visitors always commented on the fondness of the French for parties and dances. Virtually no mention or description of these exists in the eighteenth-century documents. Here diaries or letters would illuminate the picture. Estate inventories and other documents describe fine clothing; were these worn for dances? What kinds of musical instruments were used? Fiddles do not occur in the inventories. Why? Were these visualized as such personal items that they did not need to be listed as part of the estate? These and many other questions remain unanswered.

This study is called a social history; it involves two academic disciplines, history and anthropology. It is historical in relating past events and developments; anthropological in being concerned with the processes of change. History often has been focused on major events and personages—wars and rulers. Social history differs from conventional history by examining not just the elite, the wealthy, or politically prominent, but the ordinary people in a society. Social history is the story of those people who are largely invisible in the written stories of nations.[2]

Eighteenth-century French Illinois is not well known to the general public. United States history books concentrate on the East Coast colonists and tend to mention the French only in the context of the fur trade. The French customs, institutions, laws, architecture, and agricultural practices were different from those of the British colonies. These distinctions were reflected also in the values and attitudes of the society as well. For this reason the first section of the study focuses on providing images of the French life and society in the eighteenth century. For Prairie du Rocher's history this is necessary. That was the culture which formed its people and influenced their actions.

The French colonial period in the Middle Mississippi Valley has had nowhere near the quantity of publications that have been produced about the British area. Natalia Belting's early overview of the village of Kaskaskia remains a classic, but she saw the Illinois colony as a reflection of Canadian society.[3] Ekberg's excellent study of Ste. Genevieve begins later, when that settlement was formed, and extends into the nineteenth century. Ekberg also has produced other thorough scholarly studies of French society and culture.[4] Several dissertations have considered aspects of the colonial experience but they remain unpublished.[5] French Cahokia has yet to have an in-depth analysis produced, although some good short articles exist.[6]

Existing studies of the French area deal mainly with the colonial period. Communities of different ethnic backgrounds that developed in the nineteenth century in Illinois are discussed in other works but none cover the range of time from the colonial regime to the present.[7] For Prairie du Rocher this time span is available. This book does not intend to portray Prairie du Rocher as representative of all French settlements, but produces the social history of one community having a background of French colonial culture. But the depiction is not only of a French colonial village; the study continues to the present time, with even a glance at a possible future. This rural community continues to be viable in a period when many small villages are either disappearing or being absorbed into expanding urban centers.

The extension of the period of examination into the nineteenth century allows some comparisons with other emigrant communities. Studies of the Midwestern American communities that sprang into being in the mid-nineteenth century show distinct differences in orientation and culture from Prairie du Rocher. These contrasts can help to give a better understanding of the formation of the state and nation. The data here enriches the extant body of information in southern Illinois about cultural change and community development.

Every society needs to control the behavior of its people to permit effectual activity and to avoid what is perceived to be disruptive or dysfunctional. By examining the concepts and methods of its social control the inner workings of the community are revealed. The major areas of focus in the study are given in the following questions:

How were the standards of behavior enforced and from where did these standards come? Were the controls overt—governmental enforcement—or internalized—peer pressure or other local action? What kind of governmental/legal relationships operated within the community, and with the various political states affecting them? The inhabitants' reactions and responses to these and other elements of the society were guided by certain values and norms—the rules under which the society lived. Certain values doubtlessly were based on the church's teachings, but others came from cultural perceptions of the way "things should be done." *What were the integrating factors within the community and how did it hold together as a unit despite all the political upheavals?* How people handle events indicates the underlying values of a society.

Bringing the study up to the present produced some tantalizing questions. *Has there been any continuity of these values over time and have these contributed to the persistance of the village? Does the French ethnic heritage still influence the community? If so, how?*

Dealing with the present leads to the consideration of the possible future of Prairie du Rocher. *As a small rural community in an age of urbanization, what does its future hold? What are the perceptions of the local people concerning this? Do these opinions reflect old or new values?* The attitudes and opinions expressed here can be compared with those in other studies of small rural communities.

Many of the questions asked about Prairie du Rocher are the same that can be asked and are asked about other villages, particularly those settled by a single ethnic group. Prairie du Rocher is one example of the many ways our nation has been formed. What took place at Prairie du Rocher was different from what occurred in other towns, since each place has a different history, but at the same time similarities of change and adjustment allow for comparison with other communities.

Notes
(Full citations for notes appear in the References)

1. The need for understanding values is discussed in MacFarlane 1977 and Stearns 1980.
2. See A. Briggs 1983; Stearns 1980; Rutman.
3. Belting 1948.
4. Ekberg 1985; 1998.
5. Austin 1982; W. Briggs 1985; Nelson 1993.
6. Gitlin 1989; Peterson 1993; 1999.
7. For example, Carr 1996; Faragher 1986.

HISTORY AS THEY LIVED IT

1

The French Regime:
The Beginnings

The formation of the small village of Prairie du Rocher resulted from events that happened far from southwestern Illinois. Around 1500 French ships began to exploit the rich fishing banks along the northeastern coast of North America. Small temporary camps sprang up where the fishermen dried the codfish to be shipped back home. While at these camps the fishermen also traded manufactured items to the local Indians for furs; beaver pelts obtained from the Indians became an increasingly important trade item. The beaver underfur with its many small barbs was excellent for felting and creating the hats then fashionable for men. Trade increased both from the French interest in furs and the Indians' attraction to beads, iron tools, and other European goods.

These commercial activities gave rise to a desire for permanent settlement and expeditions were sent out. The early explorations were funded by the king, but by the seventeenth century the rights to explore new lands had been given to individuals and companies, along with the monopoly of trade. As nearby sources of fur became depleted from excessive hunting, the traders moved farther and farther inland along the rivers.

In 1608 a post was established at Quebec, a narrow point in

the St. Lawrence River where upriver access could be controlled. Quebec surrendered for a short period to the British in 1629. The ownership reversed, however, in 1632, and settlement began anew under the monopoly of the Company of New France. From then on Quebec gradually expanded.

In 1642 Ville-Marie on Montreal Island was established as a missionary settlement. Its prime location at the junction of the Ottawa and St. Lawrence Rivers meant that within a few years its religious orientation was overlaid with commercial interests, the fur trade. With these outposts, small and frail against the wilderness, France finally had a permanent colony. In 1674 New France, as it was called, became a royal colony.[1]

Although the government attempted to encourage settlement by artisans and to promote agricultural activities in the colony, the fur trade continued to dominate the economy. Voyageurs—the men who paddled the canoes and went out to trade for furs with the Indians, and explorers—who sought the elusive riches of silver and gold and the western route to China, went deeper and deeper into the continent in their quest.

A dominant interest in exploration was the rumor of a large river west of the Great Lakes that, it was hoped, would flow westward to the Pacific Ocean and provide access to the riches of China. Not everyone thought that the river went to the Pacific; some believed it ran into the Gulf of Mexico. If it did, this would give the French access to the Caribbean islands, with their resources and possibly to gold. French claims on the river also would prevent British and Spanish expansion into the interior of the continent.

One man who felt that the river flowed to the Gulf was Sieur Louis Jolliet, who in 1673 received trading rights and formed an expedition to seek out this route. Joining him was Fr. Jacques Marquette, a Jesuit priest who desired to see the area's potential for missions. Jolliet and Marquette descended the river as far as the present state of Arkansas. Although this was the farthest extent of their trip, they were convinced that the great river did indeed go to the sea. On their return trip north they ascended the Illinois River where, opposite the promontory later known as Starved Rock, they found a village of the

Kaskaskia, a sub-group of the Illinois Indians. Marquette noted these Indians as a potential mission field.

Jolliet and Marquette's exploration was followed by that of Robert Cavelier de la Salle. In 1682 he went down the Mississippi River all the way to the Gulf of Mexico, and in April of that year claimed the whole Mississippi River basin for the king of France. This vast area with rather indefinite boundaries he called Louisiana, in honor of King Louis XIV.

France's claim was not followed up by settlement for another sixteen years however, until Pierre Le Moyne d'Iberville built a fort at Biloxi, Mississippi, in 1699. Iberville's settlement was opportune, only a few months later the English attempted to move into the area by sending a ship up the Mississippi.

Throughout these years of exploration, voyageurs from New France continued to ply the waterways west and south of Quebec and Montreal. Some of these were legitimate, with official *congés* (permits) from the governor of New France. Many more were *coureurs de bois* (literally, runners of the wood), traders without permits, who if they were caught supposedly would be subject to various penalties. But they were difficult to catch and the courts were reluctant to punish them. Many were kinsmen of the officials and their fur trading provided needed income for the colony.

Both the voyageurs and the *coureurs de bois* traded along the Illinois and Mississippi Rivers and their tributaries. They took furs back to Quebec and Montreal, and some, as the lower riverine area developed, to Louisiana. Furs also were traded to the British, from whom the voyageurs sometimes received a better price; often, too, the British had more and better trade goods. This commerce with the British, who were commercial and political rivals, was one obvious reason why New France tried to control the permits.

The missionaries also played a role in the development of permanent settlements. In 1675 Fr. Marquette returned to the Kaskaskia village and established the mission of the Immaculate Conception, the first mission in the Illinois country. In 1692 the Illinois from the Kaskaskia village moved to Lake Pimeteoui, actually a series of three shallow lakes created by the widening of the Illinois River at what is now Peoria. The mission of the Immaculate Conception, with Fr. Jacques Gravier now the priest, followed the Indians to Pimiteoui.

Although the French government desired permanent villages for control of the Mississippi Valley, these were slow to develop. The catalyst for settlement was a virtuous Indian maiden, one of the few real personalities to emerge from the documents of the period. As the story goes,[2] a voyageur, Michel Accault, or Ako as it is usually spelled, wanted to marry Marie, the daughter of the Kaskaskia chief Rouensa. An early convert, Marie was a devout Catholic and a member of the small congregation that Fr. Gravier had assembled at Pimiteoui. Her father, Rouensa, favored the marriage; being the father-in-law to a trader would give him better access to trade goods. Marie did not want the marriage. Ako had a bad reputation; he was known to have found other Indian women more willing. Fr. Gravier classified this as debauchery.

Rouensa was determined and Marie equally so. After days of standoff Marie finally came to a decision, supposedly unprompted by the priest. She told Fr. Gravier that she had decided to marry Ako, not because of any threats by her father, but because by the marriage she hoped to convert Ako and her family. Marie must have had a strong personality as she very shortly succeeded in both endeavors. Her husband, Michel, admitted to the priest that he hardly knew himself any more he was so changed. Marie's father, Rouensa, his wife, and their extended family converted to Catholicism as well.

The conversion of the Kaskaskia chief and his family had a major impact. The French now had a firm foothold in the Middle Mississippi Valley through the support of the most important village of the Illinois Indians. Not only did the majority of the Kaskaskia become Catholics, but further marriages approved by the priest took place between French traders and Indian women, creating a small but permanent French presence in the Illinois.

Then Pierre le Moyne d'Iberville, governor of the colony of Louisiana, created a plan to resettle the Indians from the Middle Mississippi River into three compact villages for easy access and supervision. Although this rather impractical plan did not develop further, when Fr. Gravier returned in 1700 from a trip to Canada, he found the

Kaskaskia ready to depart for one of Iberville's proposed settlements downriver. He persuaded the Kaskaskia not to move so far and they stopped at present-day St. Louis, Missouri, on the bank of a river soon named for the priests, the Rivière des Peres. With the Kaskaskia came the French traders, their wives and children. The Akos' eldest son, Pierre, only five years old, was sent to Quebec for his education. This must have been quite a frightening trip for a small boy from an Indian village, up miles of rivers and over portages to an urban community.

In 1703 the village was threatened with attacks by the Sioux Indians from the west, and the Kaskaskia moved again down to a peninsula between the Mississippi and what was known then as the Metchigamia River. The Metchigamia, who had a village there, were another group of the Illinois. This river is now known by the name it acquired from the new arrivals—the Kaskaskia River.[3]

This new village of Kaskaskia contained Illinois Indians, Canadians with Indian wives and their métis children.[4] The settlement was in the fertile bottomlands and the settlers began clearing fields to grow crops. Soon the local economy included agricultural pursuits as well as trade.

Along with this fairly stable and settled group there was an indefinite but substantial number of Canadian voyageurs, both legal ones and *coureurs de bois*, who made Kaskaskia one of their trading bases. The voyageurs caused disruptions when they returned after long tedious trips in the wilderness to the village, where they could find wine and women. Outside of the villages they also disturbed the authorities by creating conflicts between tribes west of the Mississippi, to obtain slaves.

But military resources for enforcement of rules were limited; in 1708 a M. d'Eraque and a handful of men came to try to bring order to the area.[5] But by 1711 Fr. Gabriel Marest, the priest in charge at Kaskaskia, again was complaining to the authorities about the behavior of the Canadian voyageurs. A sergeant and twelve soldiers were dispatched from Mobile to punish the troublesome *coureurs de bois,* who promptly lived up to their name, runners of the woods, and disappeared into the forest.

One of the soldiers, Penicaut, remained for four months and left an account of his observations on life at Kaskaskia. Kaskaskia was still an Indian village with a few resident Canadian traders. However, agriculture was increasing in importance, the motivation a few years later for the settlement at Prairie du Rocher. The Jesuits encouraged agriculture; the priests had constructed a windmill for grinding wheat flour. The Indians themselves had two horsemills. The church, serving both the French and the Indians, was large, Penicaut said, with three chapels and a bell tower. An attraction to settlers according to Fr. Marest was the availability of Christian Indian women; in 1712 he married three Frenchmen to Indian women.[6]

The hot, humid climate of lower Louisiana was not suitable for growing wheat for bread, the staple of the French diet. Lack of food was a persistent problem in Louisiana. On the other hand, the Illinois area was rich in natural resources and the land was highly productive, even with the primitive farming methods in use. All types of vegetables, fruits, and root crops were available; the wide prairies provided grazing for horses and the livestock, reported in the soldier Penicaut's account. Ducks, geese, and other birds were available along the Mississippi flyway, and fish were abundant in the streams. Indeed Penicaut felt the settlers did not lack for any of the necessities or comforts of life.[7]

The Middle Mississippi Valley was developing, but the lower part of the Louisiana colony at the Gulf struggled along; growth was not occurring as rapidly as the French court wished. The French government found the West Indies more important; the sugar trade produced greater wealth than they could obtain from Louisiana. France continued to seek mineral wealth, gold preferably, although silver was acceptable. Indeed, the ministers hoped that mines in the Illinois country would produce silver as well as lead.[8]

Despite France's desire for colonies, the continual wars in Europe distracted the French crown and ate up the financial resources that otherwise might have been used in the colonies. Although the settlements on the Mississippi River were strategically important to prevent further incursions of other nations into the heartland of the continent, the forces to maintain control were hard to supply. Over the years the policies in France vacillated between the needs for maintaining power on the continent or in the colony, and when resources were limited, the colonies suffered.[9]

There were other difficulties. British intrigues with the Indians caused constant problems. To the north, in Wisconsin and Illinois, a series of wars between the French and the Fox Indians had begun.[10]

In 1712 a wealthy merchant in France, Antoine Crozat, was given a charter for fifteen years that gave him the monopoly of trade (excluding beaver) and the right to develop mines throughout the Louisiana colony.[11] Civil government was established under Crozat. But Crozat did not find the great profits in his monopoly he had hoped for, and in 1717 he gave up his charter. At that time in France there was a severe financial crisis resulting from the huge public debt left by Louis XIV. John Law, a Scotsman who was known for his theories of economics, offered his services to the French court as a financial consultant; he was eagerly accepted. Law set forth plans for restructuring the financial institutions and within a short time controlled all the finances of France.

One of Law's financial schemes concerned Louisiana. Law reorganized the existing trade organization the Company of the West in 1717 and gave it a charter for a complete trade monopoly of Louisiana; unlike Crozat's, this monopoly included beaver. The charter imposed the *Coutume de Paris*, the Customary Law of Paris, as law. To populate the country the company was to bring to Louisiana 6000 settlers; and, as it also had a monopoly on the slave trade of Senegal, 3000 black slaves. Significantly for Illinois, under this charter the Illinois country, previously attached to Canada, was made part of the colony of Louisiana for administrative purposes.[12]

Speculation on shares of the Company of the West in Europe was extensive. Propaganda about the wealth in mines and trade to be obtained in Louisiana was published in France—but facts had little to do with it. By 1720 the "Mississippi Bubble" was collapsing and Law fled from France.

The effect on Louisiana actually was not severe, because the Company of the West, reorganized again as the Company of the Indies, continued to function. The company never was able to meet its quota of settlers as specified in its charter, but it did send many shiploads of emigrants to Louisiana; some of those who went to the Illinois ended up in Prairie du Rocher.

Despite propaganda attempts in France to glorify Louisiana, there were factors that prevented any wholesale migration. Missionary organizations, particularly the Jesuits, stimulated by the vast mission field, sent out priests. The priests' annual reports edited into the *Jesuit Relations*, were published in France; these told wondrous tales of conversion and horrible stories of torture and death at the hands of the natives.[13] The French populace was both fascinated and repelled by tales of the wilderness and the dangers to be encountered. Such reports did not inspire French peasants to leave France. Unlike the English colonists, the French did not come to escape religious persecution; there were no Huguenot settlements in Louisiana at this time.

In 1712, under Crozat's regime, when civil government was established, a Superior Council was created for the administration of civil and criminal justice.[14] As the Illinois became settled, the need for local civil government increased, not just to control the *coureurs de bois* as the priests wanted, but to regulate property, inheritance, and other legal matters important to the inhabitants.

Traveling from the posts to New Orleans for court proceedings took quite a bit of time and effort, so a local, lower level of authority, the Provincial Council, was proposed for the Mississippi Valley settlements. Of the many habitations and posts along the river between Illinois and New Orleans, only Illinois was and remained a viable and growing one. Its distinctive position was recognized in 1717 by the creation of a Provincial Council for governing the Illinois area. This council had responsibilities similar to those of the Superior Council for civil and criminal justice, and was answerable to the Superior Council, a higher court.[15]

The new Provincial Council's jurisdiction (on paper) extended from the Kansas River in the west to the Wabash in the east, and from Fort Orleans in the south to the small post at Peoria in the north, that was garrisoned by soldiers from Fort de Chartres. The Provincial Council regulated the affairs of the Royal Indies Company also.

Records of decisions on all matters were sent down to the Superior Council and if there remained a question, cases were referred to the Superior Council.

With the establishment of the Provincial Council came permanent government for the Illinois. Pierre Degué de Boisbriant, a Canadian officer and cousin of the Intendent Iberville, was made commandant, the major commanding officer of the Illinois. With a convoy of sixty-eight soldiers, *engagés,* and miners, Boisbriant left New Orleans in December 1718 and arrived at Kaskaskia in May 1719. Boisbriant's instructions were to maintain order (particularly in reference to the continuing complaints about the *coureurs de bois*), to establish a fort, and to search for mines.[16]

One of Boisbriant's first actions was to establish a fort as he had been directed. It is not clear why he placed it six leagues upriver from Kaskaskia, the main settlement. As this was a year of high water it may have been that the vacant lands near Kaskaskia were flooded. Presumably there was a good landing place on the river near the ridge on which he built the fort, a fort that he named Fort de Chartres after the duc de Chartres, son of the regent of France. About four miles downriver, between the fort and Kaskaskia, was another prairie near the tall limestone bluffs, soon to become the settlement of Prairie du Rocher.

Other settlements were created from the initial one at Kaskaskia, where there were the Kaskaskia Indians, the growing French population, and the Metchigamia Indians. To settle problems arising between the Indians and the French, Boisbriant moved the Kaskaskia Indians six miles up the Kaskaskia River, where they established a new village. The French stayed in the old village, and the Metchigamia were moved about sixteen miles up the Mississippi near the location of the new fort, on a reserve created for them. These moves probably occurred in 1720, as Charlevoix in 1721 spoke of them as recently accomplished.

In 1731 the Company of the Indies returned the Louisiana colony to the oversight of the king and his ministers, because it, too, was unable to profit from the colony. But this did not make any great changes in the life of the people.

Censuses 1723, 1725

Two censuses were taken in the early years of the colony. In 1723 Diron D'Artaguiette, the Inspector General for Louisiana, came to the Illinois, reviewed its progress and had a brief count made of the inhabitants—not including slaves. In the Fort de Chartres area there was a total of only 126 persons; this must have included a few persons in or near Prairie du Rocher. Taking in Kaskaskia and the scant dozen at Cahokia still gave a population of only 334 French and Canadian settlers, a handful in the vast Middle Mississippi Valley.[17]

Two years later a more complete census was drawn up by the Company of the Indies covering all the settlements in Louisiana. The census listed family units, the male head of family, his wife, and their children if such existed. Six other groupings were tallied—*engagés* (contractual workers), black slaves, Indian slaves, cattle, houses, and land.

Boisbriant had made land grants in 1722 in areas that were or were to become the villages of Kaskaskia, Fort de Chartres, Prairie du Rocher, and St. Philippe. In this census, families located on lands later associated with Prairie du Rocher and St. Philippe were listed with the Fort de Chartres establishment. The concentrations of population in these locations were not large enough to warrant a separate tally. In subsequent censuses, when the population had increased, Prairie du Rocher and St. Philippe were counted separately.

The enumeration probably was done by Perillau, the clerk of court; the extant census document from the archives in France is in a French copyist's hand. The census appears to have been completed by May 1725, and then forwarded to France. The reason for the assumption about this date is that Joseph Lamy and Marie Rouensa Philippe died in May and June, 1725, respectively, but were counted in the census.[18]

For Fort de Chartres and Kaskaskia the census listed 280 persons in families, thirty-seven *engagés*, and 195 black and Indian slaves, for a total of 512 persons. Omitting duplications for those who held land in both villages would give a total of 504 persons.

Although there is no actual break in the written census to

separate Kaskaskia and Fort de Chartres, the two are easily divisible through personal names and from the land records. Differences can be seen between the Fort de Chartres settlement, of which Prairie du Rocher was part, and Kaskaskia. There were 154 people at Kaskaskia and 126 at Fort de Chartres. At Kaskaskia there were only eight married couples without children; at Chartres thirteen; the twenty-seven couples at Kaskaskia had 2.4 children per couple as opposed to 1.6 at Chartres. For example, at Kaskaskia Michel Philippe and Marie Rouensa had six children, Jean Brunet and Elisabeth Deshayes had three, and Leonard Bosseron and his Indian wife had four children. At Chartres, François Hennet and Jean Baptiste Becquet each had two children. Charles Gossiaux and his wife, the earliest known residents of Prairie du Rocher, lost twins in 1724.

In all categories Kaskaskia had the numerical preponderance—1590 versus 620 arpents of land, seventy-four horses against forty-seven and, most strikingly of all, 273 cattle with only eighty-nine at Chartres. This reflects the more recent settlement of the area around the fort; the founding of Chartres village occurred fifteen years after Kaskaskia. Many settlers at Chartres were new arrivals from France; most inhabitants at Kaskaskia were Canadian in origin and many had been married to Christian Indian women for years.

Kaskaskia again had more slaves than Fort de Chartres, 119 to seventy-six. Black slaves in the Fort de Chartres area numbered fifty-nine; there were seventeen Indian slaves and one free black. The slaves were not evenly distributed among the inhabitants. Twenty-two of the black slaves were tallied under Boisbriant, the commandant, and de La Loère, the head clerk of the Company of the Indies. These slaves were used to work on company projects, particularly the agricultural development. They also were rented out to various citizens; a certain amount of their production then was returned to the company as payment.

Twenty slaves were listed with Philippe Renault's concession for the lead mines in present Missouri, and at his agricultural lands in St. Philippe. Many authors state that Renault brought in 500 slaves; the mining company might have agreed to import 500, but census data shows there were never this many in the Illinois. A few were at the mines on the Meramec River, but in 1723 it was reported that there were only about thirty workers at the mines, all French.[19] The slaves of the company and for Renault's mining business were the majority of the slaves listed in the census; only seventeen black slaves were distributed among the various habitants in the Fort de Chartres region.

The census was not complete, some people known to have received land grants were not listed. Not all the persons tallied had agricultural land, however. There were craft specialists who had a house and lot, but did not have farm land. This category included traders, voyageurs, several blacksmiths, a gunsmith, a tailor, and a roofer. The existence of these craftsmen shows that this was not a subsistence economy but a market one, and there was sufficient prosperity to support specialists.

Other non-landholders were a few of the military officers or entrepeneurs. For some reason, not all government officials appeared on the census; some who did not were Perillau; Louis Belcour the bailiff; and François Cecire the interpreter for Indian languages.

As the records reveal that 1725 census did not include the total population, an attempt was made to add additional persons identified from notarial documents and the church registers to make a more complete count. The royal notaries' files contain 370 records between 1720 to 1726 involving local persons in land sales, marriage contracts, labor contracts, trade agreements, wills, and other documents; these give the names of participants and witnesses and reveal those not mentioned in the census.

The soldiers listed in the census were those who held land in the community; these were not all of the military personnel. The garrison reported on by D'Artaguiette in 1723 was said to have consisted of two companies. A company at this time was supposed to have fifty men, but frequently units were understrength. In 1721 the garrison assigned to Fort de Chartres consisted of sixty men, and in 1724 and 1725, of sixty-eight; a small number given the extent of the Illinois jurisdiction and the numerous hostile tribes.[20] Out of these, approximately one full company was present at Fort de Chartres. The other soldiers were at posts that were garrisoned by troops from the fort—Cahokia, Peoria, the Ouabache post, the lead mines, and Fort Orleans on the Missouri. Military lists of the day do mention all these persons at the various localities and count them as assigned to the Ilinois country.[21]

Kaskaskia was a major trade center. An unknown number of voyageurs worked out of there and the other communities. In a later census (1732) fifty men are listed as transients.

At so great a distance in time removed from 1725, an accurate census is not possible. However, approximately one hundred additional individuals can be identified as being present immediately before and during the census period. The population in the Illinois in 1725 probably was about 600 persons (including slaves and transients).

The census provides basic statistics about the population; other records help to fill in details about the persons listed. The diverse origins of the Illinois inhabitants reflect the composition of the population of the colony of Louisiana. The birthplaces of some men in the Fort de Chartres area can be identified—eighty-two were born in France, sixty-two in Canada, two or three in Spain, two were Swiss, and at least three were second generation born in the Illinois country. These figures do not include the voyageurs who certainly were Canadian, but do include the soldiers, mainly French. For the women there is even less information, but wives identified were: seventeen Indians, fourteen French, nine from Canada, four born in the Illinois, one from Holland, and one from Germany.

The expectation would be that the men coming to the Illinois would tend to be young, considering the physical labor involved in paddling or farming; actually the average age is 36.5 years for the limited number for whom there is information. The population that came appears to have been quite healthy and long lived for the period. Despite the dangers of Indian attacks and poor medical treatment, the thirty-nine men in the census whose later death dates could be found averaged 51.3 years at death. *(See Figure 1, next page).*

A few physical descriptions from the ship lists or in court cases show that the males from France were between five-feet-two-inches and five-feet-six-inches tall. The Canadian and Illinois born may have been taller, both from a better diet and genetically from intermarriage with the Indians. The Illinois Indians from a slightly later Metchigamia Indian village averaged for females, five-feet-five-inches and the males, five-feet-seven-inches in height. The French tended to use the word "tall" in their descriptions of the Illinois Indians suggesting they were taller than the majority of the habitants.

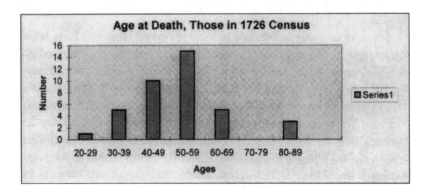

It is difficult to go beyond the statistical and descriptive levels to see what caused these people to consider coming to the Illinois. Their motivations are hard to analyze. People were not obliging enough to leave behind personal letters or diaries, although this would have been possible. Literacy was not widespread in the eighteenth century, but the Illinois country was not as raw and untutored as often considered; for example, Jacque Turpin of Prairie du Rocher possessed eight small books of devotions and a catechism.[22]

The ability to write showed a fairly significant difference between French and Canadian settlers; sixty percent of the French could write, but only forty-five percent of the Canadians. About half of the male inhabitants would meet the basic standard of literacy—they could sign their names. A good many signed with a flourish that showed them comfortable with a quill pen, and documents exist in the handwriting of individuals as well as in the notary's hand. For some, writing their name was probably the extent of their knowledge as their careful wavering printing suggests.

Beyond the statistics what do we know about the people who came here? Where did they come from and why? Biographical sketches were constructed for a few of the emigrants to help to visualize the population and to show some of the culture. The data is limited and restricted to events in their lives; these bring out facts but show little of their ambitions, interests, and thoughts. Not all of these described settled in Prairie du Rocher, but the lives of all the villagers were intertwined through kinship, intermarriage, and the community cooperation necessary to stay alive in the wilderness.

The Canadians

The earliest settlers were the Canadians. Their families came from France originally of course, but they had been in New France for two or three generations and they were truly a North American breed. Their knowledge of the wilderness, of Indian languages and customs, and of the water networks was essential for the survival of the isolated communities.

The Canadians came to the Illinois country as traders and created a base from which to continue their trading east and west. Most of these were licensed traders, possessing *congés* from Montreal or Quebec. The voyageurs and traders were self-sufficient, independent, and avoided governmental restrictions as much as possible. Although they might be out trading in the wilderness for months, they were not totally loners. They returned to their homes and kin in Canada, and when able participated in the church's observances. Family ties were important; wherever one person settled, others were likely to follow. As the traders began to make the villages in the Illinois the permanent center of their trade, members of the same extended family—nephews, cousins, and relatives by marriage—frequently ended up in the same locales.

The Illinois, with its access to many rivers, was a good location for trade. By the 1720s many traders were resident in Kaskaskia, carrying on a prosperous business. Furs and hides were taken north to Canada, and *pirogues* (dugout canoes) went downriver to lower Louisiana with meat, flour, and other supplies; trade goods were brought back from both places.

In addition to its favorable situation for trade, another motivation for settlement in the Illinois was the abundant land. Good arable land along the rivers in Canada had become more scarce as the population grew. The fertile soil and relatively mild climate of the Illinois country made settlement appealing and drew many south. As it became obvious that agricultural products were highly desirable and necessary items that could be traded in the southern part of the Louisiana colony, interest in agriculture increased.

One of the Canadians who came to the Illinois, was Etienne Philippe *dit* (called) Dulongpré. In 1717 while on a trading venture, he was captured by hostile Indians at the Wabash River. He was able to escape from them and fled to the British in the Carolinas, by whom he was taken to Santo Domingo. From there he obtained passage on a ship back to Louisiana. This brief account probably hides adventures that could be made into an action movie, but there are no details, only the bare facts.

He came to the Illinois and married a Christian Indian woman, probably an Illinois Indian, Marie Marouenceous, by whom he had four children; one died in infancy. Dulongpré continued to trade. In 1723 Diron D'Artaguiette, the Inspector General of Louisiana, noted in his journal that a pirogue of Dulongpré's, with six men paddling, was accompanying D'Artaguiette's boat up the Mississippi from New Orleans to the Illinois.

In addition to his trading ventures Etienne also had farmland in both the Fort de Chartres/Prairie du Rocher area, where he was captain of the militia, and at Kaskaskia, his official residence. Like most of the Canadians, he had relatives in the area, including his brother, Michel Philippe, who had married the Kaskaskia chief's daughter, Marie Rouensa. Etienne lived to 1734 and was about sixty-six years of age at his death.[23]

Jean Jacques Brunet *dit* Bourbonnais was born in Montreal in 1673. He was an experienced and prosperous trader when, at thirty-two, he married Elisabeth Deshayes, who had arrived in Louisiana from France on the vessel *Pelican*. That boat carried twenty marriageable girls, "reared in virtue and piety," and selected by Monsieur St. Vallier, Bishop of Quebec. This cargo of women was one of several attempts to bring girls to the colony where there was a predominantly male population. Brunet must have been in Mobile at the time of the arrival of the ship when he chose his bride. From other accounts it appears that this was a mutual selection, as the girls were not always willing and did not have to accept a marriage offer. The couple moved to the Illinois about 1722.

In 1746 he petitioned the commandant, De Bertet, and Judge de La Loère Flaucour for permission to emancipate his black slaves, Catherine and her son Pierre, after his death, in accordance with Article 50 of *le Code Noir* (the Black Code). The slaves apparently had a long time to wait as Brunet was still living in 1751 at seventy-eight years of age. At that time he and his wife gave one of their sons-in-law, Pierre Aubuchon, all their lands and goods and forgave Aubuchon the remainder of a debt for a house that Brunet had sold him earlier. The donation was in exchange for care of the couple in their old age.[24]

Alexandre De Celle Duclos was born in Boucherville, Canada, in 1704. By the early 1720s he was at Fort de Chartres, serving as an ensign and appears in the records carrying out various military duties. He married Elisabeth Philippe, one of the daughters of Michel and Marie Rouensa. His descendants are still to be found in Prairie du Rocher.[25]

Emigrants from France

Another group of settlers came directly from France to Louisiana. As the colonizing spirit was not prevalent in France, those who volunteered to come must have been the more adventurous ones, or, as suggested by Choquette, they were accustomed to migratory movements in France and this was an extension of that movement.[26]

The trip to the New World was not a voyage to be undertaken lightly; it was a long and arduous journey that lasted two to four months, with stops at Madeira and a Caribbean port—Santo Domingo, Martinique, or Havana. The ships conveying the passengers were small, mostly with a keel length of about seventy-five feet.[27] Shipwreck was common. Ships were lost due to storms, piracy, or to warfare—a constant problem—and disease was rampant. Living conditions, food, and sanitation onboard were very poor. One diary is quoted as relating:

> Live sheep and chickens brought along for food were swept overboard or drowned on deck by storms, and the passengers were reduced to eating rice gruel, salt beef and rancid lard and beans. For much of the time, water was rationed to one pint per person per day. [28]

Deaths on the ships were common and many succumbed to illnesses after they arrived. The ships that successfully reached the Gulf put in at Dauphine Island (also called Massacre Island on account of the many bones found there). Passengers were transferred as equipment permitted to Mobile, and in later times to New Orleans. Both settlements were unhealthy, low-lying places that suffered from lack of food supplies. The trip from Dauphine Island to New Orleans was lengthy, sometimes six days by pirogue.

> There were no settlements along the river and the vegetation was so dense they had to camp on the immediate banks of the river. Among the greatest troubles were the mosquitoes...We also suffered the annoyance in the pirogue of not being able to sit, stand or kneel, or to make any movement, for the pirogue would have upset...All our baggage of mattresses and chests filled it, and we had to be on top of all that in a little heap and when the pirogue stopped we changed our positions.[29]

Having attained New Orleans the immigrants bound for the Illinois faced another long, difficult trip up the Mississippi to reach their final destination. With the varying river conditions, dangers of warfare with Indians, and the time of year, the stay in New Orleans might be quite prolonged while awaiting an opportune time to embark. The trip upriver to Illinois was in small boats, bateaux or pirogues, and the trip took three to four months depending on the condition of the river and the weather. The immigrants who survived all these journeys were hardy folks.

A convoy left New Orleans in December 1718 and arrived in Illinois in May 1719 with the commandant, Boisbriant, and about one hundred other persons. In March 1721 a convoy of 120 persons arrived at Fort de Chartres; this included soldiers, miners, and the director of the mines for the Company of the Indies, Philippe Renaudière. Also with this group were forty *engagés* who had reached the colony on the ship *Le Union* in 1719. Due to the hostilities with Spain they had had to spend a long time on the coast before coming to the Illinois. The convoy left from New Orleans in September 1720.[30]

A few selections from the journal of Diron D'Artaguiette, the inspector general, tell of a typical trip upriver to the Illinois and some of the trials experienced. This trip began at the end of December and they reached Kaskaskia in mid-April. Although D'Artaguiette did stop to do a few inspections along the way, the majority of his time was spent in travel or waiting to travel. The maximum distance traveled in a day was eight leagues, but the average was three to four leagues (eight to eleven miles).

> Feb.6 - Our men having taken their oars, we continued our journey against rather strong currents, and camped four leagues above.
>
> Feb. 9 - The rain fell all the past night and continued this morning, which obliged us to remain here.
>
> Feb. 10 - The rain having ceased, we continued our journey, and, three leagues above, we found seven pirogues loaded with meat which Canadian traders, established at the Ilinnois,[sic] are taking down to New Orleans to sell. They told us that diseases had been very prevalent among the Ilinnois, and that many Canadians had died. Rain having overtaken us in this place, we passed the night there.
>
> Feb. 14 - We set out about 7 o'clock in the morning, after having heard the mass of Father Boulanger, and arrived at a little island, which is a league above, where we waited for a certain Legras, a Canadian from the pirogue of Dulongpré, and a Yazous Indian, who had departed this morning. As these two men did not return, we were obliged to camp and to fire off a gun at intervals.

After several days of searching, the men were found floating on a raft; they had gone off to hunt to supplement the food taken with them on the voyage. About a year later Legras once again was lost in the woods during a voyage and died. (See Chapter 4 for the inventory of his belongings.)

> Feb. 21 - At day-break the Reverend Jesuit Father said mass, after which we embarked and continued our journey, killed two ducks, and camped six leagues above. Today the water rose 4 feet.
>
> Mar. 5 - Our men having taken to their oars about 6 o'clock in the morning, we continued our journey and joined the Reverend Father and Dulongpré by breakfast. The weather was bad which was the reason we made only two leagues. The water rose 6 feet last night.

Spring rains along the Wabash and Ohio Rivers were causing these swift rises in the water level. The group must have camped at night on a sand ridge or natural levee to be safely above the water level and the pirogues tied with long ropes. ·

> Mar.16 - Fine weather and a good northwest wind brought us without rowing to the Rivière à Margot, where we had dinner. In this place we had a violent and contrary wind, which was the reason we made only one league. The hour for camping having come, we put to shore and killed a cow, [buffalo] which we were not able to take, the night having overtaken us. The past night the water fell two feet.
>
> Apr. 3 - Fine weather. We set out about 5 o'clock in the morning and came to breakfast at La Petite Prairie, and from this place, in spite of heavy currents, we came to camp five leagues above.
>
> Apr. 9 - Weather clear and cold. We have been obliged to remain here so as to make oars and to give our men some rest.
>
> Apr. 13 - Fine weather. We departed about 5 o'clock in the morning and came to eat dinner 4 leagues above the Ouabache at the place where the Sioux, an Indian Nation (who live towards the head of the Mississipy, a hundred leagues above the Ilinnois), had killed a man called Desnepveus, his wife, and two of his children. They were coming from Canada to establish themselves at the Ilinnois.

The Nepveu family had halted their boats at the place mentioned and sent one of their men to get assistance from voyageurs at

Kaskaskia to help paddle the rest of the way upstream to the village. When the men returned they found the group had been attacked. The father, his nine-year-old child, and a young slave had been taken away by the Indians. All the others were dead.

D'Artaguiette's convoy reached Kaskaskia in mid-April, having been enroute for about three and one-half months. This was a fairly rapid journey.[31]

Many of the French who came were able to adapt to the new environment, a much less enervating one than the Louisiana heat, and less stressful than the Canadian winters. Undoubtedly some came looking to better themselves, tradesmen seeking their fortune in the New World, who perhaps originally intended to return to France. They were recruited from various places, but most heavily from the ports of La Rochelle and Rochefort and the environs of Paris.[32] Craftsmen and laborers ended up in the Illinois as *engagés* contracted to the company for three years' work. After this period of service they could receive land if they wanted to stay.

Many of the emigrants came from urban areas rather than being peasants from rural villages. However, "urban" in the eighteenth century, is not today's urbanism. Fields, farmland, and woods were in close proximity, and craftsmen in smaller towns would of necessity raise food crops of some type. But, perhaps having a more cosmopolitan view, these emigrants tended to be more independent and adventurous than would rural peasants.

Jean Baptiste Nicolas Becquet arrived on the ship *La Gironde* in 1720. He was a locksmith and the son of a locksmith in Paris. His wife, Catherine Bareaux, was listed as a laundress from Poitou. In the Illinois he obtained land and had the dual capacity of farmer/craftsman. He apparently was quite skilled, as a major part of his work in the Illinois was as a gunsmith. He was not just a specialist though. He was able to turn his hand to all types of blacksmithing. Becquet made locks, keys, and other items, including the metal work for the early church of Ste. Anne at Fort de Chartres. In 1725 a soldier, François Derbes, contracted with Becquet as an *engagé* to work at the forge for him. In the contract Derbes also agreed that he would arrange to have his guard duty done at Fort de Chartres at his own expense.

The trade as a locksmith/gunsmith was an important one. Becquet held a contract in 1737 to repair and maintain the guns of the troops and those in the royal storehouse. He also was to keep up the guns of the Indians, some of whom were hunters employed by the government. Later he had a partnership with a gunsmith in Kaskaskia to carry out royal contracts in gunsmithing.

Jean and Catherine had five children; in addition, Becquet adopted Pierre Texier, his wife's godson, and one of three orphaned children. Godparents had an important social role since the untimely death of parents was not uncommon with the dangers on the frontier. The relationship implied familial obligations and placed the child securely within the social structure of community. Becquet promised Texier's guardians, who were responsible for his property and person, that he would care for Pierre until he was eighteen and teach him the trade of locksmithing.

Becquet was literate and documents exist that were written in his own hand. Successful in his trade and as a farmer, Becquet raised his family at Chartres until 1741, when he moved them to Kaskaskia. If he came to improve his lot in the New World, he apparently succeeded.[33]

Jean Baptiste Barbeau and his wife, Silvie La Moine, from Poiters, sailed on *La Seine* in 1720. They settled in New Orleans and had two sons, both of whom they named Jean Baptiste. The father Jean Baptiste was killed by Indians on a trip on the lower Mississippi in 1729. His widow remarried; apparently the second marriage was not a success and records of the litigation concerning property and the rights of the sons still exist in New Orleans. Perhaps the conflict with their stepfather was what lead the two sons to move to Prairie du Rocher where their descendants still live.[34]

Philippe Bienvenu of Orleans, France, took ship in May 1718 with his fifteen-year-old son, Pierre Antoine. They were bound for the concession of Melique that was located next to Prairie du Rocher. In 1721 Pierre Antoine married Françoise Rabut, who had arrived earlier on one of the shipments of women. The eighty-eight girls on her ship were from the *Hopital-General de la Salpetriere* in Paris, and were escorted to the port by constabulary guards who made certain that the girls got on the ship. Each girl had a dowry of two suits of clothing, two skirts and petticoats, six laced bodices, six chemises, and six headdresses, plus the necessary accessories. Françoise was twenty-five years old when she arrived.[35] Pierre Antoine, generally known as Antoine, later received a grant of land in Prairie du Rocher.

The importation of women was not entirely successful. Some, like Elisabeth Deshayes, had been carefully picked, but some others were women taken from prisons and orphanages, whose morals and health were dubious. It was not easy to get women to sign up for immigration. The priests, naturally, were in favor of stable, legitimate relationships; the government was interested in these, too, since families were needed for growth in the population, and more population would better secure the colony. The casual relationships of the voyageurs with the Indian women did not please either church or government.

Of all the remedies the most sure is to send women there for with difficulty will one check the course of concubinage among the backwoodsmen and the soldiers. The Indian women are easy, the climate is stimulating, and they are young men for the most part Canadians, that is to say very vigorous.[36]

Military and Government Officials

The rank and file of military personnel signed on for a six-year tour of duty. The soldiers were of *Les Compagnies Françhes de la Marine*, the Independent Companies of the Navy. Recruited by a captain, these companies were supposed to consist of the captain, a lieutenant, one ensign, one cadet *à l'eguillette* (son of an officer or gentleman training to be an officer), a soldier cadet, two sergeants, three corporals, two drummers, and forty-one soldiers. The recruits had to be at least five feet one inch tall. For uniforms they were to receive a frock coat with eighteen brass buttons, a pair of breeches, a pair of stockings, a pair of shoes, a shirt, a wool cap, a comb, a woolen blanket, and a sailor's hammock. Some of the soldiers probably were enticed by promises of land and fortune in the New World. Soldiers who completed their tour of duty were eligible to receive grants of land and remain in the Louisiana colony, an inducement for men who were landless in France.[37]

In 1721 the ship *L'Elephant* brought two companies of soldiers for the concession of Le Blanc on the lower Mississippi; some of these men ended up in the Illinois country. A high rate of mortality among arriving soldiers and frequent desertions caused men to be shifted around to fill vacancies.

François Robert *dit* Bellerose (pretty rose) arrived on *L'Elephant* in 1721 as a soldier. By 1725 he had a grant of land in the Illinois and he lived there until at least 1738.

Antoine François Ple *dit* La Plume (the feather or pen) came in 1718 as a corporal in the Brigade of the Miners. After his service he received a grant of land and remained to pursue his trade as a pit sawyer until his death in 1744 at age sixty. He was a resident of Prairie du Rocher.[38]

The officers and functionaries of the Company who came from France intended to return after their tour of duty; the New World was seen as an opportunity for financial advancement and concomitant upward mobility. Some succeeded in this plan, but others were buried here literally.

Nicolas Michel Chassin was *garde de magasin* (storekeeper) responsible for the distribution of goods and munitions for the Company of the Indies, and a councillor on the Provincial Council. He received a land grant of seventeen *arpents* next to the Prairie du Rocher tract, part of which later was incorporated into Prairie du Rocher. Chassin was well satisfied with his status in the Illinois except for one item. As he wrote to Father Bobe in France in 1722 "...the only thing that I now lack in order to make a strong establishment in Louisiana is a certain article of furniture that one often repents of having got..." namely, a wife. However, in the same year Chassin married Agnes Philippe, the sixteen-year-old daughter of Michel Philippe and Marie Rouensa. Chassin was considerably older than Agnes; this age difference was not uncommon at the time. Madame Chassin was left with three small daughters when Chassin died in Louisiana in 1730, but with the property that she inherited she was by no means destitute.[39]

The brothers, Marc Antoine de La Loère des Ursins and Pierre Louis Auguste de La Loère Flaucour came to Louisiana in 1713 to serve Crozat's interests during his monopoly. They were sent to Natchez, Mississippi, to create a post there. Then, under the Company of the Indies Des Ursins came to Illinois in 1719 and was a member of the Provincial Council as first councillor. Seven years later he was promoted and went to New Orleans, where he was appointed to the Superior Council as fourth councillor. Since this was an important position, he had to have a certification from the vicar general that he was a practicing member of the "Catholic, Apostolic and Roman church." He later returned to the Natchez where he was killed in the Indian revolt in 1729. Pierre Louis Auguste de La Loère Flaucour replaced his brother in the Illinois around 1735 and was judge of the council until his death in 1746.[40]

The military officers were both French and Canadian. Many Canadians served in the Marine in France and were sent back to the New World as officers, because it was felt they had a better understanding of warfare and diplomacy in the North American wilderness.[41]

Nicolas Pelletier de Franchomme, an ensign from France, was single when he arrived in 1719. He married an Indian woman, Marguerite Onoquamoquema. Marguerite was the widow of a well-to-do trader, Jacque Bourdon. As Bourdon's widow, Marguerite inherited her portion of Bourdon's estate. After Franchomme married her, he undertook several legal actions about Marguerite's inheritance, obtaining a new division of Bourdon's property that more greatly benefited his wife and probably himself. To be sure that he had all his rights, Franchomme petitioned to obtain a new copy of his marriage contract with Marguerite. For some reason the old contract had been found under the flooring of the storehouse gnawed by rats. A duplicate was made by the notary. An important clause in this was the donation to him by Marguerite of a large amount of money, 20,000 *livres*.[42]

Despite the financial settlement the marriage had many problems. Marguerite ran away in 1725 and an inventory of their house was done. She apparently returned, for when Franchomme wrote his will in 1728 he carefully separated his and her property and asked her to be kind to their slaves, both black and Indian. Franchomme then went off to the Fox war and was killed that same year.[43]

Another French officer, Pierre Melique of Paris, was a lieutenant in D'Artaguiette's company. He was the owner of the land concession of fourteen arpents by three quarters of a league known as the Prairie Melique, part of which became attached to Prairie du Rocher. He had *engagés* to work the land, to whom he agreed to give their necessary livelihood and 1400 *livres* wages for three years of service. At the completion of the terms of the *engagés*, Melique leased his land to tenants. Melique was unmarried. Chassin wrote in his letter to Fr. Bobe that Melique desired to marry Chassin's sister; however, their parents were unwilling for her to make the trip to Louisiana. Whether or not the parental Chassins would have relented in time it was soon too late: Melique was killed by Indians in the spring of 1727 at age 52, leaving as his heir a natural daughter Françoise, probably a *métis*.[44]

The new world was more kindly to some officers. The family of St. Ange, the father and his two sons, Pierre and Louis de Bellerive, served for a long time in the Illinois country. The father, Robert Groston de St. Ange, was born in Chatillon, on the Seine in Champagne, France. He sailed to Canada where he married. His military career went well, and in 1723 St. Ange was a lieutenant in the company of Dutisne. In 1725 he was the commandant of the militia, and for a few years in the 1730s he served as commandant at Fort de Chartres.

In 1725 St. Ange purchased an expensive dress for his wife, a secondhand one, from the widow Lamy. The outfit was of striped pink satin lined with rose colored taffeta with silk hose, shoes, and mitts. The cost was 800 *livres*, more than the cost of a pirogue and more than a year's wages for an *engagé*.[45]

One of his sons, Louis de Bellerive, became the last commandant of the French regime and surrendered Fort de Chartres to the British. After this Louis moved to the new post of St. Louis and was a prominent leader there under the Spanish for many years.

Other Settlers

The main influx of colonists from France came between 1717 and 1721. After the Law debacle it became more difficult to find people willing to go to Louisiana. Because of the problems that the Company of the Indies had in filling their quota of settlers, they also recruited outside France to increase their numbers. Swiss settlers were brought; one of whom was François Hennet, twenty-nine years old, a roofer, and his wife, Marianne Charpin. A roofer did not just shingle roofs, he was a highly skilled worker who could construct the complex so-called Norman trusses used for the framework of the house roofs. Hennet farmed land near Fort de Chartres and also plied his trade as a roofer. His son, Jean François, followed his father's trade and made the roofs of the buildings of the stone Fort de Chartres in the 1750s.[46]

There were Spanish workers also, Antoine L'Espagnol was captured in the siege of Pensacola in Spanish Florida and brought as a miner to the area. Joseph L'Espagnol, or Quebado, also took part in the mining. An Italian known to the French as Jean Montare *dit* Toussaint signed his name as Giovanni Montari Tutti Santi.[47] Many Germans were recruited and were settled on the lower Mississippi; in time a few of these appeared in the Illinois.

Some *engagés* were from other countries as well, but most were from France. Thirty-seven *engagés* were tallied in the 1726 census, and from contracts remaining in the Kaskaskia Manuscripts, some can be identified. One was Jean Martin, who made a contract with Philippe Renault to do manual labor. As part of the contract, Martin's wife, Renée Charbonnet, was to be fed and to be employed to sew.

Another *engagé* was Jean Baptiste André, who contracted with Melique to be a domestic servant for one year for a calf; he was listed on the census as an *engagé* and held land. From the census list and the summary phrase on the notarial file of his contract with Melique, it appears that André was a free black.[48]

In addition to these people there were immigrants who had little choice in the matter; they were shipped out of France. They were thieves, vagabonds, prostitutes, smugglers, deserters, or merely the urban unemployed. Their condemnation by the courts in France to the galleys was commuted to life in Louisiana. The transportation of criminals began about 1717. This had a double objective—the elimination of criminals from France, particularly from Paris and vicinity, and the peopling of the colony.

The largest group of these consisted of the contraband salt dealers (*faux sauniers*). Salt was a severely regulated and heavily taxed item in France, with strict laws concerning its sale, which people tried to evade. The offenders were sentenced for three years and provided for their trip to the New World with hose, shoes, two shirts, a suit consisting of breeches and jacket, a *capot* with a hood (specified as Canadian in style), all of the cheapest material.[49] Their wives were allowed to accompany them. Chained on board, they had the worst conditions of passage on the ships, and many did not live to arrive in Louisiana.[50]

Between 1717 and 1721 thousands of criminals arrested in France were sentenced to be deported, but only about 900 ever reached Louisiana. Many died or escaped before the trip, died on ships that sank, or succumbed to disease, and those who arrived often did not make the best colonists. Many of the these immigrants were not interested in agriculture; they had already moved from the countryside to Paris and other urban centers before being sent to the New World.[51] Frequently the vagabonds and other convicts were not disposed to perform the hard labor required to open up fields and develop settlements.

So the transportation of convicts was not a success. In New Orleans at the end of 1721 only thirty convicts were said to be still alive; only five had been there more than a year.[52] In France there were objections to the transportation of criminals and in 1720 a ruling was made to end it. The last shipments of convicts arrived in Louisiana in 1721. Not only were the convicts themselves not always beneficial to the colony, but their very presence was a deterrent to immigration by honest peasants. The topic of criminals exiled to the Mississippi was a favorite one for plays in the Italian and French theater, reinforcing the populace's disinclination to go to Louisiana.[53]

Although the convicts were considered in France as dangerous criminals and undesirables, many who ended up in the Illinois became hardworking, virtuous citizens. When one recalls the crimes for which people could be condemned to the galleys (*viz.*, Jean Valjean in *Les Miserables*), it is clear that the convicts might not all be hardened criminals.

New Orleans had little success with the convicts, but in the Illinois a large number became integrated into the society. At least fifteen or sixteen transportees can be identified with certainty in the Illinois. François Poupart *dit* Rencontre, a deserter, was sent over in 1719. Later he had a house at Fort de Chartres, of which he donated half to his godson. Poupart appears to have been redeemed and reinstated in the marines, for he was referred to subsequently as a sergeant in the troops.

Pancrasse Obremon, from Strasbourg, also was deported, listed under "deserters and such" on the ship list. He married at Fort de Chartres and had at least five children; he died about 1734.

Ambroise Moreau and his wife, Jeanne Paule, were shipped out from France, classified on the ship list under "deserters and other sorts." They lived, however, to virtuous old age in Prairie du Rocher. Ambroise was eighty years old at his death in 1760.[54]

The ship registers sometimes gave the place of origin, age, and even physical descriptions of the convicts providing rare physical descriptions of the early inhabitants. Claude Chetivau, forty-five years old, five feet three inches tall with gray hair and beard, was from Soissons. He arrived in 1719 on *Les Deux Frères* as did several others: Antoine Camus from Paris, forty-one years old, five feet tall with black hair; Louis D'espagne, also from Paris, twenty-one years old, five feet three inches tall and blond; and Germain Boule from Comté, thirty-five years old, five feet three inches tall with blonde hair. All were *faux sauniers*.

After serving his time for the company, Antoine Camus had a home at Fort de Chartres; Louis Levasseur *dit* D'espagne married and lived at Prairie du Rocher; and Germain Boule received a concession from Renault and settled in St. Philippe. Claude Chetivau, although he owned a house at the village by Fort de Chartres for a time, was not as virtuous; he soon reappeared in the court records at

Fort de Chartres.[55]

On this same boatload of convicts were three women taken in fraud—Blanche Vigernon, Jeanne L'enfant, and Marie Jeanne Gaudie. Marianne Tabouret and Marie Marguerite Moule were deported from Paris in 1719 on the ill-named ship *La Mutiné*; René Charbonnet came from the poorhouse in La Rochelle. All of them married men in the Illinois and lived out their lives there.

These people became an integral part of the colony; they intermarried with the other settlers and their children married in the colony. For them there was a new life in the New World, a world that held more opportunities for them than the urban poverty of France.

There was one other unwilling group of emigrants, the black slaves who originated from the African coasts—Caye, Gorée, Juida, Manega, Senegal, and Guinea. From the derivation of their names it appears that some of the blacks were Muslim—Galefat from Khalife, chief or boss; Malique for Malik, king; Mouca from Messa, Moses; Savez from Sabah, an Arabic personal name; and Mamarou from Mamadu, Mahmoud.[56] Slaves were a valuable part of the economic life since there was always a shortage of manpower. They were important for the prosperity of the colony and generally were treated well.

Blacks who were free had the same rights and responsibilities as the other French inhabitants. Charles Balesi quotes Article LII of *le Code Noir* (the Black Code) in stating that freed slaves "enjoy the privileges of the native born subjects of our kingdom, lands, and countries within our sovereignty..."[57] Theoretically, they had the right to participate in the village assemblies. The *Code Noir* protected the rights of slaves, too; it is discussed in Chapter 2.

Although there is little detail about lives of the slaves, it is possible to give a biography of one of the free blacks. In 1739, Jacques Duverger, a free voyageur originally from New Orleans, purchased a house and lot in Kaskaskia for 800 *livres*, which sum he had paid in full by October 1740. Several documents remain concerning Duverger, contracts that he made with other voyageurs and contracts for the transportation of goods to and from New Orleans. These indicate that he was a voyageur/merchant of sufficient standing to hire and send people out on his business while he remained in Kaskaskia.

Duverger was not only an enterprising merchant, he had other talents. He was referred to as a surgeon in some records and received payment from a Frenchman for medical treatment. Duverger died in 1743. He was married, but his wife was still a minor when he died, so the important Kaskaskia citizen, Antoine Bienvenu, was appointed as guardian for her and his estate, the standard procedure for French citizens under the *Coutume de Paris*.[58]

Indian slaves were captured from western tribes by the Illinois Indians and procured by traders from other tribes. Many slaves at an early period came from the Pawnee tribe (called Panis by the French), and this became a generic name for Indian slaves. Never a very large proportion of the slave population, very little is known about the Indian slaves. The majority of the Indian slaves were women; often they were in the households of single men serving in the kitchen and elsewhere.

The 1725 census gave a profile of the colony at the end of the period of immigration. After that with the cessation of major influxes of personnel from France, growth depended upon natural increase. Emigration from Canada continued but again, the population there was augmented mainly by births. The lack of a continued influx of new settlers led to population imbalance between the French and English colonies, to the disadvantage of the French.

Notes

1. For more detailed information on early development of Canada and · trade *see* Eccles 1969, 1972; Balesi 1992; Peyser 1992.
2. Thwaites 1896-1901. 64: 195-211; Ekberg nd.
3. Temple 1966; M. Brown 1979; Thwaites 1896-1901, vol. 64, 65; Kas. Church Rec.; Palm 1931.
4. Half-French, half-Indian.
5. Balesi 1992: 138.
6. Palm 1931, 139; Margary 5: 488; French 1875, 107; McWilliams 1953.
7. McWilliams 1953, 137-38.
8. Balesi 1992: 139.
9. Farrell 1988; Miquelon 1993.

10. Rowland and Sanders 3:405.
11. Balesi 1992:140.
12. Belting 1975:16; Giraud 3:2-27; Archives Nationales des Colonies (hereafter referred to as ANC) C 13 B 39:459; Balesi 1992:142.
13. Thwaites 1896-1901.
14. ANC B38:292-294.
15. ANC B43,103-107.
16. Giraud 3, 372.
17. ANC C13A 8, 226.
18. Dean and Brown 1981, 26:2:26:1; Ekberg nd, 15; ANC G 1 464 1/1/1726; Ako had died and Marie had married Michel Philippe.
19. Rowland and Sanders 2, 154.
20. Mereness 1916, 69; Rowland and Sanders 2, 258; AG, AI:2592; ANC, B43:459; ANC, B43:570.
21. ANC, B43, 570.
22. Dean and Brown 1981, 23:7:4:1.
23. The *dit* Dulongpre is probably from "a place of the long prairie;" 10 May 1717 ANC C13 10 May 1717; Mereness 1916, 40; Dean and Brown 1981, 25:4:30:1.
24. Lessard et al. 1986: Table pg. 2; Dean and Brown 1981, 46:10:8:1; 51:11:18:2; Higginbotham 1977, 133; ANC GI 464 1706.
25. Menard, Ruth 1997, 125.
26. Fr. Col. Hist. Soc. 2002, 19.
27. Proulx 1984, 25.
28. Norall 1988, 39, 40.
29. Dunn 1902, 272-73.
30. Giraud 3:372, 374-75.
31. Mereness 1916, 40-49.
32. Fr. Col. Hist. Soc. 2002, 3.
33. Dean and Brown 1981, 25:2:19:1; 37:3:30:1; 38:4:30:2; 40:5:18:1; 40:11:15:1;41:1:5:1.
34. Menard, Ruth 1997, 86; Letter Kathrine Seineke, Ap. 12, 1976.
35. Menard, Ruth 1994, 8, 168.
36. Rowland and Sanders 2, 72; (D'Artarguiette to Ponchartrain, Memoir to prevent libertinism in Louisiana as far as possible, 1712).
37. Deville 1973, x-xi.
38. Brown and Dean 1977: D67.
39. Dean and Brown 1981, 24:11:13:1; Rowland and Sanders 2, 279.

40. *Louisiana Historical Quarterly* (hereafter *LHQ*) 3:(3), 444-445; Dean and Brown 1981, 46:12:10:1; ONeill 1966, 235.
41. Eccles 1972, 111.
42. A *livre* is a monetary unit equaling 20 *sous*.
43. Rowland and Sanders 2, 278; *LHQ* 3, (4), 511.
44. Giraud 3, 234; Rowland and Sanders 2, 278.
45. ANC B43:347-3 51; Dean and Brown 1981, 25:10:13:1.
46. ANC G 1464; Dean and Brown 1981, 55:9:15:1.
47. Charlevoix 2, 220; Dean and Brown 1981, 32:1:14:1.
48. Dean and Brown 1981, 23:8:21:1; 25:3:12:1.
49. A *capot* was a blanket coat with a short cape that could form a hood.
50. ANC C13, 5; C15, 170, 1.
51. Moogk 1992.
52. Hardy 1966, 220.
53. Giraud 4, 177, 190; Moogk 1992, 24.
54. Brown and Dean 1977, K405, K24; D360; Dean and Brown 1981 34:10:18:1.
55. Dean and Brown 1981, 1722-32:50; 26:1:3 1:1.
56. Collet 1908, 232; Briggs nd, 21.
57. Balesi 1992, 249.
58. Dean and Brown 1981, 3 9:4:9:1; 40:10:26:1, 2; 40:10:29:1; 43:1:28:1.

Drawing of Renault. Early 18th century graffito by De La Loère, Judge of the Provincial Council, depicting Philippe Renault, Director of the Concession of the Mines, copied from the cover of one of the early record books in the archives of the Randolph County (Ill.) Courthouse.

2

Governance in the Illinois

The people who came to the Illinois were from diverse backgrounds, different socio-economic groups, and many geographical regions, but in general they shared a culture. They brought with them from France customs, values, and manners. Although there were adaptations to the new environment, these often were adaptations that attempted to make the New World conform to the perceived comforts of the old, particularly in areas that concerned them the most—family ties, security of property and inheritance, religion, justice, and order.

Under the Superior Council and the Provincial Council, a legal framework was established to provide the inhabitants with all the benefits of law as in the home country. In France, various sets of laws or customs prevailed in different areas, but by ruling of the king, the law to be followed in the colony was *la Coutume de la Prévosté et Vicomté de Paris*, the customary law of the prevostship and viscounty of Paris, generally shortened to *la Coutume de Paris*. Additionally, French legislation passed after 1717 was applicable to the colony when it was registered with the Superior Council.[1]

With the laws came the orderly keeping of records. In the

Illinois country the meetings of the Provincial Council were recorded in the "Register of Deliberations and Judgments of the Provincial Council." The clerk, André Perillau, was supposed to send copies of this back to France by the first available ship. Unfortunately only a few scattered leaves of the register exist today; the loss obscures our understanding of the activities of the Provincial Council.

In addition to that record, the clerk was to keep other registers—the "Register of Lands Conceded" (concessions made to individuals by the government); the "Register of Responses to Requests from the Inhabitants" (the court's replies to cases filed with them); the "Register of Donations" (gifts given in formal legal documents in various situations), and the "Land Register" (a listing of all land transactions). The Register of Donations is still extant and is in the Illinois State Archives, Perrin Collection.[2] Fragments of the others are preserved at the Randolph County Courthouse.

Marriage Contracts

One of the most important aspects of law for the inhabitants was making the proper arrangements for the inheritance of property. Although there were written wills, for married couples this method mostly was superceded by the marriage contract; it was one of the main sources for the regulation of inheritance. Everyone in French Illinois except slaves would have had, or would have wanted to have, a marriage contract, because of its importance in the transmittal of property. Supposedly the contract had to be made before the marriage to be valid, as the agreement could not be changed after marriage. However, because of the lack of notaries or priests sufficiently grounded in legal matters, there were occasions in the colony when it was done long after the marriage and still was considered genuine.

The marriage contract regulated the inheritance of the partners in property real and personal, or as stated in the documents *immeubles et meubles*. Article 220 of the *Coutume de Paris* stated that: "Men and women joined together by marriage are common in immovable goods and in the assets acquired during the said marriage."[3] The community of goods of a marriage did not include the immovable property that either party had acquired before marriage. This ruling had an effect on the status of women in the Illinois, for it meant a house and/or land a woman held before marriage did not become her husband's but remained hers.

The marriage contract followed a standard format; the marriage contract for Louis Pilet and Marie Barbeau is an example. Although this contract was drawn up after the end of the French regime in 1767, it was selected because it concerned a Prairie du Rocher couple; it follows the model of earlier contracts.[4]

The initial clause of the contract listed the persons involved, their names, the names of their parents, their place of birth or residence, and the witnesses for each person.

> Before the notaries in the Illinois, residing in New Chartres, in the presence of the witnesses hereafter named, were present Louis Pillet *dit* La Sonde, bachelor, residing in the village of Prairie du Rocher, parish of Ste. Anne, son of Pierre Pillet *dit* La Sonde and of Marie Magdelaine Baron, his father and mother, residing at Kaskaskia, parish of Our Lady of the Immaculate Conception, Diocese of Quebec in Canada, attended by the said Sieur his father and by Monsieur Dechaufour Louvière, captain of the militia stipulating for him; and of Mademoiselle Marie Barbeau, daughter of the late Barbeau and of Catherine Allard, her father and mother, stipulating for her, the said Dame her mother and the Sieur Ayme Le Comte her stepfather, Jean Bte. Barbeau, her paternal uncle and Jean Pierre, her uncle.

Louis Pillet was born in the Illinois of a Canadian family who lived in Kaskaskia. The family also held land at Prairie du Rocher, and as Louis grew to be an adult, he became a resident there and farmed the land. Marie Barbeau's family had come from France to New Orleans, and then Illinois.

The next clause stated that the couple would marry in the Roman Catholic Church as required; the marriage contract came into force only upon the church marriage.

> Which parties and in the presence and with the consent of their

> relatives and friends, the said Louis Pillet *dit* La Sonde and Mademoiselle Marie Barbeau have promised and hereby promise to take each other in the name and laws of legitimate marriage and to have it celebrated before our mother, the holy Catholic, Apostolic and Roman church, as soon as it is possible and advised by the said relatives and friends, and when it shall be agreed and determined between them.

Marriage not only involved the couple, but their immediate family, more distant relatives, and friends. All of the persons involved here, the couple, family, and witnesses, were of the more well-to-do, prominent citizens of the villages. Marriage ties were part of the formation of the social web of the communities.

In the next section they indicated their choice of property law; specifying the *Coutume de Paris* was necessary because this would continue in force even if the couple moved back to France, where there were many *coutumes*.

> The said future spouses shall be one and common in all their property, real and personal, acquisitions and personal acquests, according to the most advantageous custom [*coutume*] for the said community, to which they submit and shall regulate all their interests, even if they were to transfer their residence to another country or there make acquisitions.

Under the law a husband was considered responsible for all his wife's debts and the wife for half of the husband's debts even if they were incurred before marriage, unless this responsibility was specifically renounced by the contract. So generally this was stated explicitly; then neither party was responsible for the preexisting debts of the other party. Those debts could not be paid from community property; the individual (man or woman) would have to pay them. The reasons for this are obvious, no surprises. One could not conceal a debt, marry, and then get the new partner to be responsible for it. Although this was a protection for both parties, it was more significant for the woman; it prevented an impecunious man from taking advantage of a woman with considerable property.

> They shall not be responsible for the debts created by either of
> them before the celebration of the future marriage. The debts shall be
> settled by and upon the property of the one who contracted them.

Although the woman's economic security was protected under the *Coutume de Paris*, married women had inferior legal status.
Despite this lesser status that in the Illinois was not particularly no-
ticeable, the contract gave the woman security. Each party in the marriage brought property (real, personal, or money) to the marriage and
it became community property to be administered by the husband.
But a husband could not alienate a wife's property without her permission, and he could not dispose of specifically designated items at
all. The arrangement gave a woman more protection and real status
than the laws in Britain at the time; there the man had full control of
his wife's property. In the Illinois, single women and widowed women
had legal and financial autonomy and could administer their own property.

The next clause in the contract dealt with the donation of
property. Donation of property between spouses was not permitted
after marriage; another security for the woman as it prevented the
husband from exerting undue pressure on his wife to acquire her property by gift. Any donations between the couple therefore were specified in the contract. Sometimes one of the persons might make a gift
of land, money, or other property to the other, but more commonly
the donation clause was in lieu of a will, and stated the rights of the
surviving spouse.

The clause generally was reciprocal, the survivor receiving
all of the community property. This was contingent upon no children
being born to the marriage, otherwise alternate regulations of the
Coutume took precedent.

> Because of the great friendship which the said future husband
> and wife feel for each other they make and have made by these pre-
> sents, a mutual and reciprocal donation to the survivor of them of the
> property, real and personal which shall be found on the day of the
> decease of the first to die, accepting the said donation forever irrevo-

cable, to be enjoyed by the survivor in complete ownership, provided there are no children born of the said marriage, in which case the said donation shall be wholly void.

If there were children, a division of the whole was made between the spouse and the children. If the man died the wife received half of the property and the children divided the other part.

As an example, Louis Vasseur *dit* Despagne's estate in Prairie du Rocher was divided into two lots. His heirs were his widow, Janette Renoux Leveille, and three sons, Louis, Ambroise, and Joseph. The widow received one-half and the other half was divided between the children. At the death of a Prairie du Rocher widower, François Bastien, his estate was divided into two lots—one for his son, Pierre, and the other for Jean Baptiste Morain, the widower of his daughter Marie Bastien and guardian of their children.

When a child received property in such an estate division, this property remained his and did not become part of the community of any new marriage of his mother. This inheritance was then held for him until his majority. Sometimes there were complaints from the wife that her second husband was not administering the child's inheritance properly. She could take her complaints to the court and receive changes to benefit the child. The surviving parent might manage the estate, even a woman. Jeanne Germain, widow of Ignace Legras, of Prairie du Rocher, requested and obtained permission from the judge to retain possession of her minor daughter's share of the property and to enjoy the revenue from it in exchange for caring for the girl. In this case the mother was keeping her own half of the property intact and using the receipts from the other half for maintaining the daughter; perhaps this was necessary to adequately support the family.[5]

The next clause in the marriage contract dealt with dower rights; the dower was given from the husband's property. In case the husband died first this allowed his widow to subsist after his death without deprivation. A stipulated dower, the *douaire préfix*, was given and in many cases also the *préciput*, the right of a spouse to specific amounts or objects in case of predecease.

> The said future husband has endowed and endows the future wife with the sum of one hundred pistoles in dower from the finest and best of the property of the said future husband at the choice of the said future wife, who shall not be obliged to request it at law.
>
> The survivor of the said future spouses shall take as préciput and before the division is made of the property of their community, the sum of five hundred livres in personal property of the said community, or the said sum in funds.

The stipulation here that the widow would not be required to request her dower at law, probably reflects the period in which this contract was written. The English law system was being brought into use at this time and the parties wanted to be sure that it would not be necessary to go through the English court in order for her to receive her dower.

Following this in the standard contract was the statement of the right to the renunciation of the community by the wife or children. If the estate had too many debts this could be done; it occurred occasionally. Catherine Alarie, widow of Jacques Outelas and wife of Raphael Beauvais at the time of her request, renounced her interest in the community property she had shared with Outelas "finding it more burdensome than profitable."[6] This renunciation did not, however, prevent the wife from recovering what she had brought to the marriage or the dower; these were guaranteed to her.

> In case of the decease of the future husband, the future wife may accept the community or renounce it, taking out of it unreservedly, that which had been brought to it, such as the douaire and préciput as mentioned above, those clothes, personal belongings, under linen, rings, jewels for her use, her beds and their furnishings, and generally everything which may have fallen to her either by donation or otherwise, without being held liable for the debts of the said community, even though she may have been so required and ordered.

Then the document was attested by the notary and witnesses. To be valid it had to be registered in the Register of Donations.

And in order to register these presents at the record office of this jurisdiction, they have constituted as their proxy, the bearer of these presents and do give the power to do this in their name. For thus has been agreed between the parties, promising, undertaking, renouncing. Done and executed at Prairie du Rocher in the house of the said Sieur Ayme Le Comte in the year one thousand seven hundred sixty-seven, on the second day of September in the presence of the Sieurs Joseph Decelle and Gerard Langlois, the requisite witnesses who have signed with us; the said future husband and wife, Jean Pierre, Dame Catherine Allard have declared they do not know how to sign.[7]

As can be seen, the marriage contract gave great protection to the woman. She was not left destitute upon her husband's death even if he had been improvident. She was entitled to what she brought to the marriage, her personal belongings and whatever dower had been agreed on. Her rights outweighed those of any other debtors to the estate.

The marriage contract promoted stability in families and the preservation from generation to generation of family property. Although the legal status of a woman was considered to be subordinate to the man, the marriage contract was a document of mutual consent between equals. But the equality was in the family, not the individuals; the family and its property were the significant unit. These were the cultural values of the community.

Because of the scarcity of women in the Illinois and arranged marriages, some brides were young, and marriage to an older man was acceptable. A young woman probably found marriage a satisfactory arrangement; it gave her a fair amount of freedom. Married women could act independently in business, and if she were widowed she had even more independence. A widow could accept or reject a marriage offer in view of what seemed most favorable for her and her children. Widows generally remarried though, accepting propertied males who had family connections.

The *Coutume* was not only used for marriage contracts, but was cited for decisions on other legal questions as well. In one case Marie Rose Texier felt that as the full sister of deceased Paul Texier, she should receive three-quarters of his estate rather than dividing it in two lots with their half brother, Marc Antoine Lalande. Judge de La Loere Flaucour decided against her, citing Article 340 of the *Coutume* in his decision.[8]

In 1725 Marie Rouensa Philippe dictated her will. She and Michel Philippe must not have written a marriage contract prior to their marriage or this would not have been necessary. Obviously it was assumed she had the right to dispose of her property herself. In the will she stipulated that the *Coutume* should be used so that her husband, Michel Philippe, would inherit one-half of her estate and all her children would inherit the other half of her property equally with one exception. This exception was that Michel, her second son by Michel Ako, was disinherited because of his bad conduct. Michel had married an Illinois Indian woman against Marie's wishes and apparently had "gone native."

Marie made a request to the Provincial Council for approval of this provision which was given. However her Christian training or her maternal feelings finally lead her to add a codicil reinstating Michel's inheritance.

I have pity for my son Michel Aco, who has chagrined me with his folly and his flight, and I no longer wish to deprive him absolutely and forever of his claim to my possessions. Should he return and repent, my wish is that he should have the right to his possessions.

She stipulated that his siblings would hold his portion in trust until such time as he should repent and leave the Indians. He actually did return later and received his inheritance.[9]

Litigation

The French court system did not include juries; the concept of a jury of peers did not exist in French legal practices.[10] For hearings on civil cases three persons were required, the judge and two suitable citizens; most frequently these were the other members of the council. In criminal cases five persons were involved and additional citizens were called in; generally these were military officers. The members of the court were the more important, better educated men who listened to the statements given and expressed their opinions on the case to the judge who gave the final decision based on their advice and his interpretation of the evidence.

No lawyers were allowed in the colony; lawyers were felt to generate too much unnecessary legal activity. "Experience has shown only too clearly how dangerous people of this sort are to the colonies..."[11] The non-contentious position of the French notary fulfilled many of the duties of lawyers. Although the present function of a notary public in verifying the authority of a document was handled by the notary, the latter's responsibilities were more far-reaching. He wrote out and verified multiple copies of work contracts, acknowledgments of debt, marriage contracts, land sales, dispositions, and other legal documents. In each transaction a copy of the document was given to the principal participants and the notary kept an official one in his office. The records of the notary constituted a body of legal documents similar to those found today in a county courthouse with the exception of vital statistics. The church maintained those. The notaries' copies, the lists of their acts, and the remaining pages from the registers are preserved in the Randolph County Courthouse; these constitute the Kaskaskia Manuscript Collection.

Not all the notaries in the Illinois were well trained in their profession. Some indeed were not actually notaries at all, but acted as such when no one else was available. Perillau, the clerk, does not appear to have been a notary but did numerous acts in his role as clerk. One of the Kaskaskia notaries, Leonard Billeron, was not well educated and his written French was spelled phonetically, creating an interesting problem for translators. The less skillful notaries could follow standard written models for various types of transactions. Several examples appear in the Kaskaskia records and in Louisiana archives.[12]

The colonists have been called a litigious people because of the quantity of legal documents preserved, but few of these were lawsuits or disputes. The management of estates, leases of property by guardians, inventories, and sales made up a large volume of the legal papers. Because of the importance of property in the society, the management of estate matters involved a lot of legal activity and often participation by the council and the judge. Some estates were quite complex; the inventory and estate details for Louis Dutisne and Thérèse Nepveu ran for eleven hand-written pages.[13]

Upon the death of a settler, the property was sealed by an official. An inventory of goods, lands, and possessions was taken; following this a division was made between the spouse and children. These matters were generally done by the royal attorney and approved by the judge. A guardian and deputy guardian were appointed for the children and the guardians' subsequent handling of the property—leases or sales—were reviewed and approved.

Guardians administered the children's property until they came of age, which was twenty-five years. At that time a male could request enfranchisement and be responsible for his own property. The property received by a female, whether from her father's estate or from marriage, was under guardianship until twenty-five also. Generally, by age twenty-five, women were married, so disposition of their property was handled through the marriage contract.

Other than estate documents there were legal agreements contracting for work of one type or another, property being sold, trade partnerships being formed, and other necessary legal matters. One study estimated that only thirty-six cases in the Kaskaskia Manuscripts dealt with actual disputes; fourteen of those were criminal cases.[14] A definite figure is difficult to obtain; some cases are indicated only by brief descriptive phrases on the notarial lists. Criminal cases were few, though, and generally these involved persons somewhat peripheral to the society—voyageurs and soldiers; desertions by soldiers were classed as criminal cases. More litigation undoubtedly existed than has been preserved, but what remains most likely reflects proportionally the original quantity and variety of actions.

The habitants were neither confrontational nor contentious; most often problems were reconciled by arbitration. They were accustomed to bureaucracy; all actions to be official had to be done by the notary and generally approved by the judge. Despite living in the wilderness of the New World, they kept the forms and careful legal practices they were accustomed to in France.

Some cases preserved were domestic problems such as adultery, illegitimate children, and separations; there was even a question of whether a man had beaten his wife to death. Her body was exhumed and examined and the conclusion was he had not, but probably there had been some previous incidents that caused suspicion.

Quarrels, fights, and insults gave rise to some complaints. Marie Maurice Medard claimed that:

> she has been insulted in an outrageous and prejudicial manner by one Blanche, wife of Antoine, drummer, and since the insult and likewise the calumny reflect and will reflect not only upon the petitioner, but also upon her children…she has recourse to the authority of justice in order that the said Blanche might have to prove the reproach…that is, that she had been beaten and branded by the executioner of criminal sentences.

Marie Medard does not appear on the ship lists so whether she came as a deportee is not known.

In another case Madame Richard indignantly said that she had been insulted by Sanschagrin, who accused her of "taking a walk in the prairie" with Dany, a euphemism for sexual dalliance.[15]

One civil case that involved the Provincial Council was the trial of Claude Chetivau for desertion. Chetivau had arrived in the New World in 1719, deported as a *faux saunier* (a contraband salt dealer). When he appeared in the Illinois, the Superior Council had sentenced him to ten years of work for the company at the mines or in the Fort de Chartres area. In 1725 Chetivau stated he was fifty-five years old. He hailed from Soissons originally and said his trade was as a cook (one might suspect this was not *cordon bleu* but the eighteenth-century equivalent of short-order). He was charged with planning to desert and trying to get an Indian to help him go to Canada. He claimed he had been told there were better opportunities for his trade as cook there.

Judge Chassin took depositions from several people and Chetivau was found guilty. The judgment was that he was not to leave the vicinity of Fort de Chartres or he would suffer six weeks' imprisonment. Perhaps he was to be more closely supervised; also his goods were seized, that left him without resources to obtain an Indian guide.[16] Chetivau was the only one of the convicts shipped from France who reappeared in the court as a wrongdoer in the Illinois. For most of them, the new start in the New World was successful.

Cases that no doubt caused much gossip were paternity cases. In one, Guillaume Liberge was fined 300 *livres* to be donated to the church, and he was directed to rear and care for the child born to Perrine Pivert. He also was ordered to pay 3000 *livres* in damages. The amount may have been this large because Perrine's husband La Renaudrière was an important personage, the director of the mines.

In another case, Jacque Bernard *dit* St. Jacques came before the judge to request that Pierre Hullin claim and support the child born to Bernard's wife conceived during Bernard's absence on a voyage. Voyages might last four to six months, and Mme. Bernard may have been lonely. The amount of damages is not given in the document preserved.[17]

In the above cases no action was taken against the wife although the *Coutume* allowed for the erring wife to be put in a convent for two years, perhaps for enforced celibacy. The children that resulted may have been why nothing was done, as children were important for the growth of the colony. It was different in another case where a child was not involved. Sieur Faffard *dit* Boisjoly complained that his wife Marguerite Anskekae (obviously Indian) had left and committed adultery. Witnesses were called; the judge agreed she was guilty and Marguerite was convicted (in absentia apparently). However, sentences in the Illinois were less easily carried out than in France, particularly with an Indian wife who was not restricted by temperament and knowledge to the villages. The judge ruled that she should be punished if:

> Faffard is able to have her taken into custody, to be shut away wherever the said Sieur shall find appropriate and to remain there for the period of two years, during which time the Sieur Faffard may take her back if he pleases.

There is no indication in the records that she ever returned.[18]

Although these cases show interesting facets of early Illinois life, their scarcity also reflects a society that kept most problems within families and resolved conflicts internally, rather than through official avenues.

Some cases were referred to the Superior Council; in this event the persons were accompanied by soldiers and with all the documents involved in the case, were sent down to New Orleans.

One such case occurred with André Perico. Perico had been a free black in New Orleans when he committed a crime and was sentenced as a convict to serve the company. In June of 1725 Perico was assigned to Antoine Ple *dit* La Plume, master pit sawyer, to work for three years; the company would receive in exchange a third of the wood he cut. But Perico again committed a crime. In August he broke into the king's storehouse and stole goods; he intended to desert to the Indians with his goods.

Perico was sentenced to be hanged on a gallows to be constructed in the parade ground at Fort de Chartres. At this point the records become confusing. At nine A.M. on the thirty-first of August in the prison at Fort de Chartres, Perico said he would appeal to the Superior Council. At two P.M. the court met again and stated they had decided to proceed with the execution

> since it is absolutely necessary to make an example of him in order to intimidate those who might count on a lengthy delay in punishment for misdeeds.

This has a very modern sound of complaint to it; appeals delayed punishment. Indeed, it seems the appeal worked since in 1730 Perico surfaced in New Orleans again being charged with theft from the storehouse.[19] The fact that he was black did not enter into any part of the case. As a free black he had all the rights of any French citizen until he broke the law; then he was subject to the same rules and penalties as all others.

A similar chain of events of appeal to the Superior Council occurred in the crime of Jean Ducoutray *dit* Poulailler, a soldier, twenty-eight years old in 1752. While he was supposed to be on sentry duty, he broke into a henhouse and stole eight chickens. He took the chickens back to the barracks and put them in the common pot to share with the other soldiers. This gesture was generous but indicated a certain lack of intelligence on Ducoutray's part. When confronted with his crime he admitted he had sufficient food, but stealing was his weakness. He had been convicted of theft before and "V" (for *voleur*, thief) was branded on his shoulder already.

Proceedings were instituted by the military first, and a court martial was held. Then he was turned over to the civil authorities for trial and punishment in accordance with the provisions of criminal law. Joesph Buchet, with the resounding titles of Chief Clerk of the Marine, Subdelegate of the Commissioner General of the Marine, Ordainer at Louisiana, and Judge in the Illinois, found him guilty and since it was his second offense he was sentenced to be a galley slave for life.

Ducoutray appealed to the Superior Council as was his right; all the papers and he were shipped down to New Orleans in the care of Ensign Alexandre Duclos of Prairie du Rocher. The final judgment of the Superior Council was that he be branded on the left shoulder with a *fleur-de-lis*, flogged in the city streets, and be a galley slave for life.[20] Was he shipped back to France or was he used in boats in Louisiana? It may have been a sentence that was not carried out. It was stated that in Canada "It is certain that the penalty of the galleys scarcely makes an impression..."[21]

Only two violent deaths were recorded in detail in the records, a duel and a manslaughter case. While D'Artaguiette was visiting Fort de Chartres in 1723 he reported that one afternoon in April Perillau ran Morin, a drummer, through with his sword for having spoken impertinently to him. Morin was mortally wounded in this duel and died a few minutes after being struck. This is the only duel known to have been fought in the Illinois until the American period, and then the combatants were American.

Perillau was arrested and put in chains. Although no court records remain, apparently a trial was held at which D'Artaguiette and other witnesses testified; the decision was the death sentence.

Hearing about this, the chiefs of the Kaskaskia Indians came to the fort with a band of thirty men, an impressive force, to ask for Perillau's pardon. The chief Kiraoueria was definitely against capital punishment and he asked,

> Would you, my father, M. de Boisbriant, and you my fathers, MM Diron, De La Loere, Dartaguiette, and de L'isle, spill the blood of a Frenchman to blot out the blood of another and would you add to the loss of one man the loss of another?

Because of the villages' dependence on the Illinois Indians, the commandant, Boisbriant, was in an awkward position. He was supposed to obey the French laws but he did not want to alienate the Indians. He tried to equivocate:

> We are touched by the services you have rendered and wish to render to the French…but, for fear that other Frenchmen might commit similar crimes [*follies*], we feel that the warehouse-keeper must still remain in chains.

Finally, Boisbriant said that he would send all the information on the case, including the words of the Indians, to the commissioners in France. Having passed the buck, he was able to maintain the appearance of justice and to satisfy those upon whose goodwill and support the small colony depended, telling the Indians:

> Rest assured, that no other nation but you would have obtained what has been granted to you. You see by that how much I esteem and love you. I listen to your words because you listen to mine.

It is not clear whether Perillau remained in the Illinois or was sent back to France, but in March the following year he requested that his papers of remission obtained from the chancellor in France be accepted. Apparently the French government realized, too, the importance of keeping the goodwill of the Illinois Indians. Perillau's pardon was accepted and he continued to act as clerk of the court in the mid-1720s.[22]

In the other case a group of voyageurs—Richard, the settler, Richard *dit* le Parisien, Pierre Blot, and Guillaume Liberge—were having a convivial drinking evening at Henri Catin's house when tempers flared, insults were given, and a fight broke out. At some point one or both of the Richards picked up an axe and an ash shovel and struck Catin several times, mortally wounding him.

Catin lingered on for a few days while accusations went back and forth about which Richard did it; then Catin died of his wounds. The witness, Blot, was not clear on who had done what; he likely was in his cups. On the recommendation of the king's attorney, Buchet, Judge de La Loere Flaucour fined both Richards to pay 100 *sous* to the church.[23]

Very few other violent deaths occurred during the French regime, other than deaths due to Indian attack. With the exception of Perillau's duel, all criminal cases known involved soldiers or voyageurs, the more marginal persons in the society.[24] The French habitants were not an aggressive people. They were solid peasants whose litigable actions were centered on property and the family. These cases show the attitudes and values of the society in which the village of Prairie du Rocher, and the other villages participated.

The Black Code

Another set of laws that was part of the legal package for the colony was *le Code Noir*, the Black Code. It defined the rights of the slaves and the duties of their owners. The code gave the slaves a degree of legal status. Under its directives the slaves were to be fed and clothed properly, families could not be sold apart until the children were of age, and slaves could not be condemned to death or prison without action of the courts. Slaves were to be instructed in the Catholic faith, baptized and married in the church, and elderly or sick slaves were to be cared for. A slave was able theoretically to have his owner brought before the court for breach of the code.[25]

The French habitants felt no need to justify slavery; slavery was something that existed in the culture and was accepted by all.

Indian slaves were owned not only by the French but by the Illinois Indians as well. The scarcity of black slaves in the Illinois and their importance to the economic activities meant that they were valuable and their treatment reflected this. The price of a healthy slave was equivalent to the amount for purchase of a house and lot. This economic significance and the Black Code gave the Illinois slaves a secure place in the community and a certain degree of social standing. Although punishment by various brutal methods (cutting ears off, hamstringing, branding, and death) was allowed by the code for various misdeeds; economic considerations, if not humane attitudes, prevented such actions in the Illinois country.

A slave, Jean Baxe, struck and bit one of Bienvenu's overseers, François Bastien, in his efforts to avoid being beaten by Bastien. Under the code, Baxe merited death; here again one of the Indians intervened; Manatousensas, one of the Kaskaskia chiefs, pleaded for his life. Baxe was sentenced to be whipped three times and to bow down before Bastien when he met him in public. The second part of the sentence is surprising as Briggs points out, "...the purpose of a public apology was to humiliate the culprit. How do you "humiliate" a slave? Jean Baxe must have had enough status to have some to lose." The punishment was similar to a public apology required from a Frenchman who had been found guilty of slander.

The value of slaves is further pointed up in a case in which a Frenchman broke a black's arm claiming the slave had insulted him. The Frenchman, La Croix, was required to furnish a man to take the place of the slave while he could not work, and to pay for all the medical and surgeon's costs. This of course was because the slave was valuable property and the loss of his services affected the prosperity of his owner, but in many places the slave would have merited severe punishment for his verbal abuse. These cases indicate that the slaves in the Illinois did indeed have status, that is, they were not just chattel.[26]

The inhabitants generally took seriously the admonition that their slaves should be baptized and married in the church. The church records contained many references to this; for example in 1746 on the eighteenth of June, Fr. Gagnon baptized a child born the same day of the lawful marriage of Giles Senegal Negro, a slave belonging to Mr. Marin, and of Marie Thérèse, his father and mother. He was given the name of Charles Marie. The godfather was Charles Benoist, son of the Surgeon-Major of the troops at Montreal, and the godmother Françoise Millet, wife of Gabriel Dodier, blacksmith, residing in this parish.

In the same year two blacks belonging to Ignace Hebert, *syndic* of the village of Chartres, were baptized on the fifth of June and named Jean François and Marianne. Then they were married by Fr. Gagnon who

received the mutual consent to marriage of Jean François Banbara, Negro slave belonging to Sieur Hebert, and Marianne, Negress, also belonging to Sieur Hebert, with the ceremonies prescribed by our Mother the Holy Church...[27]

For the French population the marriage records gave the names and frequently the place of residence of the parents of the nuptial couple. In the case of black couples, the earliest marriage records generally did not list the parents' names, not because of their status but because the parents back in Africa were not Christian; only Catholic marriages were recognized by the church. The records though sometimes provided information on the original home of the slaves—the Barbary Coast, Manega, Senegal, and, for the majority, Guinea.

The notarial records provide minimal data for the blacks. In general even the free blacks did not draw up marriage contracts and wills, nor were inventories taken of community property upon the death of a spouse.

Emancipation occurred occasionally, increasing the small number of free blacks in the community. The majority of the manumissions were to occur upon the death of the current elderly owner; thus these slaves could not be sold as part of the estate. Antoine Ple *dit* La Plume of Prairie du Rocher promised to free Joseph and Marie upon his death, and Jean Brunet and his wife, Elisabeth, sought confirmation from the commandant of their wish to emancipate

Catherine and her son, Jean, after their deaths.[28]

Family studies were done for some of the black families. The starting point for most is 1770; apparently at this time the priest of St. Joseph's church urged the local people to obey the *Code Noir* and to have their slaves baptized and married in the church. The two major slave-holding families in Prairie du Rocher were the Louvières and the Barbeaus; each family had about twenty slaves. Of the marriages listed in 1770, four couples belonged to the Louvières, and another four to the Barbeaus. Almost all of the individuals are noted as being from Guinea; the males ranged in age from twenty-three to thirty-two. The women, where ages were given, were mostly in their early teens, a marriage pattern typical of the French community also.

One of the Louvière's slaves can be identified from even earlier records. In 1737 the estate of the deceased Jacque Bougnolle and Catherine Bechet was divided. Their daughter Jeanne Bougnolle was given as part of her inheritance a *negre piece d'inde*[29] called Leveille, who was twenty years old. Jeanne Bougnolle married Michel d'Amour de Louvière.

In 1770 the death of a two-year-old girl, Elizabeth, the daughter of Leveille and Pompon, was recorded in the church register. Pompon was listed as a heathen. Leveille apparently had been inherited by Jeanne and Michel Louvière's son, Pierre, since the couple were then the property of the widow of Pierre Louvière. Also written in the register in 1770 was the marriage of Leveille to Thérèse, who was baptized prior to their marriage. Leveille, who was born in Guinea, is now designated as Philippe Leveille. It is not clear if Thérèse is the same as Pompon, but it seems likely.

After the death of Madame Pierre Louvière the couple was given to her son, Antoine. Antoine's first wife died in 1775, at which time an inventory of community property was taken; in this, Leveille and a daughter, Catherine, three years old, appear. Thérèse is not listed; apparently she had died. Unfortunately, this is as far as the family of Leveille can be traced.[30] Some other family histories will be related later.

Supposedly, slaves were not able to carry on business or to engage in trade for themselves, but in the Illinois they apparently did.

In a list of Henri Carpentier's estate debts was the amount of seventeen *livres* of tobacco, owed to his black slave. Either the slave was trading on his own or Carpentier was paying wages to his slave. A later record mentions:

> ...the labour which Masters allows their slaves, according to ancient custom on Sundays and stated hours of other days for their own private profit.[31]

Carpentier's slave probably had taken advantage of this opportunity for private trade. The accumulation of resources could have allowed slaves to purchase their freedom. Although the eighteenth century records do not contain this type of emancipation, purchasing freedom did occur in the early nineteenth century. The possibility of doing this may have existed earlier as well.

Care was given to ill or aged persons, including the slaves, since they were viewed in the communities as part of the familial structure. An epileptic slave is mentioned, as is an elderly slave, who had been freed at the death of his master, and who then received care at another person's home until his own death. Another slave, Pierre Conairy, was said to have been ninety-eight years old at his death; he obviously would not have been in his productive years.[32]

Overall, the treatment of the black slaves was not harsh; they were well cared for. The black slaves worked in the fields, in the homes, and in the pirogues, and so did the French. Family units were not separated. Since married couples and underage children were kept together, even when an owner died and his assets were divided, the whole family of slaves would shift as a unit from one portion of the French family to another. Dissatisfied slaves sometimes deserted to the Indians, who were favorable towards them. If the slaves wanted to leave, there was no real way to keep them down on the farm; they were not chained or confined, and if brought back from the Indians could have left again. Since remaining in the villages was not because of coercive methods, it can be assumed that most were reasonably content with their lot, or at least felt a greater uncertainty about life with the Indians and preferred the relative safety and comfort of the villages.

Local Government

The main local governing activity for the *habitants* was the assembly held after high mass outside the church door. All adult males could participate in these, and widows may have had a voice in certain matters. A *syndic*, or civil agent, for the parish was elected there; he was the representative for civil matters. The *syndic* presided when the assembly debated upon matters of a civil nature; the priest when religious questions were considered. The *syndic* was an office brought from France, where he would have represented the village in lawsuits, but in the Illinois there was little need for this function of the position. Very little information about his duties in the Illinois exist. In Kaskaskia, where Antoine Bienvenu was elected *syndic*, one of his stated responsibilities was to review the condition of the commons fence; this aspect of the office continued for many years. Bienvenu took an oath "to well and faithfully administer his office for the profit and the interests of the parish." At Chartres-Prairie du Rocher, around the same time, Jean Baptiste Lalande was the *syndic*.

The assemblies also acted to select the militia captain and lieutenant. Each village had a militia unit; the initial ones were established by D'Artaguiette on his visit in 1723. Prominent citizens were elected as officers, but all able-bodied males served in the militia. Danger from Indian attacks was ever present. The militia was not limited to a defensive role, they also accompanied the regular troops and the Illinois Indian auxiliaries on campaigns against other Indians or against the British.

The popular impression of the differences between the French and the British colonies is that the French rule was autocratic and hierarchical and in New England there was complete democracy. In both cases the view is erroneous. French government in France was extremely hierarchical and autocratic; some of this spilled over into the administrative centers of New Orleans, Montreal, and Quebec, but Illinois only participated peripherally in those centers.

The French actually had about as much experience in managing their civil affairs as did the New England colonists. All adult men (twenty-five and over) seem to have been able to participate, and free blacks and widows may have, too. The franchise may have been less restrictive in the Illinois than in New England.

The villagers decided most actions in their civil life. Decisions were made by a majority of the voting citizens, *pluralité de voix*. In the assemblies, besides electing the *syndic* and militia officers, they agreed on the dates for the opening and closing of the commonfield. Official action on these dates by the commandant might be needed because of recalcitrant citizens; dates even had to be modified because of lack of cooperation. Physical coercion of dilatory persons did not occur, although threats of fines were made and probably enforced. Peer pressure brought about final action. For the commonfield system to succeed, all had to participate (this is discussed further in Chapter 3).[33]

The villagers reflected their cultural attitudes towards government; they were not used to operating in a democratic, representative fashion beyond the local level. The French Revolution was still a long way off and the existence of the king and his rule was an accepted and assumed fact of life. The commandant was a representative of the king and as such he was respected and his ordinances obeyed—most of the time. The voyageurs, ex-voyageurs, and ex-*coureurs de bois* now settled in the agricultural settlements, were quite independent and fairly skilled at avoiding undesirable governmental interference in their lives. They obeyed the rules and regulations in the villages, at least as a necessity for a smoothly operating community. Nonetheless, the settlers who were adventurous enough to emigrate to the New World maintained an attitude of independence and self-determination. This attitude extended to the women as well. This independence was tempered by the need to cooperate in many ways, the agricultural system, trade networks, and in maintaining the safety of the communities.

The Fox Wars

The constant participation of the civilian militia was needed as the garrison at the fort was always understrength. The local Illinois Indians were faithful, but groups associated with them, the Miami and Piankasaw for example, tended to favor the British. Other tribes, particularly the Fox and Sioux, raided into the area frequently, causing difficulties in the trade activities. To the south on the Mississippi River, the Chickasaw and the Natchez endangered the convoys that moved to and from New Orleans, but these were mainly protected by the regular troops.

Major strife existed with the Fox Indians from the early 1700s to 1730. The Fox made almost continual attacks on the French and Illinois Indian villages. In 1716 a major expedition was mounted by the Canadian government against the Fox, who were defeated. However,

> M. De Louvigny...who was ready to blow them up but accepted the peace, a present of 30 packages of skins and fifteen slaves which made them to understand the advantage there was in making war since one pays in beaver skins for the blood one has shed when one is not strong enough.[34]

These terms were so easy that the Fox interpreted this as weakness; the defeat had little lasting effect.

In October 1722 word came to Fort de Chartres that the Fox had attacked the Illinois Indians in northern Illinois and were besieging them. The commandant, Boisbriant, and 100 men departed in boats and pirogues to go to their rescue. Boisbriant ordered Bourdon, the militia captain of Kaskaskia, to take forty Frenchmen and some Illinois Indians, and to proceed by land to Pimetoui. Shortly after that a messenger arrived with the information that the Fox had withdrawn, so Boisbriant's troops returned. Bourdon and his group came back in a few days, but D'Artaguiette commented sourly that they were

> in pitiable condition, having suffered severely from hunger on account of the bad leadership of Bourdon who is not fit for this sort of employment and is more skillful at goading oxen than in leading a troop of warriors.

Bourdon was not the ignorant worker as implied by the disgusted D'Artaguiette; he was well-to-do and literate. He married an Indian woman who also brought wealth to the marriage and good connections to Indian groups for trade. Militia captains were elected for other qualities than military prowess; they belonged to the higher socio-economic group, and so were considered worthy for leadership.

In June 1723, while D'Artaguiette was still at the fort, a canoe was seen drifting in the middle of the river. In it was a soldier who had been killed and scalped by Indians. The canoe also held a vest of Louis St. Ange, with letters in the pocket warning the fort that the Fox were coming to attack Cahokia. Receiving this message, the commandant immediately put the troops under arms and they cut brush around Fort de Chartres to eliminate hiding places. Apparently the fort was treated more as an administrative center than a military base, and protective measures were taken only when needed. All feared that St. Ange also was dead, but he arrived soon afterwards.[36]

In the following year, commandant Boisbriant wrote:

> The Fox lie in wait around our French and Indian settlements every summer, or rather, almost all year long. This means that the habitants do not dare venture out except in groups...

In 1725 Joseph Danis, a church warden at Kaskaskia, was killed only "two steps" from the village.[37]

The Canadian government did conclude a peace between the Fox and some of the tribes with whom they had been warring in 1724, but despite attempts to incorporate the Illinois in the treaty, it did not include them. The Fox claimed that the Illinois Indians still held Fox slaves. Dutisne, then the commandant at Fort de Chartres, heard of this peace agreement in January 1725, and complained that the Fox continued to kill the French in the Illinois country. He accused the traders from Canada of involvement, feeling that commercial competition influenced them. Some Canadian traders were not too sorry to have the Illinois voyaguers attacked by the Fox, because Illinois was drawing off furs from the trade of New France. "If the ruin of this colony is desired, that is the way to succeed," he wrote to Governor de Vaudreuil in Quebec.[38]

In 1725 Fr. Nicolas Ignace Beaubois, Superior General of Missions for the Company of the Indies in Louisiana, took five Indian chiefs to France. Fr. Beaubois sought to obtain aid from the French government to protect the Illinois country and to defeat the Fox. He used the Indians in pleading his cause. It may have been in response to this visit that the French government determined finally to eradicate the Fox. A government expedition from Canada in 1728 led by Marchand de Lignery burned Fox villages and their crops, but failed to capture many warriors. Deliette, then commandant at Fort de Chartres, led a group of soldiers and militia to join this war. The Fort de Chartres contingent went as far as Chicago, where they defeated a band of Fox and Kickapoo, and then returned home.

In 1730 many of the Fox, feeling the continuing pressure of French threats, decided to move east to join the Iroquois Indians. The Fox halted southeast of Starved Rock and hastily built a fort. Lieutenant Robert Groston de St. Ange came from Fort de Chartres with a force said to number 500 men and an additional 200 Indians; other reinforcements also arrived. From St. Ange's arrival on August 17 to the night of September 8, the Fox were besieged in their fort. On the night of the eighth under the cover of a severe thunderstorm, they slipped out and attempted to escape. Followed by the French forces and their Indian allies they were located and almost all the Fox were killed or captured. Thus ended the major threat of the Fox wars.[39]

The extermination of the Fox, though, had repercussions with other Indians, many of whom were sympathetic to the Fox and disturbed at their harsh treatment. They feared that the French would turn on other tribes and eliminate them as well. Although in popular opinion the French always had good relations with and were sympathetic to the Indians, this was not the actuality. The extermination of the Fox and the revolt of the Natchez in 1729 bring this out clearly. The Natchez on the lower Mississippi River, both liked the French because of their trade goods, and disliked them because of their settlement and fort by the Indian village. The nearby British traders encouraged this hostility. The highhanded manner of the commandant in 1729, Sieur de Chopart, who wanted to acquire more land in the village, brought matters to a head. In November 1729 the Natchez revolted and killed nearly the entire civilian and military French population there. Retaliation was swift by the French. The remnants of the Natchez fled to the Chickasaw, who were already antagonistic to the French, and they continued to harass convoys on the Mississippi.[40]

Fort de Chartres

The Indian wars that produced such problems for the Illinois inhabitants were the real reason that Fort de Chartres was maintained by the French government. Initially it was the threat from the Fox, who were endangering the trade, and then the Natchez war that lead to the continuation of the garrison. Maintenance of the fort and supplying it with soldiers was a major cost for the French government. Despite the apparent success of the Illinois colony and its role in providing provisions for the lower Mississippi valley, back at the French court Illinois often seemed an expense that it would be best to eliminate.

The fort, built in 1719, served as the military post and administrative center for civil government. This fortification was built by Boisbriant on the Mississippi, about sixteen miles upstream from Kaskaskia. The only contemporary description of this first Fort de Chartres was that of the Inspector General D'Artaguiette, who in 1723 stated that it was "a fort of piles the size of one's leg, square in shape, having two bastions, which command all of the curtains." No dimensions were given. D'Artaguiette mentions two companies of infantry at the garrison. The chapel, he commented in his journal, was outside the fort as was the house occupied by the Jesuit priest, Fr. Kereben, who served as chaplain for the troops. The census in 1726 lists one fort and four houses as property of the Company of the Indies; the houses may or may not all have been within the fort.

The site of this fort was located by Terry Norris on a 1928 U.S. Army Corps of Engineers aerial photograph, and archaeological testing verified the location. The archaeological tests revealed that the first fort was a square *arpent*—a lineal *arpent* was about 192 feet.

The curtain wall was a single row of posts; on the basis of the depth of the post holes the wall would have been twelve to sixteen feet high. Structural remains were located on the interior but it was not possible to determine their size or former use in the brief archaeological program.[41]

The first fort was not in use for long; a replacement was begun in 1725. In March of that year soldiers from the garrison were hired to dig trenches three feet deep for a new palisade. The new curtain wall was apparently a double wall of posts. Surprisingly enough the second fort was smaller than first, twenty-five *toises* on a side, rather than one *arpent* (thirty *toises*). The fort now had four bastions whose size is not given, but each contained a building ten by ten feet.[42]

In November 1725, Chassin, for the Company of the Indies, contracted with Jean Pradel to furnish "as soon as possible" forty pieces of squared lumber ten feet long, twelve rafters, and joists of the same length for the construction of a powder magazine. So construction was going on eight months later and continued for some time.[43]

The Company of the Indies did not keep possession of this second fort for very many years; in 1732 they returned the Louisiana colony to the king's jurisdiction. An inventory of the contents of the storeroom there shows the stock— uniforms were kept there, as well as articles for non-military purchasers, such as brass and iron kettles, hinges, locks, nails, shingles, saws, axes, and knives. The inhabitants of the Fort de Chartres village and Prairie du Rocher would have acquired manufactured items here. Outside the fort was the chapel, thirty by twenty feet, roofed with straw. Within were an altar, a tabernacle, a step, and a small armoire, in which the vestments were kept. There was also a bell.[44]

The location of this second fort has yet to be determined. Various documents suggest that it was near the site of the first but closer to the river. If that is correct, it is likely to have been wiped out by later channel changes of the Mississippi River.

The official personnel, too, changed over time. Boisbriant was commandant until the latter half of 1724, when he left for New

Orleans. Charles Claude Dutisne became commandant for a few months, but in mid-1725 he was transferred to the Natchez post. Pierre DeLiette was appointed, but until he could arrive Jean Pradel became acting commandant.

The other commandants had kept things running smoothly, but Pradel ran into problems. He nearly caused a riot when he arrested Antoine Ple *dit* La Plume of Prairie du Rocher. The details of the case are not known. Some problem with lumber perhaps. La Plume had a contract with Dutisne to supply lumber but Pradel received the contract for the powder magazine. Whatever it was, La Plume was popular and Pradel was not.[45]

Deliette was commandant until his death in 1729, when Dutisne returned as interim until Robert Groston de St. Ange was made commandant. St. Ange remained in that position until 1733.

For most of the French regime the area was fortunate in its commandants and judges. The commandants showed great skill in dealing with the Indians, a talent always necessary for security. Maintaining the friendship of tribes was difficult; supplies of gifts and trade goods failed to arrive regularly from France. The judges, Chassin and Flaucour for this early period and Buchet for much of the remaining time, seem to have been conscientious about their job. The authority of the commandant and the judge was used wisely and the system suited the colonists well.

In the eyes of the inhabitants the judicial system was equitable and adequate. The officials in the Illinois were on the whole competent and honest; the commandant and the other officials appeared to work together without strife. This was not the case in New Orleans, where accusations always were flying around and governmental office holders disagreed. Illinois was fortunate in its personnel and the inhabitants saw the smoothness of the system as the proper way to run a French colony, and possibly came to see this as their right and due. In general they seemed to feel that the justice system and the government served their interests. Indeed it probably benefitted and favored the ordinary citizens more than did the government back in France.

Notes

1. Arnold 1985,12.
2. Dean and Brown 1981 and *see* M. Brown 1980.
3. Baker *et al.* 1983, 10.
4. Dean and Brown 1981, 67:9:2:1, trans.by Lawrie Dean.
5. Dean and Brown 1981, 83:7:23:2; 63:6:19:1; 40:1:22:1.
6. Dean and Brown 1981, 37:10:8:2.
7. Baker *et al.* 1983; Baade 1979.
8. Dean and Brown 1981, 44:1:29:1.
9. Dean and Brown 1981, 25:6:13:1; Ekberg nd.
10. Palm 1931, 49; Charlevoix 1966.
11. Alvord 1965, 195 citing a letter Minister to Bienville ANC B, 57:797.
12. Baade 1979, 12; Dean and Brown 1981, 38:1:1:1; 38:1:12:1; 50:2:8:2.
13. Dean and Brown 1981, 40:1:17:1.
14. Alvord 1965, 195; Briggs 1985, 184.
15. Brown and Dean 1977, K378; Dean and Brown 1981, 40:8:1:1; 48:2:29:1.
16. Dean and Brown 1981, 25:3:1:1.
17. Dean and Brown 1981, 26:5:23:1; 25:12:1:1.
18. Baker *et al.* 1983, 12; Brown and Dean 1977, K349.
19. Dean and Brown 1981, 25:8:27:1; La. St. Mus. Ar. 30/132A July 1730.
20. Pease 1940, 700; La. St. Mus. Ar. 52-110 1752, July.
21. Peyser 1992, 90.
22. Mereness 1916, 75; Dean and Brown 1981, 24:3:15:1; ANC B43:378: Schlarman 1929, 226, 229, 231.
23. Dean and Brown 1981, 38:12:20:1.
24. Dean and Brown, 1981, 31:6:21:1; Pease and Jenison 1940, 410; 878; Ekberg 1998, 259.
25. Eccles 1972, 152; Balesi 1992, 248.
26. Dean and Brown 1981, 30:12:20:1; 48:3:3:1; Briggs nd, 27; 38:8:20:1.
27. Brown and Dean 1977, D121; D122; D123.
28. Dean and Brown 1981, 30:-:-:1; 46:10:8:1.
29. "standard value of a complete negro, that is seventeen years or over without bodily defects, or a negress without bodily defects, of fifteen to thirty years, or three children of eight to ten years in

age." (Belting 1975, 38).

30. Dean and Brown 1981, 37:1:17:1; 75:-:-:1.
31. Dean and Brown 1981, 57:3:22:1; Alvord 1909, 575, "Inhabitants accuse Fr. Valinière," Sept. 21, 1787.
32. Dean and Brown 1981, 25:2:9:1; St. Joseph Ch. Rec. 7/3/1793.
33. For an excellent discussion of this *see* Ekberg, 1998.
34. Rowland and Sanders 3, 405.
35. Balesi 1992, 158.
36. Mereness 1916, 32, 78.
37. Jelks *et al.* 1989, 10; Kas. Church Rec., May 16, 1725.
38. Thwaites 1902, 451.
39. A controversy has existed for years about the location of this fort. Recently additional evidence has resolved the problem. *See* Peyser 1980; Peyser 1992; Edmunds and Peyser 1993.
40. Balesi 1991,179 ff.
41. Mereness 1916, 69; ANC G1A1 464 1/1/1726; Jelks *et al.* 1989.
42. Dean and Brown 1981, 25:3:12:2.
43. Brown and Dean 1977, K391.
44. ANC C13B 15 June 1732.
45. Rowland and Saunders 2, 498-9.

3

Land, Life, and Labor

T he bottomlands of Illinois held vast fertile acres, or *arpents* as the French inhabitants visualized them. These alluvial lands of the Middle Mississippi River Valley in Illinois, in later years called the American Bottom, extend between the present cities of Cahokia in the north and Chester in the south. The width of the valley varies, but for much of its area it is about four miles wide. High limestone cliffs separate the bottoms from the uplands. In the eighteenth century lowland prairies covered the drier portions of the land—tall grass prairies with groves of trees and shrubs. The lowland meadows yielded to the primitive plows and the land produced abundantly. Trees grew tall in the well watered land—walnut, poplar, various kinds of oaks, pecans, mulberry, hickory, and others—and they were available for lumber to construct houses, barns, fences and furniture. Marshes, shallow lakes, and old oxbows of the river called coulees, held water seasonally or year-round, providing extensive feeding grounds for the waterfowl that migrated through the Mississippi Flyway.

    The Illinois country provided the settlers with a fairly high standard of living for the eighteenth century. The richness of the natural resources and the suitability of the climate for agriculture made for

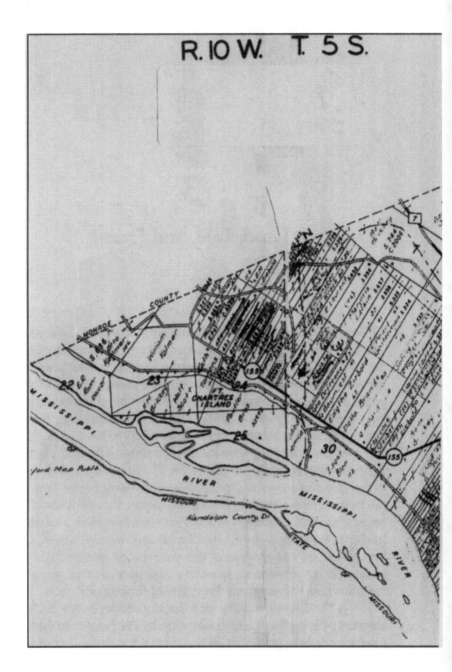

Land map produced by the efforts of the Land Commissioners to settle

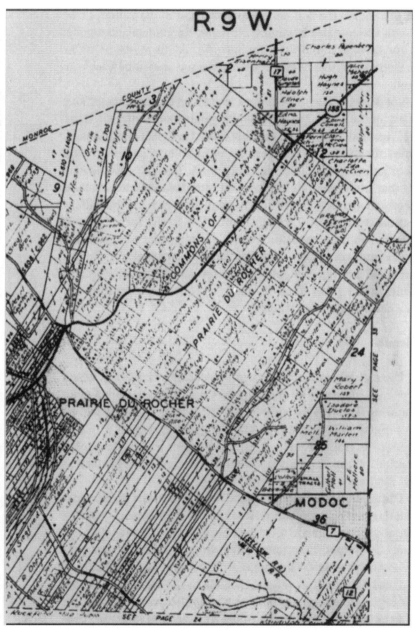

Archives, Randolph County Circuit Court

land claims in the Fort de Chartres-Prairie du Rocher area.

an easier life than in the hot, humid southern part of the colony, or in Canada with its long, harsh winters. Illinois was not dependent upon imports for survival, famine was not a worry, and the diversity of the diet was better than that available to the average person in France at the period.

Not all was Eden. Mosquitoes also loved the marshlands and it took hard physical labor to break up the prairie and to prepare it for farming. Trees had to be felled, the logs shaped and made into houses, clay hauled for plastering between the upright logs, and enormous amounts of prairie grass cut for thatching roofs. But one great advantage was that it all was free. Before the introduced domestic stock reproduced and increased in sufficient numbers to provide food, there was plentiful wild game. Through instruction by the local Indians, native plants could be used for food. Coin might be scarce, but a barter economy was viable—clearing land in exchange for cutting boards, making a pirogue of cottonwood for land, or paying for land with bacon, brandy, and flour. In many ways it was a paradise for land-poor immigrants and laborers.

Land Grants

The early Canadian settlers in Kaskaskia took up land wherever they liked, cleared it for farming, and built homes within fenced lots. Acquiring land by appropriation in this fashion was satisfactory until the official government moved in; then those claims needed to be recognized as grants from the king. Land grants became an important function of the Provincial Council and land was granted at Chartres, Prairie du Rocher, and St. Philippe.

The grants in the Illinois were different from many in Canada. In Canada large blocks of land were given by the company holding the monopoly to individuals, who then became the seigneur (lord) of a seigniory. By establishing these large seigniories the government hoped eventually to see some benefit as the proprietor brought in settlers, cleared the land, grew crops, and improved the fur trade base.[1] To encourage settlement, the seigneur assigned parcels to settlers without a purchase price. The user of the land paid the seigneur "*cens et rentes*"—tax and rent; this gave recognition of the seigneur as the actual owner of the land.[2] In the colony of Louisiana, by ordinance of the king, lands were not to be granted as seigniories, but to individuals in parcels two to four *arpents* wide and forty to sixty *arpents* long.[3] In the Fort de Chartres area in the early days however, there were a few large concessions that were visualized, at least by the acquirer, as seigniories.

One of these was a grant to Boisbriant. He later assigned this to his nephew, Ste. Thérèse Langloisière. The land was referred to as *la belle prairie du rocher*. On either side of this concession Nicolas Chassin and Pierre Melique acquired large grants of land.

All of these large grants were subdivided through concessions to other individuals. Although supposedly they were not seigniories, the land concessions seem to have been framed in terms of the seigniorial system. Philippe Renault, who was in charge of the lead mines, had grants in the lead mining area and also was given farmland near Fort de Chartres to raise food crops for the mining effort. Renault's concession on the east bank, known as St. Philippe, was parcelled out by Renault to various individuals.

Two *arpents* granted by Renault to Louis Poulé stipulated a rent of three capons for the property, and rent was required also for the two lots conceded to him. The only extant grant for Prairie du Rocher, that to Joseph Buchet, specified a rent of one capon and a half *minot* of wheat per *arpent* width for the agricultural land, and one capon per year for the village lot.[4]

Despite this appearance of apparent seignorial taxes and dues, no receipts for rent appear in the records. Although this lack is not conclusive, in combination with other evidence it makes it doubtful that rent actually was paid. Later land transactions contained comments such as, "the land being of the domain of the St. Philippe Concession and charged towards it the taxes, rent or dues of which the vender cannot tell the amount, nevertheless, having been free up to this day."[5] Another indication is that when a grantee sold the property to another person the sale did not require paying a fee to the original grantor. In the case of true seigniorial grants a fee payment would have been necessary. In actuality, the land was owned by an individual in a manner similar to ownership today, and the person could use it or sell it without restriction.

Smaller grants were made directly to individuals also, in sizes more in accordance with the king's ordinance. This land conceded was given outright. The seigneur was the king. Although taxes were not paid, the land if unused, abandoned, or left without heirs, reverted to the crown. This enabled the land to be reassigned for cultivation, as increases in cropland and population were desired. Land rights throughout the French regime were contingent upon personal usage of property. In 1745 Jean Baptiste Lalande had to petition to obtain a variance from the ordinance that required residence on and cultivation of property; he was granted his request. He apparently was in danger of losing land, part of which was in Prairie du Rocher.

The widow Chassin petitioned the judge in 1737 to request that the grantees in the Prairie Chassin, part of which was in Prairie du Rocher, be required to farm the land. Chassin's concession had been divided into one and two *arpent* strips. Obviously Madame Chassin was not able to enforce any seignorial rights and depended upon the land rules that covered all inhabitants.[6]

In Canada lands were granted in long, narrow strips running back from the St. Lawrence River. This same rectilinear pattern was used in the Illinois and in all the early French settlements; it is visible even today on topographical maps. In the Fort de Chartres area, Boisbriant, following the king's ordinance, granted land to the inhabitants in strips one to two *arpents* wide and about fifty *arpents* in length. The land sales and transfers of the period gave the bounds of the land as "running from the Mississippi to the hills," but the actual boundaries of the concessions were from a baseline near the river to another line near the bluffs. In the Fort de Chartres vicinity, the present Highway 155 is roughly the lower line, and the railroad tracks near the bluffs the upper line.

Because the river bends—it does not flow north/south in this area but more nearly west/southeast—the Prairie du Rocher commonfield strips are at an angle to the Fort de Chartres ones. The Prairie du Rocher commonfields do run from the river to the bluffs in a roughly northeast/southwest orientation.

Contemporary photo by the author of the 100-foot-high lime-stone bluffs that form the background of the village of Prairie du Rocher, and give the town its name—prairie of the rock.

Land was abundant in the Illinois country, unlike in France. There, division and sub-division of land between heirs had occurred until sometimes the tracts could no longer support a family. Even in the New England colonies in the early eighteenth century, arable land was at a premium within the settled communities, resulting in the presence of a number of landless young men.[7] In the Illinois, if the adult son of a settler needed land, the commandant could make a grant to him. In 1743 Jeanne Legras, wife of Jean Chabot of Prairie du Rocher, made a request to the commandant for grants for her two grown sons; it was approved.[8]

Common and Commonfield

Two important elements of the French colonial settlement

pattern were the common and the commonfield. The common, the summer pasture for the animals, was conceded to a village as communal property. The lands granted to persons for agricultural purposes formed what was called the commonfield. The long strips were owned individually, farmed individually, and the crops largely determined by the owner, but there were certain communal restrictions. Any inhabitant who had land in the commonfield had to build and maintain the portion of the commonfield fence bordering his property. The purpose of the fence was to include or exclude cattle and other grazing animals. After the harvest, animals were let into the commonfield to graze; then they were removed at planting time.

The dates for opening and closing the fields to animals were decided collectively in an assembly after Mass, and an order was issued by the commandant to enforce this decision.

> Public order of Alfonse de La Buissonière and de la Loere Flaucour that livestock may not be allowed to roam freely until after All Saint's, that all settlers must maintain their part of the common fence on pain of 100 livres fine payable to the hospital, that livestock must be enclosed on April 1.[9]

All Saints is, of course, November 1; all crops would be out of the fields then and the stock could graze on the residue.

The commonfield system was part of the cultural baggage of the French peasants who settled in the Illinois. Hoffman points out that the commonfield system in Europe included three features—the open fields (not divided by property lines), the practice of common pasturing, and regulation by assembly.[10] All of these were present in the Illinois. Commonfield agriculture had been closely associated with village settlement for a long time in Europe. There the system may have arisen because of pressure from land shortages; it was transferred to the Illinois despite the abundance of vacant land. Its continuance probably was due to the values of the settlers who felt it essential for the community. The system affected not only the agricultural life, but also the entire social fabric.

Communal cooperation was required to make the system work. The settlers who farmed there had to make collective decisions and conform to certain rules. To maintain the commonfield that was vital for their livelihood, it was important to keep contention between individuals at a low level; disagreements had to be resolved without disruptive behavior. Agreement had to be reached on the maintenance of the fence, the date for putting cattle into the fields, and the time to remove their animals so that they could begin the spring planting.

Ekberg feels that the pressures of the system favored a communal mindset leading in part to nonviolent resolution of conflict within the community, and that in addition to the agricultural interests, this attitude carried over into other aspects of the culture.[11] The French villagers did tend to settle differences by arbitration and legal action, rather than by violence. The court cases concerning actual civil disobedience, personal or property damage are few in number.

The Villages

The French did not settle in individual homesteads on their farms, but in villages. This was different from Canada, where people built homes on the ends of their strips along the waterways or roads. Although in the mid-seventeenth century the Canadian government encouraged the formation of villages, the Canadians did not change.[12] But in the Illinois country, as in France, the settlements were villages; security for protection may have been one reason.[13]

The original settlement at Fort de Chartres appears to have had individual homes strung out along the river, but shortly a more compact village developed, placed between the river and the lower line of the agricultural strips. Later the small village of St. Philippe formed around Renault's estate a few miles upriver from the fort, past the Metchigamia Indian reserve. Early in the settlement of the area, Prairie du Rocher began to form four miles downstream from the fort, and built closer to the bluffs, with the agricultural fields running down from it towards the Mississippi.

It is important to recognize that although the settlements were *loci* of habitation, they were not separate legal entities, as are villages today. The legal entity—the government—was the commandant at Fort de Chartres. The settlement of Prairie du Rocher was a separate and recognizable entity, but all of its activities and personnel were intertwined with the other villages, their inhabitants, and the fort. The "community" of Prairie du Rocher, the socially and economically interacting unit, was much larger than the residential boundary.

Physically the villages were small pieces of France set down in the wilderness. They offered the inhabitants a secure and social place. Here men could gather and go out to the fields as a group; women could visit, and children could play. The French did not want the isolated, independent farmsteads that the later American pioneers preferred; they desired a gregarious environment.

John C. Wild, *Valley of the Mississippi Illustrated*

Old Cahokia

Each village was focused on a church, a small wooden structure with its thatched roof surmounted by a cross. A belfry contained a bell for sounding the Angelus and for calling the inhabitants to services. Streets divided a village into roughly equal blocks; the average lot size was between twenty-five *toises* and one *arpent* square (an *arpent* equals thirty *toises*). The lots were bordered by post fences that marked out the property boundaries, kept in the resident's animals and kept out anyone else's. A house sold at Kaskaskia included a thousand fence posts; one at Fort de Chartres had seven hundred posts six and a half *pieds* long.[14] Outbuildings were grouped around the house—a stable, a chicken house, a well, a bake oven, a pigeon house (pigeons were raised for food); also in this compound was a kitchen garden and an orchard. Most of the food for the household, other than grain, was raised in the gardens—all types of fresh vegetables, beans, peas, okra, cucumbers, onions, melons, and herbs for flavoring. All these homes used wood for cooking, heating, and for baking bread; there must have been a haze of wood smoke in the air in the early morning and in the evening.

Most houses were constructed of wood, with upright posts set either in the ground (*poteaux en terre*) or on a sill (*poteaux sur sol*) with the interstices filled with clay and small rocks mixed with a variety of substances for temper. Also, structures were made *pièce sur pièce* with horizontal logs. Unlike the later American structures, the logs were not round but trimmed and squared with the ends shaped to fit into a groove on the frame. The squared logs were slid into the vertical groove and stacked up to form the wall, a very solid construction that frequently was used for barns. Barns, substantial structures often forty by twenty-four *pieds* in size, were located near the agricultural fields.

The average size of the houses was between twenty by sixteen *pieds* and thirty by twenty *pieds*. Usually there were two main rooms with a double chimney to accommodate a fireplace in each room—the kitchen/sitting room and the bed chamber.

The houses were a story and a half high; they were floored with boards and had a board ceiling that formed the floor of a loft above. The loft could be used for storage or as sleeping quarters. The interior walls of the house were plastered and whitewashed. Mullioned casement windows with small panes of glass let light into the interior. Glass was shipped in crates from France.[15] Steep roofs with thatch or wooden shingles overhung the house on each end or on all four sides and formed porch or gallery roofs.[16]

One home was described in a sale as having a main room, a hall, a double-stone chimney, two bed closets, a cellar, and a gallery all around. A bed closet was exactly what it sounds like, a very small room partitioned off for sleeping quarters. This house was shingled and had a garden with a separate kitchen house, a shed, a henhouse, a barn, and a well. Louis Levasseur of Prairie du Rocher sold a house twenty-five by twenty *pieds*, of upright posts, shingled, and floored both downstairs and up in the loft. A small building near the house was covered with boards and two sheds were attached to the house.[17]

Wells were lined with stone or wood. Directions stated that the sides of a good well should be raised at least two and a half *pieds* above the surface of the ground. A well represented an investment of labor and time, and so was valued. Often more than one property shared the rights to draw water from the well, and these rights were sold with the property. In one sale the contract stated, "it shall be allowed to the acquirer, his heirs and assigns, to draw water from the well of the said vender, built on the lot he has reserved, adjoining the lot here sold." Mathurin Charveau sold lot, house, and other amenities including "a well with a shed covered with shingles, a pulley and a rope for drawing water [he reserved the right to have water] during his lifetime [and the buyer]...shall give passage to Dame Dutrou." Madame Dutrou on a lot nearby had rights to the well, so she was to be permitted egress for drawing water. Without a well, water could be taken from the small creeks and the river, these were pure and drinkable, but less convenient.[18]

The village of Chartres seems to have had only wooden structures. Such structures were said to rot within twenty years in the damp bottomlands; this probably would be the *poteaux en terre* ones. However, the Mellière house, a *poteaux sur sol* structure built in the 1760s, is still standing in Prairie du Rocher. Buildings were made of stone too; the house of Renault's concession in St. Philippe was of masonry construction and several homes in Prairie du Rocher were of stone. In 1737 Gossiaux, a mason, made a contract to construct a stone barn in Prairie du Rocher for Urban Gervais.[19]

Inns were kept in the villages in one large room of a house. A separate room was built on some houses to hold a billiard table; billiards was a popular game. A voyageur was hired at Pierre Lacourse's billiard hall as scorekeeper and attendant.

There was a hospital in the village of Chartres. Throughout the French regime a surgeon major (the royal surgeon) was appointed from France. He provided medical care for both the troops and civilians from all the villages. The hospital building was thirty-nine by sixteen *pieds* of post-in-the-ground construction with a straw roof.[20] Although the quality of medical treatment at the time might be questionable today, the contracts made with Reneé Drouin and René Roy show attention to basic health. Reneé Drouin agreed to launder the linens from the hospital, including sheets, shirts, and bandages. René Roy, who was also the surgeon, was to provide light, heat, and food—eggs, milk, fresh meat, and vegetables. On the other hand, a list of some medicines of the period supplied in New Orleans included some of dubious value.

> Epson Salt, Gooseberry Syrup, Dragon's Blood, Oil of Sweet Almonds, Syrup of Lemon, Syrup of Licorice, Blistering Ointment, Rhubarb, Ipecac-Quinine, Turpentine, Syrup of Chicory, Essence of Juniper-berry, Extract of Hyacinthe, Flower of Camomile, Balm of Fern, Senna, Salpetre, Laudamun, Camphor, Ammonia Salt, Rattle-snake oil, Oil of Vitriol.[21]

Scalpels and various other surgeon's tools have been found in archaeological work in the area, and a surgeon's case was listed in the inventory of materials at the stone fort in 1765.[22]

The village streets between the blocks of houses were maintained by the persons bordering them. Bienvenu lived in Kaskaskia but also had a plantation at Prairie du Rocher; so in 1729 he hired Rollet to build a road there for him. Rollet received fifty livres for this work.[23] In addition to the village streets there were the royal roads running between the settlements; all inhabitants were required to work several days a year on these. The main one was the *Chemin du Roi*, the King's Road, extending from St. Philippe through the village of Chartres, to Prairie du Rocher, and on to Kaskaskia.

Bridges were built where necessary along this road. In 1748 bids were requested for the construction of a bridge on the property of Pierre St. Ange at Prairie du Rocher, to cross the stream at the entrance to the Prairie du Rocher woods, at the edge of the Grand Prairie. The specifications were:

> ...three good bridging joists of oak, sound and well seasoned and one post in the center of each joist of the same wood. The bridge shall be put in a place where the ground is good and very firm so that mires are not easily formed. The poles for covering the bridge shall be new wood of the best quality which may be found on the site.

This would have been a "corduroy" bridge. The low bidder was Michel Danis for 150 *livres*.[24]

The village with its social life and the fenced lots reflected two aspects of the *habitant's* culture, their desire for social interaction and the need for property and family integrity.

The buildings and other man-made surroundings created compact villages that provided the villagers with familiar secure spaces. Here they recreated the village life they had left behind, and found assurance in it amidst the wilderness.

Economic Life

Although the Illinois country owed its beginnings to the fur trade, its economy soon became more diversified. Beaver furs were not as thick and dark in the southern region as in the north. The fur trade in the Illinois mainly involved buffalo and deer hides, bobcat skins, and other furs. At first, most of the trade in furs continued to move north to Canada, but as lower Louisiana was settled, hides and furs went south as well. Trade with other French settlements below on the Mississippi River developed, and as this increased a shift occurred in production towards items necessary for that trade rather than purely for shipment to France. As early as 1726 Bienville commented that:

the voyageurs formerly obtained beaver, raccoon, deer, buffalo and bear skins but for six or seven years the French have been obliging them to produce oil, tallow and meat for which they trade with them.

Food products became Illinois' most important exports. Flour, peas, maize, okra, and onions were shipped downriver. Meats were important—buffalo meat (particularly tongues) and venison, and from domestic produce, beef and hams. Bear oil was deemed a good substitute for olive oil and pots of this were traded. The amount of oil rendered from a bear is given by Bossu in one case as 120 *pots*. In 1735 prices for goods from the Illinois country were:

> flour - 2 *sols* a *livre* (weight);
> hams - 4 *livres* (money);
> bear's oil - 40 *sols* a *pot*;
> frogs - 2 *livres* each;
> tobacco - 2 *livres* per *livre*;
> salt - 14 *livres* a *minot*.[27]

Contracts made in lower Louisiana indicate some of the quantities required for supply to the various posts downriver from Illinois. Judge Salmon in New Orleans made a contract with La Croix of Illinois, for him to furnish 8715 *livres* of flour and 215 *livres* of bacon to New Orleans. On his way down, La Croix was to supply the Natchez post with 2715 *livres* of flour and 215 *livres* of bacon; the Arkansas post needed 6000 *livres* of flour. This 17,430 *livres* of flour and 430 *livres* of bacon could have been transported in a couple of bateaux, or three pirogues (see below).

In another contract Judge Salmon arranged for Thomas Chauvin to bring 5905 *livres* of flour to Natchez from Illinois. Jacques de la Boucherie was to furnish to New Orleans 8148 *livres* of salted beef and thirty-five tongues, and Jean Chauvin was to bring 3088 *livres* of buffalo meat and sixty salted tongues. These were individual pirogue loads.[28]

As Illinois was a prime supplier of flour and other products to lower Louisiana, official government convoys of boats were sent downriver with the supplies. People took advantage of the official convoys to go down in their own boats, and merchants might send several pirogues and bateaux; there was safety in numbers and in the presence of the soldiers. Soldiers and hired voyageurs paddled these boats; slaves were never numerous enough to be the only ones employed for this task.

> The king's negroes are most of them too old and neither strong nor numerous enough to undertake this service [rowing bateaux]. Never has more than one been placed in each bateau...The soldiers have always rowed, and up to twenty-four are necessary for each boat.[29]

Pirogues, dugout canoes, were made from the large trees of the virgin forest; the center of the tree was burnt, cut, and chiseled out. A contract for the construction of a pirogue for Pierre Derousse (later of Prairie du Rocher) and Jacques Bernard specifies that it is to be made of black poplar wood forty feet long and three feet wide, able to carry a burden of 7-8000 *livres* (weight). The boat was to be supplied with a rudder, three oars, and one paddle.[30]

The bateaux were built of planks and held more goods; apparently there was a standard size for bateaux, forty by nine *pieds*.[31] A walnut bateau with a burden of 30,000 *livres* was contracted for construction by the partners Michel Vien and Michel Le Jeune. Jean Baptiste Aubuchon, who listed his occupation as boat builder, agreed to construct two bateaux, each capable of carrying 17,000 weight in addition to men and supplies. Another boat carried 12,000 *livres* of screened flour and had a total of 14-15,000 *livres* burden. This boat was fully rigged and had a cover for the flour.[32]

The dates on voyageur contracts reflect the seasonal activities of the trade. The majority of the contracts for voyages to New Orleans were made between April and June.[33] In the spring the water was so high that the river flooded adjacent lands. The flooding made surprise attacks by Indians along the way more difficult. The trip to New Orleans was swift—twelve to twenty-five days—but the journey upriver took three to four months.[34]

The trip was hazardous. The river itself was treacherous

enough with snags, sawyers, currents, and mosquitoes (a major complaint), but the greatest danger along the route was from hostile Indians, particularly the Chickasaw, who were affiliated with the English. Many accounts tell of death or capture by the Indians. This was an ever-present threat to the men who went out and a dread for the women who remained in the villages.

The convoys were important for the downriver settlements and for New Orleans, where supplies of goods did not always arrive promptly from France. Although the soldiers might lack for uniforms and the pay for soldiers, officers, and officials was slow in coming from France, the Illinois country was self sufficient for food. Illinois did import a great deal from France—all cloth was imported (no weaving was done here), in addition to wine, brandy, prunes, limes, rope, nails, soap, candlesticks, glass goblets, cork, long saws, linen, laces, silk stockings, and other goods. Items were imported for trade with the Indians too.[35]

In his letters to the Sieur Rossard in New Orleans, Terisse de Ternan shows the multiple economic interests that were typical of most colonists. He sent bushels of onions, hams, okra, beaver skins, and tobacco downriver, which he asked Rossard to trade for him in New Orleans to procure merchandise. The trade goods he wanted were, "knives of all kinds, brass kettles, yellow limberg, vermilion, powder, lead, etc." In addition to these items destined for the Indian trade, he was interested in items to trade or barter with other settlers.

> If you can, find stockings of all kinds send them, for they are scarce here, as well as women's shoes, ribbons, muslins and other trifles, on which there is more to gain than on large bolts. ... Send me, if you can, a jar of about 15 lbs. of sugar. If by chance you should find a pair of billiard balls for sale you would please me by sending them to me.

His items were not always ready to send down to Rossard. He related that he was having difficulty getting the walnut boards that Rossard had requested as "no one saws at present, each individual being busy sowing." That letter was written in March. The hams Rossard desired were not available yet, but "pray do not worry if I do not send your hams, they are still in the pasture and from one day to the other will be put in the salt tub."[36]

Although at first glance the economic system seems very simple, actually it was fairly complex. Trade was not just a linear exchange, but a series of triangular interrelationships. The fur trade itself moved between Canada, Illinois, and New Orleans. Voyageurs went out to the hinterland to trade with Indians and to procure meat and hides (either by their own efforts or by trade), and then through sale of these, obtained merchandise either downstream at New Orleans, upriver in Canada, or from merchants in the trading center of Kaskaskia.

The *habitants* themselves had a choice of markets. They could barter with the Indians for meat or other items, they could barter with other farmers/tradesmen for goods, products, or land, or their produce could be taken to the king's storehouse to pay debts owed or to purchase items brought from France. If inclined they could take the produce to New Orleans themselves or hire someone to do that, and in New Orleans they could obtain goods for their own use or for trade with the Indians. As early as 1723 D'Artaguiette describes this:

> The trade of the inhabitants of the Illinois, who are Canadians, French or discharged soldiers, consists in selling their wheat and other products to the company for the subsistence of the troops in exchange for merchandize (which they are obliged to fetch from New Orleans) which they trade to the Indians for quarters of buffalo, bear oil and other meats, which serve them for food or which they exchange for merchandize. They also trade in skins such as beaver, buck and deer, buffalo and bearskins, and other peltries, which they get very cheap from the Indians and which they sell at a very high price to the traders who come down from Canada every spring and autumn and who give them merchandize in exchange.[37]

Diversification was necessary. Crops could fail and that source of income be reduced; shipments might be lost due to dangers of the river or to hostile Indians.

The colony did not produce many materials desired in France

in return for all the supplies imported. The greatest problem that the crown had in maintaining the colony was that it did not make money. Lower Louisiana sent rice, indigo, lumber, tar, cotton, and tobacco. For shipment back to France, Illinois' main production was furs, hides, and some lead. Lead from Renault's mines was formed into sheets for transport. The maximum lead production was 40,000 *livres* annually; in 1743, 30,000 *livres* were shipped to France as ballast. The predominant interest of the French government in promoting the lead mines had been the hope that silver would be found. This did not happen. None of the products exported were of sufficient value to offset the expenses of the colony.[38]

The most important product of Illinois was flour. Bread was definitely the staff of life for the French. The standard used to estimate needs was that one bushel of wheat would make enough flour to provide a person with a two-pound loaf of bread each day for a month.[39] The understanding was that this was a normal and necessary ration. The climate in the lower part of the Louisiana colony was not suitable for the growth of wheat, and supplies were irregular in arrival from France. Louisiana was heavily dependent upon the Illinois country for its flour.

The first commandant, Boisbriant, recommended that the *habitants* grow winter wheat, sown in the fall and harvested sometime in June or July. The records indicate that spring wheat shortly became the more common crop. Payments in flour cluster in the late fall, after the harvest.[40]

Land was readily available and the extent of cultivated land in the Illinois was limited only by the number of persons available to work for the ten days or so that the wheat could be harvested by hand. A man could harvest about one acre per day; for the harvest period this would be about ten acres per adult male.[41] Most family farms had only the adult male, children, and perhaps one worker or slave. The larger plantations with more *engagés* and slaves would have been able to have greater production.

The equipment used in farming was simple; they were the same tools used in France.[42] The planting methods were primitive; the seed was broadcast and cultivating was nil. There is no indication of crop rotation; haphazard manuring was accomplished by turning the animals into the common field in the winter months. The land was rich, though, and spring floods rejuvenated the fields occasionally. Since the banks of the river were high and its bed deep, flooding generally was not severe; the inhabitants accepted the temporary inconvenience in exchange for its benefits.

The amount of seed used for planting is not given, although one record lists fifty *minots* of wheat that were to be used to sow three *arpents* of leased land. The three *arpents* probably are the width of the strip rather than surficial *arpents*; that would equal less than three acres. The depth of the strip is variable. Estimating use of about half a *minot* of wheat (about half a bushel) to seed one surficial *arpent* (a little less than an acre) suggests about one hundred surficial *arpents* under wheat cultivation. The land being sown was one of the larger plantations, not a family farm. As it is not known how thickly the seed was broadcast, this amount of seed could have been planned for less acreage.[43]

Production quantities are not given. One inventory lists 530 sheaves in a barn.[44] No information could be obtained on how many bushels this might represent. It has been estimated that eight to ten acres of wheat in Pennsylvania would yield eighty to a hundred bushels.[45] The bottomlands might have had a higher yield as Briggs (below) suggests.

In his thesis Briggs took the reported amounts of flour exported and extrapolated to obtain the possible acreage farmed. Using the figure of 400,000 *livres* of exported flour to New Orleans, providing an equal amount for use in the Illinois, with a small quantity for supplying other posts downriver, and saving seed for the next year, he felt would require about 1470 acres under wheat cultivation, given a yield of thirteen and three-quarters bushel per acre by his calculations.[46] Natalia Belting suggested some figures at a ten-fold production per acre that arranged to correspond with Briggs' method yields slightly more acreage, 2250.[47]

Briggs suggested a total of 272 producing farms, including Ste. Genevieve and Cahokia. Eliminating the twenty-five farms he assigned to Ste. Genevieve (since the amount of flour given is before

1750) gives 247 farms, that would indicate six or six and six-tenths acres of wheat per farm. This acreage was only part of the cultivated land, as there would have been maize and other crops as well.

This estimate is only that, an estimate. Undoubtedly there was great variation in the quantity of land farmed. It does show the possibilities for the "average" farm strip, and that the production of this quantity of flour was well within the capability of the inhabitants, of course including the Prairie du Rocher farmers.

The production of flour required mills. All the mills in the Illinois were privately owned, unlike in Canada, where they were the property of the seigneur. The largest number of mills were horse mills; the horse providing the energy to turn the millstones. It is impossible to tell how many of these existed at one time, as the horse mills appear in the records only when being sold or inherited. There must have been several to produce the quantity of flour needed.

One windmill is known to have been near Prairie du Rocher, and another by Fort de Chartres. Watermills are mentioned several times. One was built on "the stream between Fort de Chartres and Prairie du Rocher," probably the stream coming out from between the bluffs that crosses the highway near the entrance to town.[48]

Millstones probably were produced locally. There is only one mention of them, when Charles Neau agreed to supply millstones for a horse mill in 1735. The flour was processed also in a bolting mill. Bolting screened the bran from the flour and made a fine grade of white flour. Bolting cloths of silk are mentioned. A bolting mill seems to have been associated with the fort.[49]

Indian corn (maize) grew well in the bottomlands then, as it does now. One inventory mentioned ten to twelve *arpents* of corn in the field.[50] Page du Pratz listed the types of corn in use:

> Flourmaiz which is white, with a flat shrivelled surface, and is the softest of all the kinds; Homony corn, which is round, hard, and shining; of this there are four sorts, the white, the yellow, the red, and the blue;...We have besides the small corn, or small Maiz, so called because it is smaller than the other kinds.[51]

Beer was made locally with maize. One man had a copper kettle of a hundred *pots* volume for making beer (a *pot* is equal to about half a gallon). Production required eight *minots* of corn per year.[52] Wine was produced from wild grapes and cultivation of vines was practiced too. A vine dresser's pick and a clipper for working vines were listed in inventories.[53] Interesting enough, wine does not appear in inventories. Like some of the other items missing from these lists, wine apparently was considered personal or basic, and so not counted as property. Brandy, being a trade commodity, was listed.

An officer, Terisse de Ternan, in a letter to New Orleans commented on the wine he had made in the Illinois.

> I already mentioned that I had made a cask and a quarter of wine of this country with the firm resolution that I would not open it until next Spring, but having continually under foot that same "wine" in a cellar into which I often descend to see that no accident happens, I yielded for the quarter only on St. Martin's day though it is still very tart, but the cask will rest against all temptation until Easter. I only fear King's day and Saint Mardi Gras, I intend at that time to absent myself so that I may not break my word. I shall tell you in the course of time how I have behaved myself on this subject. [Postscript] Thinking of it, the quarter lasted five days, that you may not think it was drunk in one.[54]

The diversified economy, combining the Indian trade with the internal and external agricultural trade, permitted individuals to accumulate wealth, but certain elements prevented large disparities from developing. Enterprises in which to invest capital in Louisiana, such as manufacturing, did not exist due to the monopolies first of Crozat, then of the Company of the Indies, and because of the lack of French entrepreneurs' interest.

Little or no coinage was available in the country to convert to wealth for hoarding. Most coins that arrived were sent back to France as payment for debts. The monetary system was very unstable. The government in Louisiana was forced to issue various kinds of paper money, including card money—playing cards with notations of denomination. Paper money fluctuated in value, counterfeiting was prevalent. In an effort to control this, new issues were made frequently, so saving was risky.

Spanish coins obtained through Florida also were used as currency. The relative value of Spanish *piastres* versus the French money is shown in a few documents. A debt of 666 *livres*, ten *sols* to Joseph Liberville *dit* Joson, trader of Kaskaskia, was to be paid in *piastres* at 100 *sols* to the *piastre*. Boutin received a letter of exchange from Charles Braseaux for 3000 *livres* or 600 *piastres*.

Notes of debt were another form of "currency," IOUs that could be transferred from one individual to another. They were a medium of payment and exchange. These notes also are listed in inventories cited as money due to the deceased, or debts of the estate. The following IOU sounds a little complicated but if worked through the logic appears.

> Order by Joseph Buchet, Royal Attorney, that Louis Trudeau pay 1505 livres to Jacques Godefroy of Kaskaskia, in payment of a note made by Jacques Boutin in that amount to Godefroy on Feb. 7, 1746. Because Boutin is now permanently in New Orleans and because Trudeau is obligated to Boutin for 2060 livres, Trudeau is ordered to pay Godefroy, thus reducing his debt to Boutin by the amount paid to Godefroy.[55]

Investment in land was not highly useful for wealth, without having workers to farm it. Some persons did accumulate a number of properties but most of the holders of large tracts were either officers who received it by grant, or farmers in Kaskaskia who had appropriated blocks of land in the early years. A grant from the government was available to anyone who wanted to work it. Even those who rented houses, such as the voyageurs, could have a secure future; there was free for the taking—deer, waterfowl, fish, native plants for food, and firewood for cutting. All of this meant that there were neither extremely wealthy nor greatly impoverished individuals.

Colonial Society

The settlers came from a hierarchical society in France, where there were three distinct classes—clergy, nobles, and the rest of the population. Detached from this society, the colonists found themselves in an environment that allowed for advancement for all classes. Day laborers could become land holders and merchants; craftsmen who would have struggled with competition in France found their field wide open in the Illinois and prospered. Social structure in the Illinois colony lacked sharp divisions of class. It was a fairly egalitarian community.

Minor nobility appeared in the Illinois occasionally, but generally they gravitated towards the centers of power in New Orleans, Montreal, and Quebec. The awarding of major government contracts and trading permits was done in New Orleans and Canada. Fort de Chartres was a second line of authority. The ultimate source of power was not there. The top of the pyramid was cut off. Persons desiring status and recognition went elsewhere.

This does not mean there were no social distinctions, but the segregation that marked social intercourse in France was not carried over into the frontier society. A reflection of this is found in the church baptismal registers. Officials—Boisbriant or Deliette for example—stood as godparents for the children of other people's slaves, and would have been expected to perform the duties of godparents. In the Chetivau desertion case, Commandant Dutisne testified he had heard that Chetivau had a featherbed to sell so he went to inquire about it. In France this would never have happened; a servant would have been sent. A commandant would not have chatted with a convict on a street corner.

Fr. Gagnon, on the other hand, was very careful whom he listed as Monsieur, Sieur, or Madame, terms that had significant social meaning in France. The notaries were much freer in their use of those terms, indicating the greater ease in the local society for assuming these titles.[56]

In Canada rules for social distinctions included such prerogatives as the right to carry a sword or to wear a hat. Seating by rank in church also was important. None of these seem to have carried much social weight in the Illinois. Certain rules may have existed but they did not have sufficient import to enter into any of the documents, unlike in Canada or in the British colonies, where such matters were brought up, debated, and recorded.[57]

Although the society was not rigid, social groupings did exist in the Illinois as they do in any society, and marriage patterns reveal five general groups. The highest status one was that of the functionaries of the Company of the Indies, the officers and the wealthier local citizens. The merchant/craftsman/*habitant* were the next group, and then the *engagés* and the voyageurs. Free blacks, black slaves, and Indian slaves formed another group. The Illinois Indians and various related groups, such as the Miami, constituted a unit. However, these groupings were neither immutable nor constant; mobility occurred between groups.

Marriage with Indian women was common in the early period; Marie Rouensa was a prime example of a high status Indian woman. Such marriages did not appear to have any negative bearing on social standing. The métis children intermarried at all levels. Few of the officials from France married Indians. Some had brought wives with them, but most planned to return to France, having bettered their fortunes in the colony and perhaps with hopes of a good marriage there.

Although in the earlier years marriages with Indian women were encouraged, later there was official disapproval of these mixed marriages. The government believed the children would take up the Indian ways rather than becoming agricultural settlers. One of the officials in New Orleans commented:

> Few Indian girls want to enter into a permanent, stable marriage with Frenchmen. If there are cases in the Illinois country, it is more because the Frenchman has taken to the Indian way of Life. Even there— and the missionaries have not succeeded in correcting the practice— the girl is likely to go off later on with an Indian.[58]

Marriage with Indians became less common in the later years

of the French regime, but because of the earlier ones many of the French and Canadian inhabitants had Indian relatives.

The use of terms in the records to designate a person's status/ occupation was different from the usage in Canada. The term *habitant* in the local records was used commonly for the settled agriculturists in contrast to the voyageurs. Its use in Canada frequently made *habitant* equivalent to peasant, a lower class in France, a connotation that it did not have in the Illinois and one that would have been resented by the villagers.[59] Even in Canada, though, where the class lines were more distinct, *habitant* did not always indicate a class but merely a resident of the colony.[60]

In Canada the use of bourgeois as an appellation seems to refer to commercial activity and sometimes to minor nobility; the term is rarely used in the Illinois.[61] The terms *negociant* and *marchand* for the merchants were used interchangeably and frequently in combination with trader or voyageur. The combining of terms indicates the social flexibility. A voyageur could become a voyageur/trader, moving up from just being a hired paddle to doing trade on his own. A trader/merchant was beginning to supply trade goods to other persons going out on trading voyages. Commercial activities did not imply low status as it generally did in France. Since land was easily available, concessions of land did not cause the formation of a propertied elite class.

The notarial documents always list the craftsmen in the Illinois as master carpenter, master mason, master cabinetmaker, or master tailor—designations that had significance within an apprentice/master framework in France. Possibly a few of these craftsmen would not have qualified in France as masters, but in the Illinois country they did. Here they were able to practice their craft and be recognized for their skills.

The opportunities for improvement of a person's socio-economic position were not limited by his current social status. In property there might be a disparity in the amount of land and goods owned by a prosperous farmer/trader and an *engagé* or voyageur, but in some ways this was a difference between individuals at a point of time in their lives. After their initial contracted service was over, many of the *engagés* became landholders and farmers. Furthermore, some of the soldiers (French marines) who signed on for six years of service purchased homes and took up trades while they were still in the military. They had the option after their term was up of receiving grants and settling on their land.

Pierre Louvière was a voyageur who worked his way up to voyageur/trader status and became a landholder. In 1743 he took his boat downriver with two voyageurs hired for him by an associate named Colet. He carried 1000 *livres* of flour and ten hams. The agreement was that he was to bring back 1400-1500 *livres* of merchandise for Colet, including 200 *pots* of brandy and 100 *livres* of gunpowder. Pierre probably was considered a voyageur/trader at this point, although it is not specified in the records. Later, in the 1760s, he was the militia captain at Prairie du Rocher, an important post.[62]

Officials and officers who hoped to be raised to higher social status in France upon their return, did not seem to have met with much success. Illinois simply did not provide opportunities for advancement, even for those who survived to go back to France (a small number).

Status of Women

Women enjoyed a fairly high status in Illinois society. The marriage contract, by protecting the property rights of the family, also protected the woman.[63] Throughout the eighteenth century a disparity existed in the relative numbers of men and women, with men outnumbering the women. Because of the scarcity many women married at a young age, fourteen to sixteen years; frequently the man was much older. For example, Antoine Rivière, who farmed near Prairie du Rocher, was thirty-seven years old when he married Magdalene Robillard, who was fourteen. This dissimilarity in ages also meant that many women were widowed at a young age. Magdalene was seventeen when Rivière died; less than a year later she married again.

The societal convention was that women were known by their maiden name even after their marriage; notaries would list François Gilbert and Marie Langlois, his wife, in a document. However, when widowed, women became known by their husband's surname as the widow "so-and-so". Marie above would have been Widow Gilbert.

Probably the most married and a very independent woman was Renée Drouin. She was from Brittany and was already married to Jean Baptiste Blondel *dit* La Forme, a soldier, when they came over from France in 1729. Blondel purchased a house and lot in the village as most married soldiers did. It was during this marriage Renée made the contract to launder the linens from the hospital.

Blondel died and Renée remarried in 1740 to Nicolas Olle Pierrot *dit* La Sonde, a sergeant in Grandpré's company, who also had property in the village. Renée Drouin was now an innkeeper at Fort de Chartres (*aubergiste*). In 1744 De Populus acknowledged a debt owed to Renée Drouin for 240 *pots* of brandy. The debt was not to her husband but to her, so she must have been active in trade as this was more than a few drinks at her inn.[64]

After La Sonde's death in 1745 she married a neighbor, Charles Hervy, a month later. Hervy had arrived from Paris in 1720 and his profession listed on the ship was gardener, but he was a sergeant too. Hervy had ample property in the village. As they had no children when he died in 1759, his widow inherited all and was quite well off. She bought and sold pieces of property in the village. Two years later she married for a fourth time to another sergeant, François Ripère; sergeants seem to have been her interest.

Women, even married women, could initiate legal action. Marianne Govreau, the wife of Charles Gossiaux of Prairie du Rocher, filed several requests with the judge, including separation of her property from that of Gossiaux. Marianne also purchased a house for herself. Jeanne Legras of Prairie du Rocher, although married to Jean Chabot, submitted a request herself to the commandant for land grants for her two grown sons from her previous marriage.

The men were often away from the settlements either as military personnel on duty, or in trade. The women were left to carry on the day-to-day business, and consequently were involved in all economic activities of the colony. Jean Baptiste Lalande descended the river to New Orleans and decided to take up permanent residence there. He gave his wife, Charlotte Marchand, a power of attorney to settle their affairs and dispose of their property in the Illinois. While Louis Metivier was away on a voyage, his wife, Marie Faffard, was taken to court in reference to a debt Metivier owed. She was held to be responsible for the debt which was of course a debt against their community of goods. She was expected to do something about paying it before Louis returned.[65]

Women hired voyageurs and some even went out on the rivers in trade. Marie Geneviève Baudien made an agreement with a voyageur, Jean Chapron, to accompany and assist her on a journey to the Post of the Ouias to trade. Chapron was to receive 120 *livres* in buckskin for his work.[66]

Inventories

A person's economic position was important, as having property and controlling the inheritance of property were significant social values. Inventories taken at the death of an individual are the best surviving indicators of economic position; these listed their property, real estate and personal. Often the inventories are lengthy; the ones chosen here are not the longest (for the sake of space), but are typical. These documents also are one of the best ways to convey the lifestyle of the time.

The first is for a voyageur/hunter. Legras was a hunter for the Company of the Indies when he was lost in the woods and presumed dead in 1724. D'Artaguiette had mentioned him paddling in Dulongpré's pirogue a year earlier. A sale was held of his belongings; the sale record gave prices for the auctioned items showing their relative values.

> one half gallon of brandy 2310 *livres*
> a trade gun 81 *livres*
> another trade gun 83 *livres*
> a broken gun 50 *livres*
> an old blanket of dog hair 11 *livres*
> an old greatcoat of limbourg 20 *livres*
> a pair of silk hose and one of wool

two shirts of linen of Rouen 99 *livres*
a case with two razors, a small syringe, a comb, a pocket knife,
two gun worms 15 *livres,* 10 *sols*
half a bar of soap 30 *livres*
an old casket without a key and two pairs of Indian moccasins 16
    livres.

Legras did not have a large amount of possessions; he may have had more belongings back at Kaskaskia, but if so that record was not preserved. For his trip he had packed two shirts, two pairs of stockings, two pairs of moccasins and a coat. No breeches are mentioned in the sale. Presumably he had some but they may have been in too poor condition to be sold at auction or he was lost in his only pair. It appears he was conscientious about his appearance, with his razors, comb, and soap. The most valuable item he owned was the half-gallon of brandy; that must have been a very fine year to have sold for so much, if this price was not an error by the notary.[67]

An inventory for Jean Rivet, a voyageur who died while at Fort Orleans on the Missouri River, lists also items left in Kaskaskia, "An old razor, an old small pickaxe, a plate of wood, an old capot, an old waistcoat, two old shirts." Another inventory was done at Fort Orleans of the pelts, skins, and trade goods he had acquired.

269 *livre* of dry beaver at 30 *sols*
6 *livre* of fat beaver 40 *sols*
19 deerskins, male
40 ditto female
8 buffalo hides, 41 wild cat, 66 deerskins
6 livres of tobacco in a roll
12 *livre* of sheet lead, 50 *livres* in ball
a barrel of powder
a Padocah slave [Indian slave]
4 wooden handled knives
2 scrapers, a club, a dagger
5 old guns[68]

Although some of the voyageurs might have had few possessions, the *habitants* lived far better than they would have in France.
The bountiful resources of the Illinois allowed for a good, prosperous
life. The inventories taken at the death of a spouse show the quality
of life for the *habitants*.

The interiors of the homes had locally made furniture, arm-
chairs, side chairs, tables with and without leaves, armoires, and chests.
Important among the possessions was the couple's bed; this was such
a significant item that frequently the disposition of it was written into
the marriage contract. The bedstead was provided with a mattress, a
feather bed, sheets, coverlets of various types, pillows, and curtains.
The curtained bed provided privacy in a home where generally the
couple and children slept in the same room; the curtains also provided warm shelter on cold nights. The bed was symbolic of the marriage and indeed the reference to a prior marriage was *primer lit*—the
first bed.

The houses did not just hold the bare necessities for household use, nor were they plain and primitive. Although most furnishings were made in the Illinois, clothing, dishes, cooking utensils, and
other household goods were imported from France. In the more prosperous homes the glazed casement windows were curtained, and there
might even be a mirror with a curved frame hung on the white washed
walls. The table could be set with a tablecloth and serviettes, a cande-
labra, silver or crystal goblets, and faience or pewter plates. Faience
is glazed earthenware; many fragments have been found on archaeological sites in the area. Faience plates with an off-white glaze and a
narrow decorative border in blue are common. Platters and soup tu-
reens had elaborate rims and were painted with bright colors in floral
patterns.[69]

Cloth and clothing were imported from France. Although there
is a reference to linen spinners from Canada it does not appears that
homespun or locally woven fabrics were used.[70] Fine dress was important to the inhabitants; one person requested:

a complete suit of camleteen [woolen cloth woven with mohair or silk]
with silk lining, to wit: a green coat and 2 pairs of breeches, one fine

half beaver hat, 4 good and fine shirts trimmed with good cambric, a pair of silk hose of a color suitable to the rest.

This *habitant* with his knee breeches, matching silk stockings, shirt with ruffles, a smart wool coat and felt hat, and the elegant lady in silk taffeta—cited below—are hardly the usual concept of the frontier. This again points up the difference between the French settle-

Anonymous, Montreal Municipal Library
This ca. 1780 drawing shows a man dressed in Indian-style moccasins and garters.

ments patterned after towns in France and the American pioneer expansion. The French took their civilization with them; the Americans waited for it to catch up.

As could be expected, officers' wives had finer clothing, such as the "woman's outfit of striped satin lined with taffeta, rose colored, with one pair of silk hose, shoes, socks and mitts" mentioned earlier.[71] But the average *habitant* also possessed good clothes as examples taken from inventories suggest. For the gentlemen—a vest of coffee colored woolen broadcloth, half beaver hat trimmed with silver, three frock coats, a vest of camlet with silver braid and silver buttons, a pair of gloves, silk handkerchiefs, a nightcap, a Malacca cane, a pair of pocket pistols, and a cavalryman's pistol. For the ladies—three black coifs, two crimson coifs, six fichus, and a pinafore, a dressing gown and petticoat of taffeta, embroidered shoes, and a quilted petticoat.[72] The coifs or bonnets mentioned in inventories are described in greater detail from Canada.

> White satin caps embroidered with imitation silver, hoods of crepe decorated with veiling, quilted bonnets of black taffeta lined with white linen.[73]

A man in Kaskaskia was listed as master barber and wig maker; a clay curler for a wig has been found in archaeological work. Some other interesting items listed were two pairs of spectacles (one decorated with silver), a corset, a chamber pot of earthenware, a paper of pins, and (showing that not all were illiterate), one man had eight small books of devotions and a cathechism.

Native materials were in use too—buffalo robes, moccasins, mitasses (leggings) of deerskin, and a lump of calumet stone (used for carving Micmac pipes). Deerskin was used for breeches and other clothing, too. The inventories show that not only the professional traders but also the *habitants* traded with the Indians. For example, in inventories were: eleven trade type hats, five trade guns (listed separately from the other guns the person owned), four dozen glass beads, and three and one-half dozen large white beads. The goods received in exchange from the Indians are present as well— beaver, deer, buffalo, and bobcat skins.

In taking an inventory the evaluators went to the house and walked through each room listing items. A few inventories even mention what room they are in. The inventories of two *habitants* in the 1740s are reproduced here. The amount given after each group is in *livres*; these show relative cost but it is not possible to give prices in present-day terms.

The first inventory is of the community property of deceased Toussaint Loisel and Cecile Brunet; she was one of the daughters of Jean Brunet and Elisabeth Deshayes.

In a cupboard which is enclosed in the wall of the room on the west side, one quilted petticoat, one short calamanco cape and one calamanco skirt, all used—60; 3 men's shirts, trimmed and 1 of coarse cloth—60; 3 poor women's chemises—25; 2 sheets, one tablecloth and 2 old napkins—30.

In a chest were found two laundry irons—10; 2 old cotton dresses, one ditto of calico, one ditto of taffeta, one calico skirt, two short capes, one of limburg and the other of calico—200; plain coifs with their forms, including two black gauze coiffes—32.

Many terms for fabric cannot be translated; the type of cloth to which they refer to is unknown.[74] Calico was a term for any plain cotton fabric which was heavier than muslin. These coifs might have been headdresses for regional peasant dress, probably the traditional type from the province where Cecile's mother was born.

In another chest was found the following: one coat of cinnamon colored cloth, one of white beaver cloth, the whole lined, and a pair of silk stockings all used—100; one Malacca cane with silver handle and ribbed stem, 1 hat, one salt cellar of common glass, 1 shirt—90; 1 old camlet cloak—25. The two aforementioned chests in poor condition—20.

Beaver was an overcoating cloth heavily milled, one face

sheared with a raised nap finish. The material was soft to handle and was woven from fine grade wool. Camlet was introduced by the Dutch; it was first woven from camel or goat's hair but later mixed with silk or wool.

The inventories do omit items; they are not a complete list of everything owned by the householders. Possibly only those items that had market value and that were not specifically personal property were itemized. No jewelry is mentioned; it cannot be proven that Cecile had jewelry, but if it existed it would have been specified as hers in the marriage contract and so not inventoried. The haphazard survival of records makes it difficult to follow references to items such as jewelry in a contract, and then in an inventory. The marriage contract of Toussaint and Cecile is not extant.

Although a fair amount of clothing is mentioned, breeches again were missing and only one pair of stockings is given; presumably Toussaint had a few more clothes that were not tallied.

One bed furnished with a feather bed, straw mattress, cot, curtains and the tester, all old, poor blanket of white wool—120; one ditto bed without curtains, feather bed, straw mattress, cot, one old buffalo robe, two bolsters—60; 1 quilted bedspread and one robe—100.

One dresser with its walnut sideboard—80; six turned chairs, all sound—36; one turned armchair—5; one turned table—20; one folding ditto—10; one brass candlestick and one poor betty lamp; one old bottle case with 8 five chopine bottles—40.

Bottle cases appear in many inventories; these were wood cases with wooden dividers that separated the bottles from each other for greater safety in transport. A *chopine* is equal to half a liter.

The evaluators at the Loisels' then turned to the kitchen items, first the fireplace and its fittings.

4 andirons, 1 iron fire shovel, 1 large pair of iron fire tongs—70; one spit; one large earthenware dish, 14 tin plates, four spoons and 4 forks—55; four terrines and one saucepan of copper—32; two pails

with iron fittings—28; one large copper pan, one frying pan and one fork for pulling meat out of the pots, one small cauldron—30.

Two old service guns—70; one old gun—8. [the service guns presumably were military issue]

35 minots of corn 40 sous the minot—70; about fifteen pots of sweet oil and lard mixed together at 30 sous the pot—221 livres 10 sous; two salt pigs about eighteen months old—120; one barrel of oil holding 25 pots at 30 sous the pot—38.10.

A *minot* was a dry measure for grain; a *pot* was equal to half a gallon. The salt pigs refer to pork that has been salted down for preserving the meat.

One ax—7; one plow with wheels, provided with its plowshare, coulter and all of the fittings to it—100; two carts, one for wood and the other for hay, mounted on their wheels, both good and bad—100; four cartloads of hay—80.

7 pigs, 6 large and one medium—120; 4 oxen—600; 3 cows-300; 2 heifers, one fifteen mo. old, the other 8—100; 40 fowls—80.

One Indian slave named Catherine about 20 years old—1000

This is an unusually high price for an Indian slave woman. She must have been either of high status or very talented.

one stone house with its lot, well, a building which was intended to be a mill—3400; one property situated in Chassin's prairie abutting on the Prairie du Rocher common and on the other side on Bacanet, four arpents or thereabouts wide; one barn 40 x22 situated in the common on a lot of 25 toises—270.[75]

Unfortunately this was not one of the houses for which a deed of sale exists that would have listed the dimensions of the house and lot. Their farming property was on the border of the Prairie Chassin and Prairie du Rocher. The document is not specific about where the house lot was located. Probably there were only two rooms in the stone house, although it is difficult to tell from the arbitrators' description. One, the west room, was unusual in possessing a built-in cupboard. Armoires were more common for storage. Clothing was stored in the cupboard and in the two chests. The bed had its curtains; the cot was likely under the bed when not in use. The two children the couple had were adults by this time. The other room was the main living and working quarters with a dresser, chairs, an armchair, the main dining table, and a folding table for occasional use. Cooking was done in the fireplace that had its spit, terrines, saucepan, frying pan, and other culinary items.

The cattle and pigs would have been roaming in the common field at this time of year. All animals had their distinctive marks so they could be identified and counted. The farm equipment, corn, and hay were probably in the barn on the common. This inventory allows our imagination to furnish a picture of the lifestyle of Cecile and Toussaint; it would have been a satisfactory life with an adequate supply of property, provisions, and a few luxuries.

The second example of an inventory is that for Charles Heneaux, a bachelor, who farmed land at Prairie du Rocher.

> First in a chest is found the following: one pair of used stockings, one cotton shirt, one Saha cloth, one poor fichu, one skein of cotton thread, one half aune of new cloth of Crin, three pairs of breeches of munition cloth, one poor frockcoat, one vest of Pinchinat partly worn, two poor coats of cloth on silk, one poor greatcoat, one poor vest of morocco cloth, one old wool hat and one old hair purse—45

At least Monsieur Heneaux had breeches! An *aune* was a measure of cloth. Pinchinat was a coarse woolen cloth from Toulon.[76]

A mixture of tools, clothes and kitchen items came next.

> One pair of grappling irons, one glass bottle, one old pair of white flannel leggings, one old gun—30; 2 mounted scythes with rings—

30; one old scythe, one pair of old andirons, one fire shovel, one grill, two axes—50; one spade, one pickaxe, one frying pan—35.

One featherbed and the pillow—60; three buffalo robes and two doeskins—25; 7 poor chairs and one poor armchair, table with folding legs—20; one small bed with boards—10; one piece sideboard of walnut, well fitted with lock and key—50; one sea chest well fitted with lock and key—15.

The unmarried Heneaux had no fine curtained bed. His sideboard made of local walnut was the best piece of furniture he had. The sea chest probably had accompanied him from Canada. He had a few cooking items.

7 terrines, a wicker covered bottle—20; 2 platters, 8 plates, 2 bowls, one porringer and 2 spoons, the whole of pewter—30; one iron cooking pot, one iron cooking spoon, two cauldrons, the bottom part of a footed pie plate, one pair of candle snuffers with the tray—40.

Heneaux owned a billard hall (see below) and listed in the inventory were: "Two sets of billiard balls—10." Billiard balls were made of ivory and came in large and small sizes; a few have been found in archaeological work. Other items were tallied—farm equipment, real estate, slaves and livestock.

Two buckets with iron rings and one small kettle used as a drinking cup—20; two ferrules, two bolts and one plough chain—12; one poor bottle case—3; one salt box—10.

one pit saw which was lent to Jean Baptiste Lalande who has it now—15.

One big cart without wheels—20; about one and a half spans of rope—1.

One negro piece d'Inde named Trompette—1500; one female

Indian slave—350.[77]

One property located in the village of Fort de Chartres upon which is built one house with a building attached in which is a billiard table in good condition, the butts and other billiard equipment, an enclosed slave cabin and everything within—1600; one arpent of land located in the prairie of Fort de Chartres, abutting on one side to the heirs of the late Martin on the other on the heirs of the late Loisel, one end on the thicket and the other on the bluffs—80.

5 milch cows—400; 3 calves from this year—200; 4 year and a half old calves—200; 3 bulls, 3 years old, nearing four—300; one yoke of oxen—250; one milch cow—80; 10 large pigs and 13 medium and small of different ages—400; 12 chickens, one rooster and one dozen small chicks—25.

Of his sixteen cattle several were cows that seem to have been producing offspring regularly. The yoke of oxen was an important item; it was like a tractor today, for they were used for plowing the fields.

530 sheaves or thereabouts of wheat in his barn which the executor will have threshed and will add to the present inventory the number of minots which is yielded therefrom; 10-12 arpents of Indian corn in the field, the amount of which shall also be added to the present inventory by the said executor.

Owed to him by Jacques Philippe, one pair of new wheels and a cart of new wood—95.[78]

The wheat must have been harvested by Heneaux and Trompette. The maize was ten to twelve surficial *arpents* (between eight and ten acres).

Heneaux' house sounds like a bachelor's. Although there was a chest containing clothes, most of the rest of the goods were mixed, such as white flannel leggings, a spade, a frying pan, and his small kettle used as a cup. His kitchen/dining area is quite well supplied, though. Heneaux had a goodly amount of property, a slave to help in the fields, and an Indian female slave to do kitchen and laundry work. With his cattle and crops Heneaux was a prosperous *habitant* and would have been a very eligible bachelor.

The Church

The Catholic religion constituted one of the main cultural elements that the settlers brought with them. The church was an integral part of the community. Its doctrines provided the justification for the moral norms of the society. This unity of beliefs supported and influenced the integration of the community. Because the concepts were shared, there was reduction in conflict. The settlers did not come for religious freedom or change. Baptized in a Catholic parish in France, they moved to a Catholic parish in the new land. Despite the domination by the Catholic Church and the officially prohibited immigration from other religious affiliations, a few Swiss and German settlers in the Louisiana colony were Lutherans and Calvinists. There were even one or two Jews.[79]

Life revolved around the church year, the feasts and festivals, the weekly mass and the saint's days; there were twenty-seven holy days observed throughout the year.[80] The priest was an important personage in the community whose authority in ecclesiastical governing paralleled that of the commandant in the secular world. The lay organization included the *marguilliers*, the three church wardens who were elected from the congregation as the temporal administrators of the parish business under the priest. A sexton was employed to care for the church. Although the contract for one at the parish of Ste. Anne at Fort de Chartres village is not extant, an agreement at Kaskaskia with Pierre Le Bain to serve as sexton gives the duties, responsibilities, and renumeration for a position that would have been similar to the one at Ste. Anne's.

His wage shall be 100 francs per year and one minot of flour from each habitant who contributes wafers for consecration and who has a pew in the church. The churchwardens will help him obtain payment from the parishioners.[81]

    This indicates that supplying the wafers for communion was one of the duties and honors of the parishioners.

    Although seating in church was not apparently a matter of contention in the Illinois, the more important citizens probably sat closest to the front. The commandant, the judge, the council, other governmental officials, the *marguillers*, the militia captain, and *syndic* carried significant status recognized by all and would have had pews closest to the front of the church. Other affluent persons would come next and then the other *habitants*, and to the rear, probably voyageurs and slaves.

    In Kaskaskia there is a record of the sixth pew on the left being rented to Pierre Faffard, captain of the militia. The cost of Faffart's pew for his lifetime and that of his children was ten *livres* per year. The rental cost of pews did not seem to increase. Much later (1776) in Prairie du Rocher the first pew of each row was ten *livres*; those following cost from five *livres* to twenty *sols*.[82]

    Burial in the parish church was the prerogative of the most important persons. In his will, Commandant Charles Claude Dutisne requested burial in the chapel at Fort de Chartres. Such status could extend to wives and children too. Elisabeth St. Ange, wife of François Coulon de Villiers, an officer, was buried in the church; their fourteen-month-old son, François, had been buried there previously.[83] The ordinary *habitants* were buried in the cemeteries of the churches. In his will, Fr. Gagnon requested that he be buried outside the door of the church of Ste. Anne, face down.[84]

    All persons were expected to tithe. One thirteenth had been common in France on all products, but the Canadians would agree only to half of that and on wheat alone, asserting their independence.[85] Most likely this amount continued in the Illinois.

    The church maintained the records of baptisms, marriages and burials. The baptismal godparent relationship implied certain responsibilities toward a child. For the settlers this sometimes meant *in loco parentis*, as in Jean Baptiste Becquet's adoption of his wife's godson mentioned earlier. Another responsibility is shown from a document in which Jean Hubert and his wife, Jeanne Bailly, as foster parents, provided Marie Jeanne Illeret, their goddaughter, a dowry of one cow for her marriage to Nicolas Marechal.[86]

A chapel for the use of the troops was constructed outside the first Fort de Chartres. As the population expanded, new churches were needed. One of the Company of the Indies' obligations was to provide churches and priests, but they did little in that regard. As early as 1720 the colonists at Kaskaskia complained that the company was not building a church for them. Boisbriant replied that they would have to bear the expense themselves of building a church, rectory, and cemetery. The Kaskaskians must have constructed a church as one was there. Presumably the one outside the first Fort de Chartres was built by *habitants* as well.

The Illinois country came under the jurisdiction of the diocese of Quebec. The date when the missions in the Illinois country became parishes is not known.[88] By the late 1730s at least there were three parishes in the Illinois country—Cahokia with the Holy Family church, Kaskaskia with the church of the Immaculate Conception, and at Fort de Chartres, Ste. Anne's, which included Prairie du Rocher and St. Philippe.

At Kaskaskia the Jesuits served the church of the Immaculate Conception. The missionaries had come south with the Indians as they moved, and served them and the French. The early services at Kaskaskia were conducted in both the Illinois language and Latin. Penicaut describes this: "The Illinois sing a verse of a psalm or hymn in their language and the French the following verse in Latin."[89] The chapel by the fort had a Jesuit chaplain who saw to the religious needs of the soldiers and took care of the mission of St. Francis Xavier on the nearby Metchigamia Indian reserve. The priests from the fort and from Kaskaskia provided rites for the inhabitants of both Prairie du Rocher and St. Philippe. At Cahokia the mission and parish of the Holy Family was run by the priests of the Seminary of Foreign Missions.

In 1731, when the Company of the Indies returned the colony to the king, there was a flurry of construction of religious structures.

The *habitants* in the village by the fort wanted their own church, separate and larger than the fort's chapel.[90] The churchwardens, Hebert, Fabut, and Delessart, elected by the *habitants*, contracted with Mathurin Charveau of Prairie du Rocher to have a church and rectory built in the Prairie of the Establishment. Charveau was

> to make and build the framework of a church fifty feet long and thirty feet wide, eleven feet under the beams, the beams set in the posts; and the framework of a house twenty-seven feet long and twenty feet wide on sills.

The churchwardens were to furnish all the lumber and to deliver it to the site in the size and thicknesses specified by Charveau. The lumber was to be delivered by March 15 at the latest, at which time the contractor promised to begin construction. Charveau was to be paid 1000 *livres* in supplies, half in bacon and half in wheat, in two payments.[91]

Probably the chapel of St. Joseph at Prairie du Rocher was erected in the same year. The notation of the agreement is on a notary's list that covered the years 1722-32, so 1732 is the latest possible date.[92] The church wardens made an agreement with Antoine Ple for his lot on which to construct the chapel. The chapel of the Visitation at St. Philippe possibly dates from this time, too.

Shortly the church of Ste. Anne, constructed by Charveau, was ready. Now that the parish had a new church and associated chapels, the inhabitants requested a priest. Fr. de Guyenne apparently had enough to do to manage the fort and the Xavier mission; Fr. Tartarin was fully occupied with the parish at Kaskaskia. The supply of priests never was sufficient for the needs of the colony, but the Jesuits promised to provide one when more arrived from France. This indefinite wait for when a priest would become available did not please the villagers of Prairie du Rocher and Fort de Chartres. They then exhibited signs of very unconventional thinking unleashing an ecclesiastical storm. Not willing to wait for a Jesuit sometime in the future, the *habitants* contacted Fr. Mercier, the superior of the Seminary of Foreign Missions at Cahokia, asking for a priest. He, glad of the opportunity, came to perform services and also assigned a curé, Fr. Joseph Gagnon.

The new church was dedicated on Easter Sunday of 1732, as Ste. Anne's, and Fr. Mercier reported to Quebec:

> I remained there for the feast of easter and had much consolation to see the piety and fervor with which everyone approached the sacraments, because heretofore the greater number of the habitans and other people of that place, without any scruple, went on years without making their easter...of all the persons who compose that new parish, only two or three did not make their duty, but I have every reason to believe they have done so since then.[93]

The chapels at Prairie du Rocher (St. Joseph's) and at St. Philippe (Our Lady of the Visitation), since they were part of the parish, were served by the seminary priests, too. The parish of Ste. Anne, as distinct from the chapel at the fort, dates from this time. There is no information as to whether or not the chapel at the fort had been dedicated to Ste. Anne.

This invitation to the Cahokian missionaries was not the first time that a stir had been caused by the incursion of the seminary priests into what the Jesuits considered their mission field. In 1699 the seminary had established a mission in the Illinois country at the Tamarois/Cahokia Indian village. The Jesuits, although they had not constucted a chapel there, had visited the village previously and felt the location was within the purview of their letters patent for evangelization. For a time priests of both orders lived there in comparative harmony; eventually the ruling of the ecclesiatical court left the seminary priests in charge at the mission.

The Jesuits were not pleased with this new expansion of the seminary's jurisdiction and the officials in New Orleans were uncertain about its legality.

> The habitants of the Prairie of Fort de Chartres, in the Illinois, have addressed a petition to us asking for the confirmation of their choice of a priest of the Foreign Missions to assume charge of the

Church and Presbytery that they had built at their own expense. .. We remarked, however, to M. St. Ange, who commands at this post, that our opinion is, that it was not within the power of these habitants to call in a priest of the Foreign Missions.[94]

The officials sent their comments off to the minister in France who concurred with their opinion. It never has been and still is not within the power of a Catholic congregation to call a priest for their church. Fr. D'outreleau, the superior of the Jesuit missions in Illinois, filed a formal protest. The notary, Jerome, presented the official copy of this protest to the Seminary Superior Fr. Mercier at Fort de Chartres in August 1733. It produced no change.

In 1733 Pierre D'Artaguiette, nephew of the previous D'Artaguiette, was then commandant, and at the request of the Jesuit Fr. du Guyenne built or repaired the chapel at the fort so that the Jesuits could continue to conduct services there for the troops.[95] Although correspondence continued on the subject of the Jesuits vs. the seminarians for several years, the seminary priests remained. Unfortunately the church records are missing from 1726-1743; these might have given a clearer picture of the events.

Having taken their extremely unusual action, the villagers calmly accepted it and ignored the controversy, certain that in time it would go away, which it did. They had succeeded in acquiring a church and a priest to provide for the religious and social needs of their communities. To have access to the Catholic church was more important than the political question of jurisdiction. This event casts quite a different light on the relationship of the people and the church than usually depicted. They were not meek peasants overwhelmed by the authority of the church. The villagers apparently held a very modern concept, that the church was there to serve them. In France such behavior would have been suppressed, but here government was less authoritarian and they were well aware of that.

The communal activities, the governmental structure, the church, and the family ties all were formed from the culture brought from France. All inhabitants held certain expectations—the continuance of the church and its sacraments, the regulated inheritance of property, and justice under the security of the laws of France. The new land did not require a great deal of modification in the culture. Although they were living a life with different hazards and stresses than in France, the internal mechanisms of the society could deal with these without much strain. There was a common understanding of the norms and values coming from their traditions that served to form the basis for the society. The church provided the moral sanctions that underlay determination of appropriate behavior; in most cases these were followed. The family, its continuation, and control of property remained central to the villagers, and institutions and manners supported these familial values. However, the lack of close governmental supervision, affluence, and social and physical mobility developed in them self-determination for working out their lives.

Notes

1. Eccles 1972, 34.
2. Trudel 1971, 11.
3. ANC B38, 29-5-296.
4. Brown and Dean 1977, 30:4:6:1; Dean and Brown 1981, 34:2:19:1; a capon was a castrated rooster, fattened for food.
5. Brown and Dean 1977, K159.
6. Dean and Brown 1981 45:10:31:1; 37:-:-:1.
7. Henretta 1978.
8. Dean and Brown 1981: 43:3:9:2.
9. Dean and Brown 1981, 37:3:8:1.
10. Hoffman 1975, 24.
11. Ekberg 1998, 48; Hoffman 1975, 24; Ekberg 1995, 257; 263.
12. Courville n.d.
13. For an excellent and detailed discussion of the land settlement and its effects, *see* Ekberg, 1998.
14. Brown and Dean 1977, K58.
15. Rowland and Sanders 2:557.
16. Recent archaeological work at the village of Chartres revealed a two-room house with galleries, roughly 20 x 28 ft., of *poteaux en terre* construction. Gums and Witty 2000.
17. Dean and Brown 1981, 58:12:30:1; 40:8:22:1.
18. Brown and Dean 1977, K7; K161; K32.

19. Dean and Brown 1981:37:11:4:1.
20. Dean and Brown 1981, 44:8:22:1; Brown and Dean 1977, K111.
21. Dean and Brown 1981, 40:11:27:1, 2; La. Hist. Soc. Rec. July 1, 1739.
22. Keefe 1992, 43.
23. Brown and Dean 1977, K441.
24. Dean and Brown 1981, 48:9:8:1; 48:9:15:1.
25. Rowland and Sanders 2, 532.
26. Bossu 1962, 118.
27. A *minot* is a dry measure of 70 lbs., Surrey 1916, 291.
28. *Louisiana Historical Quarterly* (hereafter *LHQ*) 8:2, 290; 3:5, 381, 378.
29. Pease and Jenison 1940, 274.
30. Dean and Brown 1981, 26:8:12.
31. Ekberg 1998, 280.
32. Dean and Brown 1981, 37:12:16:1; 46:11:22:1; 33:9:2:1.
33. For further details on the voyageurs' activities *see* M. Brown 2002.
34. Surrey 1916, 46; 75.
35. Surrey 1916, 207.
36. *LHQ* 3:4, 513, 516-519.
37. Mereness 1916, 70.
38. Caldwell 1941, 47; Dean and Brown 1981, 40:7:22:1.
39. Eccles 1968, 79.
40. Jelks and Ekberg 1989, 10; Palm 1931, 44; Reynolds 1852, 68.
41. Briggs 1985, 284; Duby 1976, 18; Henretta 1978, 18.
42. For agricultural implements *see* Duby 1976; Benson 1937; Ekberg 1998, 177ff.
43. Dean and Brown 1981, 47:10:22:1; 48:2:22:1.
44. Dean and Brown 1981, 44:7:29:1.
45. Henretta 1978, 18.
46. Briggs 1985, 286. Briggs took as his base 800,000 *livres* of flour, a hearsay report related by Page du Pratz (1975, 182), who tended to exaggeration. Briggs' figures were adjusted to correspond with 400,000 *livres,* an amount that can be verified in the records.
47. Pers. comm. 1975.
48. Dean and Brown 1981, 30:8:9:2; 32:6:14:1.
49. Brown and Dean 1977, K81; Dean and Brown 1981 50:1:1:4; Pease and Jenison 1940, 430.
50. Dean and Brown 1981, 44:7:29:1.
51. Page du Pratz 1975, 226.

52. Dean and Brown 1981, 37:7:2:1.
53. Brown and Dean 1977, K388; Ekberg n.d.
54. *LHQ* 3:4, 513; 516-519.
55. Dean and Brown 1981, 46:7:30:1; 46:8:6:1; 47:5:4:1.
56. Briggs 1985; *see* discussions in Nish 1968, Couville n.d.
57. Essex County Court 111, 153. For example, a man was called to account for his wife wearing a silk scarf. He was found to have property of more than 200 pounds value, so the case was dismissed as his wife could indeed wear silk.
58. Duclos in O'Neill 1966, 251.
59. Ekberg 1998, 144.
60. Nish 1968, 183.
61. Nish 1968, 25.
62. Dean and Brown 1981, 43:5:20:1.
63. Boyle 1983.
64. Dean and Brown 1981, 40:11:27:1; 41:5:1:1; 45:6:28:5; 44:6:28:1; 1977, D302.
65. Dean and Brown 1981, various ref., *see* index; Boyle 1983.
66. Dean and Brown 1981, 41:9:22:1; 37:10:9:1.
67. Brown and Dean 1977, K355.
68. Dean and Brown 1981, 24:9:2:1; 25:1:15:1.
69. Jelks *et. al.*, 1989; Noble, 1997.
70. Pease and Jenison 1940, 307.
71. Brown and Dean 1995, 16.
72. A fichu is a small triangular shawl to cover the shoulders and neck.
73. Douville and Casanova 1968, 53.
74. Some fabrics are listed in Waugh 1968, 316; and Fiske 1975.
75. Dean and Brown 1981, 44:1:3:1.
76. pers. comm. Lawrie Dean.
77. *Piece d'Inde* was "the standard value of a complete negro, that is 17 years old or over without bodily defects, or a negress without bodily defects, of 15 to 30 years, or three children of 8 to 10 years in age." Belting 1975, 38.
78. Dean and Brown 1981, 44:7:29:1.
79. 0'Neill 1966, 280.
80. Belting 1975, 68.
81. Dean and Brown 1981, 39:12:3:1.
82. Dean and Brown 1981, 24:5:1:1; St. Jo. Ch. Rec. 31 Jan. 1776.

83. Dean and Brown 1981, 30:5:12:1; Brown and Dean 1977, D273; D37.
84. Dean and Brown 57:3:14:1.
85. Eccles 1968, 72.
86. Dean and Brown 1981, 35:8:20:1.
87. Dean and Brown 1981, 29:3:8:1.
88. Balesi 1992, 217.
89. Margry 1875-1886 5, 491.
90. ANC, Series C, 1-1, Fo. 139, 15 July 1732.
91. Dean and Brown 19 81, 31:1:7:1.
92. Dean and Brown 1981, 1722-32:62; 1722-32:45; 44:8:6:1.
93. Schlarmann 1929, 287.
94. Palm 1931, 57.
95. Palm 1931, 59.

4

Prairie du Rocher
Under the French Regime

The 1730s and early 1740s were the time when life seemed most promising for the colonists in the Illinois. It was a time of relative peace and stability; the Fox wars had ended and the European powers were not engaged in any major conflict affecting the colony. Nevertheless, the Illinois villages and their attached farmlands were small, civilized islands amidst the prairies and woods of the Mississippi Valley wilderness. The lack of continuing steady immigration from France meant that the population in Louisiana would not increase rapidly again, as it had in the mid-1720s. The population grew slowly from natural increase, emigration from Canada, and movement upriver from the less successful settlements on the lower Mississippi River.

Another official census was taken in 1732. The area of Fort de Chartres, St. Philippe, and Prairie du Rocher had 179 French and 102 black and Indian slaves totaling 281 persons. The total on the census record in 1726 for the same area had been 208, so this was not much of an increase. The village of Kaskaskia had 184 French and 170 slaves. Three officers and forty-one soldiers were listed from the garrison at Fort de Chartres. An estimated fifty voyageurs operated mainly out of Kaskaskia.[1] The French presence was spread thinly along the Mississippi River.

Clustered together in the villages, the people had a degree of security and safety, but this ended on the outskirts of town. Marauding bands of Indians occasionally struck down people in the woods and on the trails. Between Prairie du Rocher and Kaskaskia was the *Grand Bois* (the Big Woods), the scene of several deaths. The convoys, of course, were in constant danger and voyageurs were killed, captured, or had to deal with hostile Indians. "Street-wise," the voyageurs knew much about the Indian ways and used them to survive.

Living in the Illinois may have had its dangers and problems, but in general the *habitants* saw it as a secure life. Young men born in the Illinois sought new land to establish themselves, having high expectations for future expansion of the settlements. Unfortunately this optimism and relative peace did not last for long. In 1730 no one could have expected that within a generation Britain's victories in the Seven Year's War would have swept away all French rule from North America.

Land Grants in Prairie du Rocher

During the 1730s Prairie du Rocher developed sufficient population to be recognized in official correspondence as a settlement distinct from Fort de Chartres. Although the 1732 census listed only Charles Gossiaux and his wife living there, they could hardly have been the sole inhabitants. The first church of St. Joseph was constructed in 1731 or 1732, and a single family would not require nor could they afford a separate chapel. Indeed the land on which to construct the church was a lot belonging to Antoine Ple *dit* La Plume, the pit sawyer, who received another lot in exchange for it.[2] Obviously he was around, and there must have been more residents who for one reason or another did not appear on the census.

The settlement of the Prairie du Rocher area had begun earlier. Charlevoix commented in 1721 that "the French are now beginning to settle the country between this fort [Fort de Chartres] and the first mission [Kaskaskia]."[3] The concession of land that became Prairie

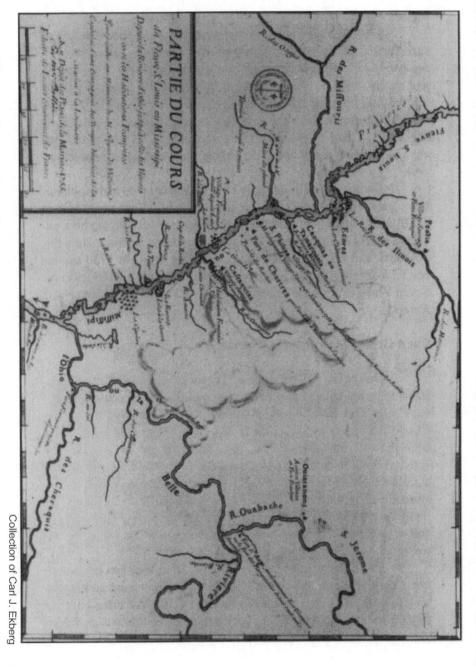

Collection of Carl J. Ekberg

This map, drawn in 1755, shows Prairie du Rocher, Fort de Chartres, and other settlements along the

du Rocher had been the commandant Boisbriant's. He transferred his nominal seignory to his nephew, Ensign Jacques-Gaspard Piot de L'Angloiserie, his sister's son.[4] The grant was adjacent to Chassin's concession, known as the Prairie Chassin, part of which later became attached to the Prairie du Rocher commonfield. On the downriver side of Prairie du Rocher was Melique's grant, and then the Grand Prairie.

Official land grants were made to individuals in Prairie du Rocher by Ste. Thérèse in 1734; he was leaving the area then to take command of Arkansas Post.[5] However, the grantees had been farming the strips for a number of years. Ten land grants to individuals made by Ste. Thérèse in February 1734 are listed in the notary's record, but only one survives today. This is the grant to Joseph Buchet. Buchet was the judge and held various positions from the 1730s through the 1750s. He received the concession of a large strip, six *arpents* wide, in the "*domaine du Rocher*," and a town lot. Buchet agreed to pay Ste. Thérèse on St. Martin's feast day half a *minot* of wheat for each *arpent* frontage, two capons for each two *arpents* frontage of non-arable land, and one capon a year for the lot. The non-arable land was swamp and wet woods, as can be determined from the location of his grant.

Nine other persons received grants: Charles Gossiaux, Jean Baptiste Beauvais, Joseph La Roche, Jean Baptiste Turpin, François Corset dit Coco, René Grude, Jacques Lalande, Ignace Legras, and Antoine Bienvenu. Ple is not mentioned; his farmland was in the Prairie Chassin section. A small village would have formed already if all of these people had lots. Ste. Thérèse's grants probably recognized and confirmed previously cultivated lands; the prior relationship with them may have been as tenant farmers.

In May Etienne Langlois, recently arrived in the Illinois, was given a grant next to Jacques Lalande. Langlois also received rights to a stream on which to build a flour mill and a sawmill. Langlois' grant was made by the commandant, Pierre D'Artaguiette. An additional grant is listed on the notary's inventory of documents to the widow Potier in 1739; the original record has not been preserved. This probably was Françoise La Brise, the widow of Jean Baptiste

Potier and mother of Marie Françoise, Buchet's wife.

Probably rents similar to those in Buchet's grant were listed in the original documents for these properties but, as mentioned previously, it is unlikely that any were paid. This supposition is reinforced by Ste. Thérèse's later grant in 1737, done in New Orleans, to Augustin Langlois, brother to Etienne. In this, Ste. Thérèse gives him land from "my domain." Ste. Thérèse stated, "…I exact nothing from the [other] settlers on the same Prairie; they are all lords and masters."[6]

In making out the grants Ste. Thérèse had reserved his seigniorial rights to the streams for a mill, but these rights shortly reverted to the domain. In 1734 three residents of Prairie Chassin and Prairie du Rocher, Onesime Delessart, Charles Gossiaux, and Antoine Bienvenu, requested and received a grant of six *arpents* below the bluffs, between Prairie du Rocher and Fort de Chartres, where they could build a water mill. The mill was to be placed near a fork in the stream; they requested both arms of the stream and the land between them. The outline of the grant still can be seen on USGS maps today. The partners received a permit from Commandant St. Ange to construct the watermill. They requested assistance from Philippe Renault, who verified that there was sufficient water in the stream for a mill. Antoine Ple *dit* La Plume contracted to build a causeway for the mill and guaranteed it against being washed away for three years.[7]

The village of Prairie du Rocher lists its founding as 1722 but how this date was determined is not certain. Charles Gossiaux may have arrived here that year, beginning the settlement. Definitely he was one of the earliest residents. In 1722, when Gossiaux was about twenty-three years old, he and Jeanne Bienvenu, sister to Antoine, made a marriage contract in the Illinois country. They were married a year later.

The document of Gossiaux' grant from Ste. Thérèse is not in existence and the exact location of Gossiaux' property can longer be determined. It must have been near what was known as the Marais Gossiaux (the Gossiaux swamp). This name continued to appear with variations in spelling on maps throughout the nineteenth century. The area is along Prairie du Rocher Creek near the present sewage lagoon.

He and Jeanne Bienvenu had twins, a boy and girl, in 1724, both of whom died in infancy. Jeanne died in 1729 and Charles married for the second time to Marie Rose Govreau, or Bonneaux, the widow of an officer, Villeneuve, who brought with her Pierre Villeneuve, her son. Marianne was unusual for a woman in being literate; she signed the marriage contract herself. Three children born to them who lived are recorded—Marie Jeanne, Marie Charlotte and Jacques Charles.

The second marriage had some ups and downs. In 1740 Marie Rose made a request to the judge, de La Loere Flaucour, to have the property of Pierre Villeneuve, her son, transfered from Gossiaux, who was the guardian, to the custody of Joseph Baron, the deputy guardian of the child. She charged that Gossiaux had mismanaged the property and had sold some improperly. The judge ordered this to be done. In 1741 though, the couple requested that they be allowed to sell two properties in Kaskaskia that belonged to Pierre, since they were too far away to manage and they would buy land in Prairie du Rocher in exchange. The court agreed. A couple of years later Marie Rose acknowledged receipt of property from Baron, having been elected as the child's guardian herself. Women could be official guardians for their children.

In 1743 there was a voluntary separation of property between Gossiaux and Marie Rose. Gossiaux was forced to sell a large house as part of the settlement of the separation of property. Then he rented a room with a fireplace for two years for himself, his wife, and children, so the marriage must have stumbled along. Apparently he had other property, for later he sold Urban Gervais land, a house, and lot in Prairie du Rocher, plus a share in a watermill located in Prairie Chassin. He received in exchange two black slaves, their three children, and 700 *livres* in flour.

Gossiaux was a mason; like most of the craftsmen he was referred to as a "master." He may have gone through the whole apprenticeship sequence in France, but whether or he had or not in the Illinois, he would be listed as a master. This rapid acquisiton of status definitely was an advantage to young men coming from France.

In one contract Gossiaux agreed to replaster the interior of a house, plaster the chimney, and plaster the front and rear faces of the house, presumably under the porch roofs. He also dug a well; someone assisted with this job. His part of the work probably was laying up the stone for the casement of the well. Gossiaux had a lime kiln for burning the limestone to make mortar. An old lime kiln still exists by the bluffs; it is possible that it dates to this period.

He and another early inhabitant, Mathurin Charveau, a carpenter, agreed to do the carpentry and stone work for a windmill in the prairie near Prairie du Rocher for Jean Baptiste Lalande. In 1737 Charveau contracted to build a stone barn in Prairie du Rocher for Urban Gervais. His fee was to be an amount of stone and wood equal to that used in the barn, to be delivered to a site in Prairie du Rocher for him.

Charles Gossiaux died in February 1751 at age fifty-two. After his death, his son through a guardian sold a lot that had on it an unfinished stone house with a vaulted cellar.[8]

Antoine Bienvenu received land from Ste. Thérèse, but lived in Kaskaskia. Bienvenu was well-to-do; he hired overseers for both his property in Kaskaskia and at Prairie du Rocher. In the 1750s he moved to New Orleans, but members of the family remained in the Illinois.[9]

Jean Baptiste Beauvais, a Canadian, lived in Kaskaskia. He was related to settlers in St. Philippe and he married a girl from there, Louise LaCroix. He sold the land he received from Ste. Thérèse to François Bastien and Antoine Rivière in 1737.[10]

Jean Joseph Laroche, born about 1696 in La Madeline, Canada, married Marie La Pointe of Fort de Chartres. He received six *arpents* from Ste. Thérèse. He sold three *arpents* of his grant to Charles Heneaux in 1737, but retained the other three as farmland for his own use. He also owned land around Fort de Chartres.[11]

Another grantee, Jean Baptiste Turpin, had many relatives from Canada living in the area. Among these was his uncle Louis, living in Kaskaskia, who assisted him in transactions when he was a minor (under twenty-five) and administered Jean Baptiste's estate after he was killed in the Chickasaw Wars.

Jean Baptiste had been married to an Indian or métis woman

and the marriage had not been successful. After Turpin's death Louis Metivier attempted to get a portion of Jean's estate because he was married to an aunt of Jean Baptiste's, who also was related to Jean's wife. In the legal hearings that followed depositions were taken from various people for information concerning the wife. Catherine Mallet stated that:

> she knows that the wife of the late Jean Baptiste Turpin had quarreled with her husband and gone off with the Ottawa Indians where she took one of them named Pintalsy as husband. The commandant at Detroit, who was M. du Buisson had her put in irons and she was shipped to her husband in punishment. Her husband later had her released from the irons through his pleas. She complained that he would not give her any clothes and he bought one hundred ecus worth for her. After this purchase she refused to have anything to do with the clothes and made her way to the Hurons.

Another witness said that Jean Baptiste had had her put in the General Hospital in Montreal and that she escaped from there and went to England. The courts in Illinois favored the uncle, Louis Turpin, as it was felt Mme. Turpin had forfeited her rights as a wife when she fled and abandoned her husband. The Metiviers appealed to the Superior Council and Louis Turpin had to go to New Orleans for the hearing on the case.[12]

René Grude *dit* Langevin, who received land from Ste. Thérèse, was from the diocese of Le Mans. He married Marie Barbe Deblee of Germany in the Illinois in 1725. Marie Barbe may have been from one of the German settlements on the lower Mississippi. Grude was a roofer; he died early in 1739. His widow then married Louis Levasseur, another resident of Prairie du Rocher. Louis Levasseur *dit* D'espagne (the Spaniard) had been deported from Paris at twenty-one years of age as a *faux saunier*. In 1731 an Indian shot him and he thought he was dying from the wound, so he wrote his will; he lived, however, to be about sixty-two years old. Like most of the convicts who came to the Illinois, he became a respected and prosperous citizen. In the new land his past was not held against him;

he kept to the norms of the society and was integrated into the community.[13]

Jacque Guillemot *dit* La Lande, generally known as Lalande, was a Canadian, a cousin of the governor of Louisiana, Bienville. He married an Indian woman, Marie Titio. Lalande died by 1737, at which time his widow sold four *arpents* probably from his grant to Pierre Pilet.[14]

Jean Baptiste Ignace LeGras *dit* Gros Jean was from Villemarie in Canada. He married Jeanne Germain, and their daughter Jeanne inherited his four-*arpent*-wide grant. She married Jean Baptiste Barbeau.

Etienne Langlois died by 1737 and his widow married Urban Gervais; Etienne's land went with her. Etienne had received the rights from Ste. Thérèse to a stream on the Prairie Chassin on which to build a water mill and a sawmill. As part of the adjudication of Langlois' estate a mill was offered for sale and was purchased by Gervais. Equipment for the unfinished mill was listed in the sale.

The square [body?] of the mill raised on twelve pieces of wood.
A completed millstone, bored which is by the door of Augustin
    Langlois'.
The main shaft, bored, near the mill.
The cogwheel[?] completed and garnished.
The iron spindle mounted, spindles.
The waterwheel completed and bored, it appears ready.

Gervais also purchased a share in the mill from Gossiaux.[15]

Augustin Langlois' land stayed in the family. Later Buchet sold nine arpents to Pierre Chabot. Buchet had acquired land in addition to his grant.[16] With all these sales, by 1740 a number of the original grantees were no longer in possession of the concessions from Ste. Thérèse. The people to whom they sold farmed the land, but not all were full-time residents of Prairie du Rocher; this did not matter. The corporate entity was not the village, but the land-holding community. This type of affiliation is contrary to our way of thinking now, but is necessary to comprehend in order to understand the colonists and their world view. Prairie du Rocher was not so much a village—a town—but a settlement of *habitants*. No matter where their residences were, the persons who owned land there were involved in decisions for the communal property—the common and commonfield.

Other Settlers

Besides those who had the original concessions there were other residents; some held lands in the adjacent Prairie Chassin or in the Fort de Chartres commonfields. Mathurin Charveau, a carpenter, came early to Prairie du Rocher. He was a craftsman and did not farm. He purchased a house in the "prairie" in 1726; this might have been in Prairie du Rocher or elsewhere. The designations for areas frequently are unclear—to us that is. They undoubtedly were plain to the residents then. He was the carpenter who built the church of Ste. Anne.[17]

Another early settler was Ambroise Moreau *dit* Sansregret. He with his wife, Jeanne Paule, had been deported from France in the early 1720s, classified as "deserters and other sorts." Moreau owned land in the Prairie du Rocher area and was a business partner with Charveau. During this partnership Pierre Petoux donated to them his property and labor for the rest of his life in exchange for agreeing to care for him in his old age. Chaveau and the Moreaus also made up a mutual donation of property in the event of the death of one of them and had it filed in the Register of Donations. Ambroise lived to be eighty years old, probably outliving Petoux and Charveau. He and his wife also were also examples of the convicts' success in the Illinois. Respected citizens, they enjoyed a better life than they would have been able to in France.[18]

François Bastien, who was Swiss, had arrived in 1719 on the ship *Le Union*, destined for Renault's concession. After being a tenant farmer, he, too, ended up in Prairie du Rocher. He bought Jean Baptiste Beauvais' grant, married, had three or four children, and died in 1763 at more than sixty years of age.

Soldiers sometimes purchased houses in the villages where they lived when not on duty. At least one, Michel Arbre, lived in

Prairie du Rocher. Detailed for duty on a convoy, he leased his house, lot, barn, and livestock to Joseph Roubeau, with the understanding that if he did not return within eighteen months it would constitute a sale.[19]

Sometime in the mid-1740s two Barbeau brothers, both named Jean Baptiste, came to Illinois. Their family was originally from Poitou. The elder brother married Catherine Allard, daughter of deceased Jean Allard and Jeanne Germain. The younger brother married Jeanne LeGras, daughter of Ignace Legras and Jeanne Germain. The widowed Jeanne Germain had married Legras for her second marriage and so, not only did the two brothers have the same name, but they had the same mother-in-law, having married half-sisters.[20] These families are an example of the complex relationships that came about between the settlers. Descendants of the Barbeaus remain in the area.

Most of the villagers were related in some way or another to other persons in the colony. Although for the French-born, these connections were limited; the Canadian settlers were highly interrelated. St. Philippe shows this the most strongly. With forty-one percent of its inhabitants of Canadian origin, many were related to each other and to the other Canadians in the region.[21]

These kinds of interrelationships made for very flexible residence patterns. Inhabitants continually moved between the various villages, setting up shop in Kaskaskia, the village of Chartres, St. Philippe, or Prairie du Rocher, as the opportunities for business in one form or another appeared. They were always near relatives.

Extensive communication and interaction existed among the settlements. Frequently farmland was owned next to a relative's land, and the assumption is that this was for cooperative working of the fields. The comings and goings for relatives' baptisms, weddings, joint trade ventures, seeding, harvesting, putting stock in and out of the commonfield and so on, made for a peripatetic lifestyle, to say nothing of possible trips to New Orleans, Canada, or up the Missouri River. Traffic was continual on roads and on the Mississippi River between the villages.

An example of the shifting residencies was Pierre Dirousse *dit* St. Pierre Laverdure, who in 1737 had a house constructed for him at Fort de Chartres by Alexandre Duclos. In 1740 he purchased land, a stone house, and half a horse mill at Prairie du Rocher from Gossiaux. In 1741 he made a request to Judge de La Loère Flaucour to be replaced as the guardian for the heirs of Donet. He was moving to Prairie du Rocher, so he would no longer be able to fulfill his duties to care for the livestock at Fort de Chartres that belonged to the heirs. At Prairie du Rocher he became an innkeeper, but in 1743 he arranged an exchange of houses with Pierre Louvier D'amour Dechaufour of Kaskaskia. Louvier moved to Prairie du Rocher and Dirousse went to Kaskaskia, where he remained at least until 1779 as an innkeeper. Although Dirousse did not move back to Prairie du Rocher, some of his descendants did.[22]

The *habitants* of Prairie du Rocher were occupied mainly as craftsmen and farmers. The businesses and artisans in Prairie du Rocher mirrored those of the other settlements—one of the Barbeaus was a master joiner. Gossiaux and Manuel were masons, Charveau a carpenter, Derousse an innkeeper, and Ple a pit sawyer. Milling was a seasonal occupation. A number of privately owned horse mills existed. Jean Baptiste Lalande seems to have been in the milling business and had several windmills built over the years. One of these, designed by Philippe Renault, was near Prairie du Rocher. Gossiaux contracted for the masonry work of the mill, Charveau for the carpentry, and Lalande agreed to provide the cloth for the sails. No records are known, however, concerning its operation, nor for the water mill mentioned earlier.[23]

Prairie du Rocher was not a fur trade center like Kaskaskia. The inhabitants engaged mainly in the produce trade and with the local Indians for meat or hides. They brought flour and other foodstuffs to the fort to exchange for imported goods. A few men who had farmland in Prairie du Rocher, such as Bienvenu and Pilet, engaged in major trading partnerships, but lived in Kaskaskia. However, some traders and voyageurs resided in the community.

François Marie Gilbert *dit* Sans Peur (without fear) was a trader originally from Detroit, but moved to Prairie du Rocher, where he held land. He married a daughter of Augustin Langlois and was accompanied at the wedding by three brothers, also traders. A

voyageur, Laderoute, was reportedly killed by Indians while returning from New Orleans. Joseph Buchet, Attorney for Vacant Lands
(one of his many titles), took back for the domain the two lots
Laderoute had owned in Prairie du Rocher.[24]

Pierre de Chaufour de Louvière was from a large family that
had lived in Quebec for three generations. Very likely he came to the
area because his brother Michel was established at the Fort de Chartres
village. In the early 1740s he was a trader upriver to Michilimackinac
and Montreal and down to New Orleans. He made an agreement with
Louis Marin of Prairie du Rocher to take to New Orleans 851 *livres*
in flour and notes and 248 *livres* of buckskin. Louvière would trade
these items for merchandise in New Orleans and deliver the goods to
Kaskaskia. He was to receive 50 *livres* in weight for each 100 *livres*
of merchandise that he managed to obtain for Marin's goods. The
similar agreement he made with Colet was mentioned earlier.

Successful as a trader/merchant, twenty years later he was
sufficiently prominent to be elected the militia captain for Prairie du
Rocher. At his death Louvière owned a two-story stone house and a
horse mill in Prairie du Rocher. His status also was indicated in the
burial record.

24 May 1768 Burial of Pierre du Chaufour de Louvière, habitant, captain of militia of His Britannic Majesty. His body was buried in the
chapel of Prairie du Rocher with all ceremonies on the left side in
front. He received all the sacraments.[25]

Although many voyageur contracts are extant in the records
for the 1740s, there are few for residents of Prairie du Rocher. The
Prairie du Rocher villagers did not in general contract out as voyageurs,
with the exception of some of the young men. The urge to travel and
the challenge of the voyages continued to appeal to the youth. Although no contracts are extant for young Prairie du Rocher males,
they probably were similar to those in other communities. At Fort de
Chartres village, Jean Henrion and his wife, Marie Barbé, contracted
with the trader, Pierre Messager, for their fourteen-year-old son, Pierrot
(little Pierre) to work with Messager for three years for a wage of 300

livres. His wages were to be paid to the parents. Pierrot was to receive food, maintenance, and religious instruction.

The Henrions not only wanted their young son to have food, clothing, and care in his profession, but as devout Catholics they wanted him to have proper knowledge of the catechism and the church's rules. Since it is unlikely much religious instruction would occur enroute between Illinois and New Orleans, this would have to be provided either in New Orleans or while wintering in the Illinois, when apparently Pierrot would be residing with Messager, rather than with his parents.

The elder Henrions received his wage for the work; they evidently hired him out to Messager as one would do with a slave or contracted laborer, maintaining complete control over his life and labor. Too few of these "appenticeship" documents exist to determine if this was a typical pattern. A contract for another youth, Jean Baptiste Neport, does not specify that the wage would go to his father, although this could have been the understanding.[26]

The age of fourteen was considered mature enough for a boy to begin training for his future occuption. The *cadet à l'eguillette,* who was the son of an officer, began his service at this age. There is no indication of any formal apprenticeship program in the Illinois, but instruction as a voyageur/trader, blacksmith, or in other crafts constituted an type of apprenticeship. In a late document Jean Baptiste Conand, twenty years old, was apprenticed by his mother under the power of attorney from her husband to Nicolas Canada, "master smith," to spend a year learning his trade.[27] This is similar to Jean Baptiste Becquet's agreeing to teach Pierre Texier the locksmith trade. For girls, fourteen was a marriageable age, although occasionally they married even younger.

Besides the training for crafts and occupations, other educational opportunities were available. In a few families literacy was important. Not only males were instructed, but female children as well. Families paid for instruction, an arrangement that may have been similar to later subscription schools. In a contract in 1760, François Cottin, a schoolmaster, agreed to teach a daughter of the Aubuchon family to read and write, and stated that she would have the ordinary two sessions per day. The implication is that schooling was throughout the whole day, although the length of the sessions is not given.

The Barbeau family of Prairie du Rocher insisted on literacy for the children, including the girls. The girls signed documents as witnesses, spelling the name "Barbau" as did Jean Baptiste, their father, a major political figure in the Illinois. The name later received an "e."

Cottin may have taught the child in the home or possibly she went to a "school." In other cases, students did come from a distance to attend classes. In the 1760s the deaths of two "students" at Prairie du Rocher were recorded in the Ste. Anne's registers; both had been boarding with local people, one with the Gossiaux family.[28]

Life in the 1740s

By the early 1740s a generation born in the Illinois settlements was growing up and wanted to establish themselves on their own land. Having property was not only an economic necessity, but also held social significance. Property allowed them to support a family and, importantly in the mentality of the society, to provide an inheritance for the next generation. Here, unlike in France, there was land to acquire.

St. Joseph's prairie, four leagues from Kaskaskia, was divided into grants for children of the *habitants* of Kaskaskia.[29] Two leagues above St. Philippe was a newly opened area for settlement in the Prairie of the Apacois (the Indian word for prairie potato). As a grant explained, this was more properly called Belle Fontaine. Lands were granted and permission was given to settle there as soon as there were sufficient settlers for safety.[30]

All the lands in the commonfield of Prairie du Rocher had been allocated. The commonfield of Prairie du Rocher extended from the village that was clustered around the church, down toward the river. Downstream towards Kaskaskia, the commonfield was bounded by *le Grand Bois* (the Big Woods), and the lands of Melique and the Grand Prairie. On the upriver side the land was intersected by small streams and the swamp. This area, bordering at some places on the Marais Gossiaux, appears to be what was called the prairie of the *Cul de Sac* or Dead End prairie, a name that appears in many land transactions. Beyond, towards the fort, was the Prairie Chassin, part of which was added to the Prairie du Rocher commonfield. The other section became part of the Fort de Chartres commonfield.

In 1734 Ste. Thérèse had made a concession of a common for pasturing animals to the Prairie du Rocher community.[31] The plat of the grant is not extant, but its shape can be seen on many early land maps—a roughly square area with a long triangular section extending from its base. On this communally-held land, lots were given for residences around the church and the cemetery (the former lot of Ple), on the eastern side of Ste. Thérèse's concession.

With the growth of the farming population at Prairie du Rocher, the number of grazing animals increased, and the common became too small for pasturing. Not a large area to begin with, the common was seasonally restricted further by high water and marsh. In 1743 the *habitants* addressed a petition to Chevalier de Bertet, commandant, and de La Loere Flaucour, principal clerk of the marine, for a grant of additional land to use as a common. The common requested was on the bluffs above the village with a frontage of two leagues along the bluffs and a depth of one league. This land was granted to the inhabitants on 7 May 1743.

The demand for property during the 1740s throughout the Illinois area produced many real estate transactions, and the quantity of these provided an opportunity to examine the relative values of lands and houses among the villages. A question was posed—were land values higher in the more important villages of Kaskaskia and Fort de Chartres, than in the small village of Prairie du Rocher?

Despite the number of documents available, values were not easy to determine. The land descriptions often were vague and lacking in specificity, sometimes the amount of land being purchased was not even given (the parties knew, so why bother!), and a frequent method of acquisition was an exchange of land or houses, one for one. As for cost, when prices were listed they might be in monetary *livres,* but more often they were in *livres* of flour (a measure of weight).

The purchase could be partly for cash and partly for goods—350 *livres* (monetary), and fifty *livres* of bacon (weight), for instance.

Louis Marin of Prairie du Rocher purchased three *arpents* of land for 200 *livres* and twenty-five *pots* of large beer; another house was sold for seven and a half *pots* of brandy and one *livre* of vermillion. In the Prairie Chassin, Antoine Heneaux sold one *arpent* for a cow, her calf, and a year-old hog; Charles Heneaux sold five and three-quarters *arpents* and two lots in Prairie du Rocher for 1150 *livres* at port prices in flour and pelts, five *aunes* of cotton, and two shirts.[33]

Despite this great variation in payment methods, the impression given is that property in Kaskaskia was slightly more expensive than in Prairie du Rocher, and property in Prairie du Rocher was slightly more valuable than in the village of Chartres. However, there is a wide range of prices within all these settlements, so the question can never be answered satisfactorily.

Government and the Church

Government in the Illinois actually functioned as a balance of power, a concept certainly not consciously recognized by the people then. The commandant usually did what the people wanted and the *habitants* usually did what the commandant wanted. The commandant could not afford to be authoritarian; even he held very little real power over the populace. It is unlikely that the soldiers at the fort could have been used to enforce any actions if the commandant had wanted to; the soldiers were too much part of the people. Despite their adherence to the forms of law and order brought with them from France, the attitudes of the people were changing, reflecting their freedom in the new land.

The concept of separation of church and state did not develop until much later, of course. Church and state were intertwined in the eighteenth century. Obligations to the civil government were also obligations to the church; offenses against the community were offenses against the church. Fines from the court at Fort de Chartres were given to the church. Perillau, the clerk, received Fr. de Kereben's receipts for thirty francs and for 500 francs from fines for the church at Fort de Chartres. Jean Baptiste Poudret, who was unable to produce ten *pots* of brandy from the estate of his deceased employer, made a request for a delay in obtaining them. The council, probably aware that Poudret had been doing some dealing on the side, granted the delay but fined him fifty *livres* for the church and ordered him to have a mass said for the deceased.[34]

The residents of the concession of Prairie du Rocher were members of the parish of Ste. Anne, and after mass would have attended the participatory meetings held outside the church. St. Joseph's at this time was a "chapel of ease," in which the main activities were baptism and burials. Most marriages seem to have taken place at Ste. Anne's, possibly because the structure was larger and had all the necessary furnishings. There was an insufficient supply of priests to allow for regular masses to be held at the chapel.

The people continued to support values of the old society, particularly of the church, and tithed. A common eighteenth century practice was for the priest to give the rights for the tithe to an individual in exchange for a sum equal to what should be collected. The collection of the tithes was then left up to this person, giving the priest a more certain source of support, and perhaps a less contentious relationship with his parishioners.

Some of the Prairie du Rocher *habitants* seem to have become dissatisfied shortly after the formation of the parish of Ste. Anne. Perhaps they felt their chapel did not get a sufficient amount of Fr. Gagnon's time, or maybe they resented the domination of the church-wardens from Chartres. Collection of the tithes from Prairie du Rocher became a problem, particularly with some individuals. In 1737 Ignace Hebert, one of the church wardens, owned the revenues from the tithes of Fort de Chartres, Prairie du Rocher, and St. Philippe. He made a request to de La Loere Flaucour, the judge at the fort, to force the citizens of Prairie du Rocher to pay their tithes for 1736 plus damages. Antoine Bienvenu was so dilatory that a writ was served on him and addition to the tithes he had to pay court costs.[35]

Two years later Fr. Gagnon was having difficulties in collecting tithes, suggesting that perhaps Hebert had given up. Fr. Gagnon petitioned Flaucour for permission to summon several *habitants* of

Prairie du Rocher for non-payment of tithes. Apparently most of them came through then. However, the judge had to order Pierre Pilet of Kaskaskia, who held farmland at Prairie du Rocher, to pay his tithe that had been due at Easter, and also court costs.

War, Indians, and Population

The 1730s and 1740s were relatively peaceful in comparison to the earlier constant harassment by the Fox and their allies, but the years were not without warfare. The major conflict during the period was the Chickasaw War. Although the battleground was far south of Illinois, it had a great impact on the villages. Local troops and militia took part, and many did not return.

The Chickasaw Indians were unfriendly to the French and open to the British traders. They had harbored fugitive Natchez Indians after the massacre of the French in 1729. Jean Baptiste le Moyne, Sieur de Bienville, the governor of Louisiana, wanting to reduce the constant threat of Chickasaw attack on the convoys, decided to mount a major campaign against them in the winter of 1735-36. The plan he designed called for him to come up from New Orleans with troops, and with support from the Illinois and Arkansas posts, to produce a three-pronged attack against the Chickasaws.

Pierre D'Artaguiette was the commandant at Fort de Chartres. He took south a group of 130 regular troops and militia, and more than 200 Illinois and Miami Indians. He ordered Tisserant de Montcharvaux to bring Indians from Cahokia and Metchigamia. François Larche de Grandpré was to bring Arkansas Indians.

Things went awry. Montcharvaux did not arrive on time and Grandpré was not aware that the march had begun. Bienville sent word that he was delayed, but the notice did not arrive until too late. D'Artaguiette's forces attacked a small Chickasaw village but were ambushed by several hundred hidden Indians. The Illinois and Miami auxiliaries fled and about forty Frenchmen were killed. The commandant, D'Artaguiette, and the officers Pierre St. Ange; Louis Dutisne, Sieur de Vincennes; and the Jesuit priest, Antoine Senat, were burned at the stake.[36]

This defeat sent waves of fear through the communities about Indian wars. People also mourned their losses. The officers killed were sons of prominent inhabitants, the elite of the villages. D'Arta-guiette, the commandant, had been a very popular leader. There was even a song made up about him after his death; the "days of D'Arta-guiette" were looked upon as a golden era.

A few names from the local militia and regular troops who were killed in this battle appear in the notary's records, when inventories were made of their belongings in the Illinois. One of the men was from Prairie du Rocher, Jean Baptiste Turpin, whose unfortunate marriage was mentioned earlier.[37]

The forty men killed severely depleted the garrison at Fort de Chartres. To bring it back up to strength Bienville sent new troops.

> The post of the Illinois being stripped of men and munitions I have dispatched the regular convoy... I have drawn forty-three of the best men of this garrison to fill the three companies.[38]

Bienville was determined to try again and to make better preparations for the war. Illinois' involvement then was on a different and less emotionally stressful level. In 1739 Bienville arranged to purchase seventy-seven yoke of oxen and eighty horses in the Illinois, and made arrangements for them to be taken down to Fort Assumption, near the site of present Memphis, Tennessee. Bateaux and pirogues were not suitable for the transportation of so many large animals; they were to go on their own four feet. Trails existed along the river, trails originally made by the Indians for trade and warfare; most likely one of these was selected for the route of the cattle and horse drive. Bienville hired forty-five Frenchmen and seventeen Indians from Illinois for the drive. None of the persons named in the contracts that have been preserved (twenty-one plus one Indian) were from Prairie du Rocher or the Fort de Chartres vicinity; all were voyageurs out of Kaskaskia.

The drives were not highly successful; the voyageurs apparently did not make good cowboys. Stock was lost enroute; eight yoke of oxen and thirty horses did not make it to their destination. More voyageurs were hired to find the livestock lost and wandering in the woods.[39]

The second campaign was not a success either, but peace was negotiated with the Chickasaw. This peace, although shaky and not long to endure, provided a breathing space for the colony.

By the mid-1740s events in Europe began to have an impact on the colony again. France and Britain became embroiled in strife—the War of the Austrian Succession (1744-48). In North America the war was mainly a maritime war and had little direct effect on the area. The loss of the fortress of Louisbourg in Nova Scotia was too far away to affect the Illinois. However, the war did make it difficult for the French to obtain merchandise for trade and gifts to the Indians, as there was a lack of available ships, and the supply line from France was no longer safe. The treaty of Aix-la-Chapelle that ended the war left the colonies in North America in about the same situation as they had been after the Treaty of Utrecht.[40]

Although the status of the colony had not changed, there were other effects from the war, particularly threats of Indian attack again. The Indians, dissatisfied with the lack of goods from the French, sought out British traders, who were all too pleased to fill the void. Trade from the Pennsylvania area and the Carolinas expanded. Additionally, the Indian tribes were concerned about what had happened to the Fox; they reasoned that if the French could annihilate the Fox, they might turn against another group and do the same. The British traders, of course, did what they could to increase this distrust.

Fortunately, the commandant during this period, de Bertet, was very able in his dealing with the Indians, but it required a constant balancing act. Rumors of attack flew around continually. The governor Vaudreuil reported in 1748,

> Last year the harvests were abundant in spite of the course which M. Bertet took at that time of assembling all the French villages into one and surrounding it with good palisades in order to put himself in a state of defense.[41]

Possibly Bertet wished to do this, but it did not occur. The local documents of 1747 do not indicate that the consolidation of the villages actually took place; the settlements continued to operate individually.

An epidemic of some sort hit the village of Chartres in 1746-47. Although Prairie du Rocher itself seems to have been spared, some of the people affected at the village of Chartres owned farmland in the commonfields of Prairie du Rocher. The records report at least seventeen deaths; de La Loere Flaucour, who had been the judge for a long time, died at this time, probably of the same disease. There is no information on what the disease was, but many deaths were said to be sudden. It also was reported in 1749 that, "...in the last two years epidemic diseases carried off a good many of the inhabitants."[42]

Because the families were interrelated and the villages were small enough so that all were acquainted, this would have been a shock for all communities. Several of these persons were prominent citizens, so the social fabric of the villages was affected by their loss.

France continued to be indifferently supportive of the Illinois settlement, but its strategic importance was recognized.

> A good settlement is necessary to make the English give up the hope of settling there and barring to us the passage between the two colonies, [Canada and Louisiana]...[43]

However, in the late 1740s, the French government raised the question again of whether Illinois should be attached to Canada or Louisiana. Citing the fact that most of the fur trade already passed to Canada, the French ministers did not see any benefits to Louisiana for the continued attachment of Illinois. The flour trade with the southern posts could continue even it was part of Canada. The royal court also found the maintenance of two companies of soldiers at the fort burdensome to the budget. Although transferring Illinois to Canada seemed to have greater benefits, it remained with Louisiana. But this discussion added uncertainty to the status of the communities and the future of their inhabitants.[44]

A census was done again in 1752; there was growth from

1732 but the increase was only about 1000 more persons. In this census Prairie du Rocher was separated from the other villages for enumeration. With the exception of the recently settled village of Ste. Geneviève on the western bank of the river with only twenty-three people, Prairie du Rocher was the smallest of the settlements, 101 persons. Close to half of this number were black and Indian slaves.[45]

Almost all the families in Prairie du Rocher had slaves, most commonly three to five slaves. The majority of the slaves though were owned by the larger landowners—Bienvenu, Langlois, and Louvier; these account for more than half of the slaves. These farms were carried on as a business investment. As mentioned previously, Bienvenu had an overseer to assist with operating his farms. The remainder of the landowners were farmers/traders/craftsmen who lived on their land and farmed it with the assistance of a few helpers (*engagés* or slaves) and probably most members of the family.

In the 1752 census, only four of the *habitants* represent the original grantees in Prairie du Rocher: Augustin Langlois, Antoine Bienvenu, and the widows of Ignace Legras and Charles Gossiaux—Jeanne Germain and Marie Anne Govreau—who held their deceased husbands' land. As before, the census does not represent all the population of Prairie du Rocher nor all who held land there, but who lived elsewhere. Charles Heneaux was listed in a document as a *habitant*, a landowner at Prairie du Rocher, but he actually resided at the village of Chartres.[46] Among the others who held farmland at Prairie du Rocher were Antoine Rivière and Joseph Laroche.

For the other villages, Chartres had 316 persons; St. Philippe, 122; and Cahokia, 135. The population for all the Illinois villages, including black and Indian slaves, was 1366. Macarty reported on five of the six companies assigned to the Illinois and indicated 225 military personnel present. This figure would make the total population 1621. Only two of the companies were said to be at Fort de Chartres; the others were spread throughout posts garrisoned by troops from the fort.[47]

The population of the Illinois was never large and the losses from both the Chickasaw War and the epidemics cut into the growth that had occurred. After the 1740s no more mention is made of expansion into new areas. This census reflects the problem that existed throughout the French colonies—too few persons to maintain a hold on the vast territory they claimed. Numerically the French colonies were at a great disadvantage to the British. In 1746 a census of the whole colony of Louisiana counted 4,100 persons including the military. The New England colonies had in 1740 a population of over 900,000.[48] Although the inhabitants of the Illinois were not aware of the disproportionate numbers, the effects would soon be felt.

Fort de Chartres

Changes occurred over time with Fort de Chartres, the center for civil government in the Illinois. However, contradictory reports about the fort in governmental correspondence make it difficult to determine the sequence of reconstructions. The first fort's size and location are known. Another fort was constructed in 1725; most likely it was closer to the river. In 1727 a report said that a summer flood had destroyed the fort.[49] In 1732 the inventory of that fort noted that the stockaded walls were collapsing. Supposedly around this time St. Ange built a new fort at some distance from the river at his own expense. In 1734 this was reported to be already partly destroyed.[50] A fort apparently continued, either in its original location or in St. Ange's, but by 1736 its condition was so poor that the commandant Buissionière had the engineer Broutin draw up plans for a site on the bluffs east of Kaskaskia.

The garrison continued to occupy the fort until 1749, when it was in such disrepair that most of the military personnel were transferred to Kaskaskia. Buchet, keeper of the royal storehouse, rented structures there from Louis Turpin, Jean Baptiste's uncle, to house the commandant, storehouse, barracks, and a bolting mill.[51] The local villagers apparently continued to keep up the fort for protection, in case of Indian attack.

During 1749 the activities of the judicial court were held both at Fort de Chartres and Kaskaskia. The notary Barrois traveled to Prairie du Rocher to write up marriage contracts. He did the contract between François Marie Gilbert *dit* Sans Peur and Marie Joseph

Langlois, and also for Jean Baptiste Barbeau and Jeanne Legras.[52]

From 1749 until Judge Buchet moved back to Fort de Chartres in August 1754, the inhabitants of Prairie du Rocher and the village of Chartres generally had to go to Kaskaskia for court hearings. The bailiff, Gerard, did go to the old fort for some functions such as the sale of a house to Marianne Gossiaux, wife of Charles. But in 1750, when Thomas Deslauriers hired out as a domestic servant and field hand for a year on Augustin Langlois' plantation in Prairie du Rocher, the document was written in Kaskaskia. Deslauriers was to receive a wage of 300 *livres* and to have his washing and mending done.

The sale to François Bastien of a house belonging to the deceased Gossiaux, and the sale of the estate of Paul Bisset of Prairie du Rocher, were executed in Kaskaskia. François Bastien carried the will of Jean Baptiste Collerat of Prairie du Rocher to Kaskaskia, to have it officially registered. Collerat requested in his will that he be buried in St. Joseph's cemetery.[53]

Few records exist in the Kaskaskia documents concerning Prairie du Rocher residents from 1750-54; traveling to Kaskaskia for contracts and agreements was inconvenient. Probably during this period Prairie du Rocher began to expand its internal methods of handling administrative and judicial needs. Minor matters could have been taken care of by the militia captain, who emerges later as a kind of "mayor." The position of *syndic* might have been held by the captain as well. This increase in local management of affairs strengthened the internal social controls of the village.

Indian problems increased. The Miami conspired with Illinois Indians to attack the French. This incursion was averted, but troubles continued. In December 1751 a number of the Piankasaw came to town, pretending friendship but intending to ambush the villagers. Near Fort de Chartres a couple of Indians tried to stop two young boys. The youths were armed with a gun and sabre. The twelve-year-old, who had the gun, fatally shot one of the Indians in panic, then ran to the fort. These Indians were from a band headed by Chief Le Loup, who had been visiting in the area the night before and staying at the house of Dodier, the interpreter of Indian languages. The dead Indian was found to possess items stolen from local homes including a *capot* taken from a boy at the Langlois home in Prairie du Rocher.

The military government was in Kaskaskia, so several men mounted up and headed there from the fort to alert the commandant. At Prairie du Rocher they encountered Augustin Langlois on horseback; he had been shot in the stomach by an Indian. A soldier sent earlier as a messenger to Kaskaskia was found scalped at the entrance to the Big Woods.

When they reached Kaskaskia a general alarm was given by acting commandant Benoist. The other Indians of Le Loup's band in town ran away, realizing that their plot to attack had been discovered. The militia killed and captured a few Indians. At this point the new commandant, Mactigue Macarty, arrived in the convoy from New Orleans with soldiers. He ordered a detachment of a hundred regular troops and militia to chase the Indians. The local militia, however, politely requested that Monsieur de Villiers be put in charge of the militia; apparently they trusted his judgment more than the new untried commandant. With Villiers in charge they went out.[54]

Alarms continued and during the Christmas season settlers were ordered to bring guns to mass. Two sentries were posted at the church door in Kaskaskia.[55] Although it is not stated, probably the same rules were in effect for the churches of Ste. Anne and the chapel of St. Joseph.

Macarty had been assigned four companies of soldiers, more troops than could be housed in the old deteriorated fort at Chartres. Since the government was presently centered in Kaskaskia, this meant that the habitants in Kaskaskia had to quarter soldiers in their homes, and at their own expense. This did not endear them to Macarty.

Sometime later Macarty visited the old fort and found that the buildings needed reinforcement. He commented that, "Every year the habitants and voyageurs furnish a certain quantity of pickets, enough to replace one curtain each year."[56]

A decision was made finally to construct a new fort. Over the next two years the location for the fort was in question. The reason for the placement of the original fort was not clear to Vaudreuil, the governor of Louisiana. At one point he stated: "The village of the

Settlement up to now has been the principal post without the reasons
for it being too well understood...". In another place his comments
suggest that the early settlement of Prairie du Rocher was part of the
reason for the location; it was constructed so that it might "cover the
settlements which began to be made at Du Rocher and Kaskaskia."[57]

In France and New Orleans the opinion was that the new
construction should be near the major town of Kaskaskia.

> [Kaskaskia] is today the most important place since it has as
> many inhabitants as the four others put together. It is the place of the
> resort of our convoys, of the voyageurs of Canada, of the couriers from
> the posts of Detroit, and of the greatest part of the Indian tribes...[58]

Various locations near Kaskaskia were examined and the reasons they were not suitable were put forth by Macarty. Some places
examined were too far from the town; the location on the heights
overlooking the river was too expensive to move goods to and from;
a location in the town was not feasible because of the irregular layout
of the streets and lots. Macarty also observed that a placement within
the town would be overlooked by the hills and was within cannon
shot of them, a tactical advantage exploited later by John Dodge.

A notation in the notary's record indicates that land was purchased at Kaskaskia for a fort in May 1753. Presumably this was the
property for a fort on the hill across the river from the town. The fort
built there, later known as Fort Kaskaskia, was never an elaborate
structure; it was designed to be available for a refuge in case of Indian attack.[59]

Governor Vaudreuil continued to give directions to Macarty
to find a place near Kaskaskia for the main fortification. However,
the final decision in December 1752 was made by the local officials
and was in favor of a locale near the old fort.

> We visited the site here with a party of army and militia officers
> and decided that the fort should be located where formerly proposed,
> that is to say about six arpents above this place.[60]

When Kerlerec succeeded Vaudreuil as governor of Louisiana in 1753, he found that plans were drawn up for a fort near the old location. Work on the fort was done by *habitants*, hired workers, and soldiers. Squads of soldiers were detailed to work on the construction at the pay of fifteen sous per day. Evidently the townspeople were expected to provide supplies and labor as part of their obligation to the government, and it is evident that they were not inclined to do so.

The engineer on the fort, François Saucier, was pessimistic.

> I do not believe, Monsieur, that it will be easy to have the work done by the inhabitants. They appear disposed to resist your intention that they supply a part of the materials, pleading their small resources and aptitudes. The voyageurs are birds of passage...
>
> However things turn out, I cannot persuade myself that there will be enough workmen to push on these undertakings; and when I remember that more than fifty workmen and laborers have been employed without interruption on the construction of the petty fortifications of Mobile for more than ten years without having finished them, I promise myself to find my grave in the Illinois;...[61]

More progress was made than Saucier expected. Work must have proceeded throughout 1753, as by July 1754 it was said that the major part of the work on the new fort was completed. Judge Buchet moved his residence back to Fort de Chartres in August 1754.

Local masons were employed on the fort; some were from Prairie du Rocher. Gossiaux had died by then, but Jean Manuel and Joseph Robeau of Prairie du Rocher would have worked on it.[62] François Hennet, born in the Illinois and son of the original Swiss settler, constructed the roofs of the fort buildings. Work on the fort continued into 1759.[63]

Throughout the time that the governmental activities centered on Kaskaskia, Prairie du Rocher remained somewhat separate. No doubt the villagers there were called on to increase their agricultural production and to work on the new fort, but they still managed to be less directly involved with the officials than inhabitants at Kaskaskia and the village of Chartres, now called Nouvelle Chartres (New

Chartres).

Macarty seems to have disrupted the balance of power that had been the accustomed unofficial form of government in the Illinois. He attempted to be more authoritarian than the previous commandants. He had orders from Vaudreuil

> to command the military, militia, habitants, and voyageurs whom we order in the king's name to recognize the said Sieur de Macarty in these capacities and to obey him in everything that shall be for the good of the service.[64]

He was determined to carry out these orders and often did so without much tact. The *habitants* were used to deciding what they were to do in cooperation with the commandant, not by being ordered. Apparently the villagers became very uncooperative. Governor Vaudreuil wrote to Macarty:

> I should not leave you ignorant of a report which is spread around here, that the insubordination of the inhabitants was carried to a point at which you had to put the troops under arms against them.[65]

Unfortunately there is no more information on this event. Life in the New World was forming ideas of self-determination and liberty for the *habitants*. Unlike the British colonists though, they had no desire to separate from the parent country. They wanted what they felt to be the best from French law and custom, and to dispense with that which confined them. Not only Macarty experienced this resistance to autocratic authority, the royal governors upholding the status quo saw it as a pernicious attitude. Denonville in Canada commented, "These Canadians are difficult to govern. They love liberty and have a loathing of authority."[66]

The problem of the *coureurs-de-bois* persisted too; they were very free souls. The government in Louisiana complained and felt it was necessary to

> take steps to restain the coureurs de bois whose number increases yearly

in the Illinois Country, and to stop the desertion of soldiers from that post,...[67]

Although a few soldiers had deserted over the previous years, during Macarty's harsh command many left, sometimes in large numbers. There was one group of ten deserters and another of twenty-one. At least eighty desertions are listed in the records. Macarty's three companies dwindled rapidly, although he did receive replacements. The militia was called out frequently to search for deserters; possibly they did not try too hard to capture any, being themselves dissatisfied with Macarty.

A literate citizen of the village of Kaskaskia wrote directly to the governor with his complaints about Macarty. After Vaudreuil received the letter, he questioned Macarty who assured him that:

No one can be gentler with the inhabitants than I have been. Most of them want to direct things themselves. They ask to be paid when they march on duty as after the deserters. I foresee difficulties when it becomes necessary to labor on public work of the fort.[68]

Obviously the problem was with Macarty. Earlier it was observed that the people replaced one wall a year of the old fort. Without coercion they worked more willingly.

Macarty had little understanding of or sympathy for the local Illinois Indians either. His method of trying to keep their allegiance was by exposing them to an attack by a party of Sauk, Sioux, and Kickapoo Indians. By this he hoped to drive them back to the French. After an attack by other Indians on the Metchigamia, no help was forthcoming from Macarty. The Metchgamia "whose cabins had been burned, were without food, furniture, clothing or arms, but they were in no way helped although intercession was made for them on all sides." They were urged to take refuge at Kaskaskia which was six leagues away. It was a cold, rainy night, and four to five hundred people reached the village drenched with rain.

The interpreter and the principal inhabitants, touched by the misery of all these fugitives, spoke and interceded for them, urged in vain that they be lodged somewhere and given food.

The inhabitants took in some and others were lodged temporarily in the church. Macarty's behavior in this and his indifference to the problems of the Indians in other alarms led the priest, Fr. Du Guyenne, to write and complain to the governor about Macarty's attitude towards the Illinois.[69]

But Macarty did have a good grasp of the basic problems that he and the colony faced—too few people and a great expanse of territory.

I have three hundred men of troops to keep three or four hundred leagues of country. We have, counting inhabitants and slaves, 1600 souls who form six villages large and small. This is all the population of the country.[70]

The continuing problems with Macarty's behavior and his wish to go to New Orleans where the action was, led to the appointment of Neyon de Villiers as commandant in 1754. Villiers was the one the militia had asked to lead them when they went out after the Piankashaw Indians. He was liked by both citizens and Indians. Kerlerac, the governor, who was also Villiers' brother-in-law, recommended him as did the Jesuits.

Nothing is impossible with these people when they love a commandant, and without partiality it can be said the M. de Neyon is of all officers in the country the one fittest to command the Illinois with dignity and success. One could even be assured that he is the only one proper in present circumstances when it is a question of regaining the confidence of our domiciled Indians which has been much abated, not to say entirely lost, by the attack which the Foxes, Sauk, Kickapoo, and Mascoutens have made upon them. We tried to persuade them that this blow was made without our knowledge, but they learned from the very people who attacked them that it had been brought about by the commandant of the Illinois.

M. de Neyon, replacing the man who caused this disgrace, will be very proper to make them forget it. They know and love that officer who, being the brother-in-law of M. the governor, would have more opportunity than ever to cultivate and increase the confidence which the inhabitants and the Indians have in him.[71]

Neyon de Villiers became commandant, although Macarty remained in the area for a time.

Macarty's original orders had directed him to oppose by force British attempts to make settlements on the Ohio or Tennessee Rivers. The British were pushing into the Ohio region, an area contested with the French who felt they had a prior claim. The British saw the strife in terms of commercial benefits, both for trade and land development. A land company, the Ohio Company, was set up by London merchants and influential Virginians—including the Washingtons—to exploit the territory beyond the Appalachians. The French colonial government, seeing a threat to their fur trade in the northwest, garrisoned forts in the Ohio Valley to resist British encroachments. The overlapping claims of the two governments, and the fortifications that the French built, made war inevitable.

French and Indian War

In 1754 a force of Virginia militia attempted to establish a fort at the junction of the Ohio and Monongahela Rivers; the French drove them out. Then Governor Dinwiddie of Virginia sent a group of British militia to the forks of the Ohio to explore and spy out the area under the command of a twenty-one-year-old provincial major, George Washington. The militia encountered a small body of French troops, and in a skirmish some Frenchmen were killed, including an officer, Coulon de Villiers, the Sieur Jumonville. The dead French soldiers were scalped by the British Indian auxiliaries. Jumonville was the brother of an officer at Fort de Chartres, François de Coulon de Villiers (no relation to Neyon).

Washington was aware that the French would retaliate for this action. For protection he constructed a fort, Fort Necessity, in a valley called Great Meadows. His troops were reinforced by Virginia and Carolina militia to about 400 men. From Fort Duquesne, Louis de Coulon de Villiers, another brother of Jumonville, with 500 French and more than 100 Indians, went to attack this fort. After a fairly short battle, in which about eighty of Washington's troops were killed, Villiers decided to ask the fort to surrender. Villiers was afraid that his Indians allies would not stay with him if it came to a seige. On 3 July, 1754, the fort capitulated. Villiers accorded the British the honors of war allowing them to leave with their personal belongings and wounded, saying, "it is never our intention to trouble the peace and harmony which reigns between our two friendly princes, but only to avenge the assassination of our officers..."[72]

A nineteenth century French article commented on the contrast between the two commandants– theVirginia militia leader who allowed (or could not prevent) the scalping of French troops, and the magnanimous French commandant who did not seek revenge—*quelle différénce,* the article commented.[73] It does not comment on whether this magnanimity met with François' approval, also.

Fort Necessity was the opening battle of the French and Indian War, or the Seven Years War, as it was known in Europe. Although war was not declared officially until May 1756, from 1754 on conflicts arose in North America and in Europe. In Europe the aim of France was the destruction of Prussian power, for Britain the defeat of the Austrian, French, and Russian alliance.

In North America, at the beginning of the undeclared war the French had great success. In the year following the taking of Fort Necessity, French troops defeated a large British force under Sir Edward Braddock that had been sent towards Fort Duquesne. But the British were successful in other parts of the empire, and France became deeply involved in the war on the continent, so French resources were concentrated elsewhere. Then, too, the French government was blind to the real importance of the colony, seeing only the profits from the Caribbean sugar islands. The British saw its vast commercial potential.

Throughout the war, Illinois was called upon to provision the troops of New France. In spring 1759, about 400 of Macarty's men were sent with Charles Philippe Aubrey to provision forts in the North-east. This army was defeated near Niagara; six officers, thirty-two soldiers, and fifty-four *habitants* were killed.[74] The notary's records do not mention any of these persons, but for that period almost all documents other than those pertaining to land transactions are missing.

Canada surrendered in 1760. Fears of British attack ran through the Illinois, and the colony made preparations for defense, but no battles were fought there. The end of the Louisiana colony came by treaty.

The negotiations for peace and the ending of the Seven Years War were completed in 1762 and the Treaty of Paris signed in February 1763. Through this all of France's possessions east of the Mississippi were ceded to Britian, with the exception of New Orleans. To compensate Spain for the loss of Florida, France ceded to her by separate secret treaty the lands west of the Mississippi.

The Treaty of Paris did contain clauses important to the inhabitants of the colony—they were allowed to practice the Roman Catholic religion, they were confirmed in their land holdings, and they were permitted to take their goods and move freely to the other side of the river or elsewhere if desired.

The Illinois country and Louisiana had been viewed as a drain to the finances of France, so the government now readily disposed of the Louisiana colony. At no time had the French government ever fully comprehended the possibilities of the area for agriculture and settlement. Agricultural produce, hides, and strategic position were not valued as highly by the court as were products such as sugar from the islands and precious metals. On the other hand, the British saw the potential in the land for expansion as well as for further commercial opportunities for trade. France's rule on the Mississippi was ended and the inhabitants of Prairie du Rocher were faced with an uncertain future.

Notes

1. ANC G1 Al 464.
2. Dean and Brown 1981, 1722-32:45; 44.8.6.1.

3. Charlevoix 1966, 21.

4. Ekberg 1998, 8.

5. Rowland and Saunders 3, 667.

6. Dean and Brown 1981, 34:2:6:1-3; 34:2:10:1; 34:2:17:1-2; 34:2:18:1; 34:2:19:1-3; 34:2:30:1; 28:4:28:1; 34:5:8:1; 39:2:19:1; *LHQ* 5, 408.

7. Dean and Brown 1981, 32:6:14:1; 34:6:4:1; 38:2:10:2.

8. Dean and Brown 1981, 22--:1; 26:5:4:2; 29:9:14:3; 30:8:9:2; 37:5:8:1; 37:11:4:1; 39:3:2:1; 40:9:9:1; 40:9:9:4; 43:1:30:1; 43:1:30:2; 43:5:15:1; Brown and Dean 1977, K421; ANC G1 412.

9. Menard, Ruth 1994, 7-9.

10. Dean and Brown 1981, 37:5:19:1; 37:6:12:1.

11. Dean and Brown 1981, 37:6:25:2.

12. Dean and Brown 1981, 41:4:28:2,3,4; *LHQ* 10:4, 567, 582.

13. Dean and Brown 1981, 25:4:11:1; 31:6:23:1.

14. Nelson 1993, 187; Dean and Brown 1981, 37.3:6:1.

15. Dean and Brown 1981, 37:2:6:1; 37:5:5:1; 37:5:8:1.

16. Dean and Brown 1981, 46:10:3:1.

17. Dean and Brown 1981, 26:6:-:1.

18. Brown and Dean 1977, D360; Dean and Brown 1981, 31:10:1:1; 38:1:31:3; 38:2:18:2.

19. Dean and Brown 1981, 56:3:11:1.

20. Pers. comm. Kathrine Seineke.

21. Nelson 1993, 96; 157-191.

22. Dean and Brown 1981, 37:1:18:1; 40:7:10:2; 41:9:25:1; 43:4:10:1; 43:6:12:1; 79:6:30:1.

23. Dean and Brown 1981, 34:6:4:1.

24. Dean and Brown 1981, 49:4:27:1; 40:6:20:1.

25. Dean and Brown 1981, 40:7:26:1; 42:12:7:1; 43:6:10:1; 43:4:10:1; 43:5:20:1; D'Amours 1974, 213; St. Jo. Ch. Rec. 24 May 1768.

26. Dean and Brown 1981, 41:1:28:1; 37:10:1:1.

27. Dean and Brown 1981, 81:4:3:1.

28. Dean and Brown 1981, 60:11:20:1; Brown and Dean 1977, D365: D408.

29. Dean and Brown 1981, 43:5:8:3, 4.

30. Dean and Brown 1981, 42:1:24:1; 43:3:19:2; 43:3:9:2.

31. Dean and Brown 1981, 34:2:19:2.

32. Auditor of Public Acts, vol. 833. Dean and Brown 1981, 43:5:7:4-5.

33. Dean and Brown 1981, 44:2:8:3; 45:10:10:1; 39:2:5:2.

34. Dean and Brown 1981, 25:9:17:3; 25:10:14:1; 25:11:12:1.
35. Dean and Brown 1981, 37:5:7:1; 40:7:3:1; 38:1:31:1.
36. Alvord 1965, 177ff; Rowland and Saunders 1, 311ff.
37. Dean and Brown 1981, 37:2:3:1.
38. Rowland and Sanders 3, 326.
39. M. Brown 1983.
40. Balesi 1992, 255; Eccles 1972, 177.
41. Pease and Jenison 1940, 55.
42. Pease and Jenison 1940, 103.
43. Pease and Jenison 1940, 277.
44. Thwaites 1908, 15.
45. Vaudreuil Papers; personal communication Kathrine Seineke.
46. Dean and Brown 1981, 40:10:20:1.
47. Pease and Jenison 1940, 431.
48. Eccles 1972, 172.
49. Alvord 1965, 159.
50. ANC C13B 1/1/15 June 1732; Rowland and Saunders 3:667.
51. Dean and Brown 1981, 49:1:1:1-4.
52. Dean and Brown 1981, 49:4:27:1; 49:4:28:1.
53. Dean and Brown 1981, 50:8:11:1; 52:9:27:1; 53:1:31:2; 50:2:5:1;
    51:9:14:1.
54. Pease and Jenison 1940, 433.
55. Bossu 1962, 71.
56. Pease and Jenison 1940, 441-442.
57. Pease and Jenison 1940, 262, 263.
58. Pease and Jenison 1940, 263.
59. Dean and Brown 1981, 53:5:20:1; Orser and Karamanski 1977.
60. Pease and Jenison 1940, 427, 445.
61. Pease and Jenison 1940, 471-2.
62. Mason's marks are preserved on a few stones found at the stone
    fort. One of these is an "M."
63. Dean and Brown 1981, 55:9:15:1; 56:3:17:1.
64. Pease and Jenison 1940, 293-4.
65. Pease and Jenison 1940, 609.
66. Douville and Casanova 1968, 69.
67. Thwaites 1902, xviii, 6.
68. Pease and Jenison 1940, 705.
69. Austin 1982, 89; Davis 1998, 51; Pease and Jenison 1940, 721, 724.
70. Pease and Jenison 1940, 481.
71. Pease and Jenison 1940, 874-5.

72. Villiers 1904, 61; Peyser 1999.
73. Villiers 1904, 63.
74. Alvord 1965, 241.

5

Under Three Flags

By June 1763 the provisions of the Treaty of Paris became known. The details arrived by ship at New Orleans and as quickly as messages could be sent, the Illinois was informed. Communication being what it was, it was not until October that the commandant of Fort de Chartres, Neyon de Villiers, sent messages to the other northern posts concerning the surrender. A number of inhabitants received permission to go down to New Orleans at this time in order to seek transportation back to France.

The lack of personal diaries and letters is particularly frustrating for this crucial time of change. Official French documents discussed the treaty with dignity and in bureaucratic blandness. What was the reaction of the populace when the official notice was read at the church door after mass? Other than the fact that many *habitants* voted with their feet and left, we have no record. The colonists had not wanted separation from France; they considered themselves still Frenchmen, yet their country had abandoned them. The British had been the enemy and their trade competitor for years. England was anti-Catholic. Although a provision in the treaty allowed the French to keep their religion, there must have been great apprehension in the population.

British Rule

Although the French villagers had to accept their dispossession by treaty, many of the Indian nations were disinclined to have British rule and they did not acknowledge the right of the European governments to decide their fate. They noted the displacement of eastern tribes by British settlers. Pontiac, chief of the Ottawa, was able to accomplish what no one previously had been able to do, to join the various tribes into a coordinated fighting force antagonistic to the British. Under his leadership the combined Indian nations went to war and drove the British out of Michilimackinac, St. Joseph, Miami, Ouiatenon, and other posts. For the Illinois country, the direct impact of Pontiac's work was that Indian opposition prevented the British from reaching Fort de Chartres and establishing their rule for two years. Although in 1764 the Indians were defeated and the rebellion broken, not all tribes had submitted to the British. Villiers, isolated in Illinois and a faithful French officer, was trying to maintain peace and to obey the treaty. Respected by both the French and Indians, he managed to keep the Illinois country fairly stable despite the turmoil around it. Because Villiers stood firm on obeying the treaty, the new post of St. Louis across the river became a center for intrigue against the British.

On June 15, 1764, Neyon de Villiers turned over the fort to Louis St. Ange de Bellerive, whom he had recalled from the post at Vincennes. Villiers left for New Orleans. Forty soldiers remained with St. Ange; the other troops and a few *habitants* went down to southern Louisiana.

If the loss of the villagers' status as Frenchmen, and if becoming subjects of their hereditary enemy were not enough, the colonists were dealt yet another blow. Antagonism against the powerful and wealthy Jesuit order in Europe had come to a head in 1761. By royal authority the order was suppressed in France and their estates confiscated, with the hope that the moneys from these would help pay the debts of the Seven Years War. In 1763 Louis XV issued directives for the colonies also to seize Jesuit lands. The Jesuit lands in New Orleans and Illinois were taken; the priests were deprived of their support and expelled from the country.[1] In November the six Jesuits in the Illinois departed for New Orleans: Philibert Watrin, Superior of the Illinois Mission; Jean Baptiste Aubert, curé at Kaskaskia; Jean Baptiste Salleneuve from Detroit; Sebastian Meurin, missionary to the Kaskaskia Indians; Jean Baptiste de la Morinie from Ste. Geneviève; and Julian Devernai from Vincennes.[2]

For the inhabitants to whom the church was the central focus of their lives, losing the priests was a blow even worse than that of being turned over to a foreign power. Although the parish of Ste. Anne would not have been affected by the ban, as it was under the seminary priests, the church had been lacking a permanent curé since the death of Fr. Gagnon in 1757. Abbé Forget Duverger and the Recollect fathers, Hypolite and Luc Collet from Cahokia, had been performing services at Ste. Anne's, St. Joseph's, and the chapel of the Visitation.[3] Forget Duverger, apprehensive about the future, sold the Cahokia church property in October of 1763, an action opposed by the citizens of Cahokia. He departed for New Orleans and France leaving the Collets alone. Fr. Luc Collet's last entries in the registers of Ste. Anne's were in August of 1765; he died in September 1765. He was buried in Ste. Anne's cemetery.[4]

The British continued their attempts to reach the Illinois country and to gain possession of the fort. In 1765 Lt. John Ross of the 34th Regiment made his way to Illinois. He wanted to obtain an agreement for Major Farmar to come up the Mississippi and officially secure the fort. St. Ange arranged a council of Kaskaskia, Peoria, Cahokia, Metchigamia, Osage, and Missouri Indians to attempt reconciliation, but the tribes continued to be hostile to Ross. Tamarois, a chief of the Kaskaskia bluntly told him:

> All the red men possess scales in which are weighed our father, the Frenchman, and the Englishman. Whenever they raise it, the Englishman wins out and always weighs more. Why? Because he is filled with wickedness and he has not the white heart like our father.

Tamarois continued, poignantly expressing his concepts on land ownership, the contrast between the Indian and European views that was to cause so much grief for the Indians from then on.

> Get out, move on as quickly as possible and tell your chief all
> you have heard, that we are the children of the French and that they are
> the only ones we want among us. Tell him that these lands are ours and
> no one claims them, not even other red men. Why do you wish to come
> here? You do not know us; we have never seen you. Tell your chief to
> remain on his lands as we do on ours.[5]

In July George Croghan, deputy Indian agent for the British, held a peace conference at Vincennes with the Indians and another at Detroit soon afterwards. At these the final resolution of Pontiac's war was accomplished. Finally in October 1765 Captain Stirling arrived in the Illinois country with a hundred men of the 42nd Regiment of foot, the Black Watch, to take possession of Fort de Chartres.

> Today the tenth of October 1765, we Louis Saint Ange de
> Bellerive, Captain of infantry, Commandant for his most Christian
> Majesty of the said fort and Joseph Lefebvre, Storekeeper for the king
> and serving in the function of commissary of the said fort in conse-
> quence of the orders which we have received from Messieurs Aubry,
> Chevalier of the royal and military order of St. Louis and commandant
> of the Province of Louisiana and Foucault Commissary Comptroller of
> the Navy and Ordonnateur in the said province, cede to Monsieur Ster-
> ling, appointed by Monsieur Gage, governor of New York and General
> commanding the troops of his Britannic Majesty in America and all the
> left side of the province of Louisiana following the seventh article of
> the treaty defining the peace concluded at Versailles the 10th February
> 1763.[6]

For two years French officers had governed an area officially British territory. Now St. Ange, Lefebvre, his officers and men departed for St. Louis in the Spanish domain.[7] St. Ange and his men were allowed to take supplies and equipment from the fort with them. Military equipment included fourteen grenadier guns, 1000 lbs. bars of lead, two old uniform coats, 1500 gun flints, eleven cannonballs, 259 gun cocks, and an old sword for a sergeant. Trade goods from the storehouse went, too: two lbs. of vermillion, 467 small bells, 640 "dog-head" knives, seventy-two combs of boxwood, sixteen pairs of scissors, five necklaces, and fifty-two lbs. of beads. Many domestic items from the residences and barracks were listed on the inventory: stew pans, coffeepot, copper kettles, chafing dish, even a chimney crane and hooks. The official life was represented by several scales, a block of copper to press paper, two fleur-de-lis stamps, sails and awnings for boats, iron shackles, and handcuffs.[8]

Not only did the troops leave but also the majority of the residents from the villages of Chartres and St. Philippe. Many Kaskaskians left for the west bank, too. These settlers wanted to stay under a Bourbon king, even if he were Spanish rather than French. The new settlement of St. Louis, the post of Laclède, benefitted from this exodus as did Ste. Geneviève. Laclède, who had wintered at Fort de Chartres in 1763, had established himself on the west bank only the previous year. Very few villagers left from Prairie du Rocher.

Informants in Prairie du Rocher gave two traditional tales (variants of the same story) about the arrival of the British and their acquisition of Fort de Chartres. One recounted that when the British came they built a huge bonfire up on the bluff and marched their men around and around in front of the fire so that the French thought there were more soldiers than they had. In the other story the British cut trees into the shapes of men and the French saw these and thought there was a whole army. These tales may be a later attempt to explain why such a substantial fort was surrendered to the enemy without a battle. The Treaty of Paris, probably always poorly understood, would have faded quickly from the remembrance of the local populace.[9]

The commander-in-chief of the British army, Gen. Thomas Gage, had sent a proclamation based on the articles of the treaty concerning the rights of the inhabitants. Following the acquisition of the fort, Capt. Thomas Stirling went to Kaskaskia and had General Gage's proclamation read in French to the inhabitants.

...that His Majesty grants to the inhabitants of the Illinois the liberty of the Catholic religion...his new Roman Catholic subjects of the Illinois may exercise the worship of their religion according to the rites of the Roman church...[they] may retire in full safety and freedom wherever they please, even to New Orleans, or any other part of Louisiana,...and they may sell their estates, provided it be to subjects of His Majesty, and transport their effects, as well as their persons, without restraint upon their emigration, under any pretence whatever, except in consequence of debts or of criminal process.[10]

Those persons staying were asked to take an oath of allegiance to Great Britain. The inhabitants requested more time to make the decision whether to stay or leave, and Stirling gave them until the first of March 1766 to decide. This delay was extended to residents of the other villages also.[11] The British renamed the fort and the village of Chartres, Cavendish, but this name did not survive for long. Even official British correspondence shortly slipped back to using Fort de Chartres.

The parliment in Britain for the next few years debated Indian policy lengthily—whether there were to be boundaries and where and what was to be the method for managing the Indian trade. These questions never were resolved completely and the need for civil government in the Illinois was ignored.[12]

So now the British had arrived and the French authorities departed, but Captain Stirling had been left with no arrangements or authority for civil government. There was a jurisdictional vacuum. To fill it, the military commander had to assume civil duties without authority. Sirling attempted to do this by appointing Jean La Grange of Kaskaskia as judge. He wrote to General Gage:

The only Judges here was one LeFevre who was Judge, King's Commissary, & Garde de Magazin, & another who acted as Procureur du Roi; All Causes were tried before them, & their Sentence confirmed or revised by the Council at N. Orleans, in case of appeal, the Commandant decided all small disputes, yet every complaint was addressed to him, & he ordered the Judge to try them; those two are gone to the Spanish side being continued in their employments there. I was therefore obliged to appoint one Mr. La Grange to decide all disputes that might arise among the Inhabitants. According to the Laws & Customs of the Country with liberty to Appeal to me, in case they were not satisfied with his decision; ... It will be necessary that Judges be sent here to administer Justice, as Mr. La Granges knowledge to the Law is not sufficient to fill that employment as it ought to be. The Captains of Militia have the same power as in Canada.[13]

La Grange referred to himself in one document as judge at Kaskaskia, and in another record acts in his role as judge ordering Capt. Philip Pittman to pay Beauvais for a contract. La Grange died in early January 1767. No other judge seems to have been appointed to succeed him.[14]

On the local village level the British left in place the captains of militia, who under the French regime had had the ability to try petty cases and to put into execution decrees given by the commandant. Under the British these duties continued. Within the village of Prairie du Rocher there was little change in social control. The internal integration allowed for continuity despite the change in external government. Pierre de Chaufour Louvière was the captain of the militia at Prairie du Rocher until his death in 1768.[15] Jean Baptiste Barbeau became the next captain. Shortly afterwards he emerges as a major political figure in the Illinois.

With the loss of the Jesuits in 1763 and the death of Fr. Collet in 1765, the entire area would have been without the benefit of the church's sacraments had it not been that Fr. Sebastien Meurin was able to return to the Illinois. Not wanting to leave the Illinois *habitants* without access to their religion, he submitted to the jurisdiction of the Capuchin order in New Orleans, which allowed him to remain in the country. He agreed to regulations from the Capuchins, constraining him to a residence on the Spanish side in Ste. Geneviève. However, he came to the east bank every springtime for Easter services, again in the autumn, and when he was called on for the sick. The care of six villages, however, was too much for one priest. In 1767 he wrote: "I am only sixty-one years old, but I am exhausted and ruined by mission work in this country for twenty-five years..."[16]

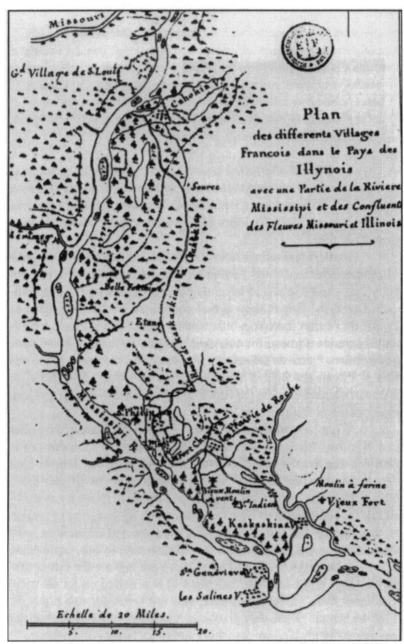

An unknown French cartographer drew this map of the Illinois country, probably in the mid-1760s.

Nevertheless, Fr. Meurin continued to try to serve the parishes. He too had problems with tithes. Ste. Geneviève felt that they supported him, so he should not be required to go to the other parishes. The other parishes felt they did not owe a tithe because he was rarely with them and lived on the Spanish side.

The church properties on the east bank were a worry to Fr. Meurin. The Jesuit land and chapel at Kaskaskia had been sold to a private individual; likewise the Cahokia property sold by Forget Duverger. The village of Chartres was deserted and the church of Ste. Anne abandoned.

> The church of Ste. Anne has, for almost a year, been without roof, doors and windows and with walls broken or badly closed, because the churchwardens have changed their home and village without informing me or having others elected; and they left the keys to the beadle who withdrew also and left them with an inhabitant and thus they pass from one to another.

The chapel of St. Joseph at Prairie du Rocher was the sole remaining representative of the parish. The village of Chartres had two male inhabitants and St. Philippe, four. Fr. Meurin wanted to remove what was left in the church of Ste. Anne and take it to St. Joseph.

> When finally I was informed I went there and demanded and obtained from the English commandant [Colonel Reed] his consent to the removal of the furniture of the church of Ste. Anne to the chapel of St. Joseph at Prairie du Rocher. I myself carried the sacred vessels...

Fr. Meurin then commissioned in writing the captain of the militia, Pierre Louvière, and three others (probably the churchwardens) to go to the church and take the furnishings. When they went, the two inhabitants of the village of Chartres opposed them. Apparently these inhabitants filed several petitions with Col. John Reed claiming that the church and furniture belonged to them personally. None of these petitions have been preserved. The inhabitants known to have been

Built in 1799, the Church of the Holy Family in Cahokia remains an excellent example of upright log construction.

still residing there were Ignace Hebert, his wife, Marie Rose, and Louis Langlois *dit* Traversy and his Indian wife. Ignace was the son of the one who had the tithes in the 1740s; apparently this Ignace felt he owned the church now.

Fr. Meurin was ordered to bring back the sacred vessels which fortunately he did not do. They are still preserved at St. Joseph's. Apparently there were further legal ramifications; Fr. Meurin related to Bishop Briand,

> I wrote in the form of a petition drawn up in the name of your chapter...
> I was obliged to stand a suit; my adversaries insisted upon I know not
> what yet; I lost your suit; I wrote again; English judges were named
> and the process will be ended when it shall please God and your high-
> ness.[17]

Church vessels from the Church of Ste. Anne are said to have been given by the king to the church. They bear French hallmarks, one of which is a Paris discharge mark for the years 1687-1691.

It would be interesting to have the records of this case but none of Fr. Meurin's petitions are preserved. In fact there is no evidence of any court existing in the Illinois at this time; the judges referred to must have been arbitrators appointed by the commandant.

A year later the church property at Chartres was endangered by the Mississippi River cutting the eastern bank, and Fr. Meurin arranged for the bodies of Fr. Gagnon and Fr. Luc Collet to be disinterred and taken to the cemetery at Prairie du Rocher.[18] Their graves and their tombstones are there today.

In recognition of his labors Bishop Briand of the Diocese of Quebec appointed Fr. Meurin vicar general for the Illinois. Supposedly he was no longer under the jurisdiction of the Diocese of Quebec, so this caused him further problems. Because Fr. Meurin had put himself under the orders of the Capuchins in Louisiana, the Spanish

Gravestone of Fr. Joseph Gagnon from the cemetery at Ste. Anne. Fr. Meurin moved the body and stone to the Prairie du Rocher cemetery in 1768 due to the encroaching Mississippi River. Fr. Luc Collet's body was moved at the same time.

commandant of Ste. Geneviève, Philippe François de Rastel de Rocheblave, considered any dealing with the British in Canada (i.e., the Diocese of Quebec) as dangerous and treasonable. He ordered Fr. Meurin seized and imprisoned, but Fr. Meurin escaped to the east side, where he made his home from then on. In 1768 in answer to pleas from the aging Fr. Meurin for assistance, Bishop Briand sent the young Fr. Pierre Gibault to the Illinois country. This provided some relief for Fr. Meurin. Fr. Gibault took over Kaskaskia and Fr. Meurin went to Cahokia. Both he and Fr. Gibault continued to travel to all the parishes when needed.

In 1769 Fr. Meurin finally retired to Prairie du Rocher, "a little village of twenty-four souls." By souls he must have meant families, as a census in the previous year counted twenty-five families.[19] The village welcomed him.

> …this little parish, all that is left of Ste. Anne at Fort de Chartres, invited me to finish my days with them, promising me to build a rectory and to furnish me all things I needed for the remainder of my life, into whatever infirmity I might fall. …They furnish me with a servant and horse and open carriage for my journey, undoubtedly that they may keep me the longer. May the divine goodness keep account of their deeds![20]

Despite his health and retirement to Prairie du Rocher Fr. Meurin continued traveling to other parishes, even into Spanish territory, where there are records of baptisms performed by him. His last recorded visit to St. Louis was in 1775.[21] He died in 1777 and was buried in the Prairie du Rocher cemetery.

In 1768 Fr. Pierre Gibault was sent to the Illinois country to assist Fr. Meurin.
Collection of Carl J. Ekberg

The opening up of the continent west to the Mississippi was for British commercial interests the equivalent of a gold rush. Companies to exploit land multiplied and major trading firms moved to Kaskaskia. The large firm of Baynton, Wharton, and Morgan set up a store in Kaskaskia, and later in Cahokia and Vincennes. Other English traders followed suit. However, settlement on the vast areas of land still was frustrated by Indian troubles. Also the British firms were not able to obtain control of the volume of trade that they had expected. The French, who operated out of St. Louis, continued to dominate the fur trade, and this trade went down to New Orleans out of the hands of the British. Not all the British felt that holding the Illinois country was to their advantage. Capt. Harry Gordon wrote:

> Our Possession of the Ilinois is only usefull at present in one respect, it Shews the Indian Nations our Superiority over the French...This is dearly bought by the Expence it is to us, and the Inconvenience of Supporting it. The French carry on the trade all around us by Land and by Water...[22]

The British were impressed with the countryside, the rich bottomlands, and the potential for settlement, but as the French maintained their prejudice towards the British, so did the British towards the French.

> It is certainly the finest Land in the known World, it Wants for nothing but inhabitants and cultivation to make it exceed any part of America I have ever been in. You would be surprised to see how Luxuriously every kind of Vegetables grows here,.. and there are such quantities of the finest Medow that the grass is in Common to all, Their Cattle run in grass so high that you may be within five yards of a very large Ox, and not see him. When the french (whom you know are a very Idle set of people..) Cut their grass its common for them to take three or four teams to the Meddow in a morning, mow all day, and bring it home at night...[23]

The quote indicates that haying was done on the common and perhaps part of the commonfield where there was native prairie. However, the soldier Butricke, who wrote that report, probably had not had much experience with haying if he felt the people were idle. Cutting prairie grass with a scythe and forking on to the horse-drawn wagons all day was not a job for a lazy person.

Major Farmar also expressed his opinion of the land and the

French farmers:

> The Soil of this Country is in General very good & fertile, and
> with proper industry and Cultivation it would I make no Doubt in a few
> Years produce sufficient Grain for the Maintenance of the Troops and
> Inhabitants; but the present Inhabitants are and always have been too
> indolent and lazy to bestow any Pains upon cultivating their Lands,
> especially since the Country has been ceded to the Crown of Great
> Britain...[24]

Probably the last sentence gives the real reason for lack of
cultivation. Much of the land had been abandoned when people left
for the west bank; prior to the coming of the British the area had had
no difficulty feeding itself and exporting large amounts of food.

Distaste for the nearby British presence had emptied the village of Chartres. Prairie du Rocher was far enough away to avoid
daily contact with the military, even though people continued to farm
within the Fort de Chartres commonfield. The village was looked
upon as too small and unimportant to have English traders establish
themselves there.

The first two British commandants, Stirling and Farmar, were
fairly well regarded. The later ones, Reed and Wilkins, were more
interested in acquiring money for themselves. Fr. Meurin reported
that the last two commandants had forbidden him to celebrate a marriage ceremony without a license, for which Reed charged six *piastres*, five for himself and one for his secretary.[25] Wilkins was said to
charge only for the secretary.

In January 1770 Fr. Meurin received the permission of Colonel Wilkins for the marriage of Frenchman with an Indian woman.
Jean Baptiste Jacquemin of Prairie du Rocher married Thérèse Ricara,
presumably a Christian Arikara Indian.[26] Such mixed marriages had
fallen into disfavor even in the French regime, and Vaudreuil's instructions to Macarty had included the need for the commandant's
permission for such marriages. Apparently the British continued this.
There were no restrictions, governmental or social, on marriage with
métis, of which there were a fairly large number.

The greatest complaint of the inhabitants against the British was the lack of civil government. Government under the military rule was dependent upon the character and inclinations of the commandant. Although the French were accustomed to and liked the concept of the final authority being a paternalistic commandant, they were also used to having this commandant and a set of officials act in accordance with known customs and civil laws. Not only were British customs alien to the French, but because it was a military outpost they were not even under the British civil law.

In 1768 Colonel Wilkins, on his own authority, created a Court of the Judicatory to hear cases on debts and property. His motivations were largely for his own benefit. He was helping the merchants Morgan and Wharton to get repayment on debts. He would receive a kickback from them. The court was to levy fines and to impose punishment as any other court under the laws of England, but Wilkins disallowed trial by jury on the grounds that there were too few inhabitants and that they did not have knowledge of the laws and customs of England.

The court consisted of six justices. The initial court had three British, all associates of Morgan: James Rumsey, James Campbell, and James McMillan. There were also three French, Jean Baptiste Barbeau, representing Prairie du Rocher; Pierre Girardot, from St. Philippe; and Louis Viviat, from Kaskaskia. Wilkins appointed George Morgan as president of the court. This appointment offended the French, who disliked Morgan intensely, recognizing his association with Wilkins. When Morgan and Wharton decided to cease paying him, Wilkins expanded the court's prerogatives to hear criminal cases and changed the court personnel. All justices except Morgan were French—Barbeau, Girardot, Viviat, Joseph Charleville, and Antoine Louvière (the last also was from Prairie du Rocher).[27]

The court met at fairly frequent intervals, although the meetings were irregularly spaced. The hearings were held more or less alternately at the villages of Chartres and Kaskaskia. The village of Chartres now had been deserted by all the French. Hebert had died and was buried in the cemetery at Prairie du Rocher. His widow, Marie Rose, sold their land to the British; Louis Langlois Traversy also died and his wife sold the property.[28] The court hearings must have been held at Fort de Chartres, but it does not appear that the commandant was willing to provide shelter and food for the justices. Apparently Prairie du Rocher did not have at this time an inn able to accommodate the group.

In the latter part of 1770 the court made a decision about the hearings, probably at the instigation of Morgan:

> The Court taking into Consideration the great Expenses & Inconveniences attending the Inhabitants being obliged to go to Fort Chartres should the Court be in future held there where there are no Houses of Entertainment or other Places they can be supplied with Provisions & Lodgings at, or Oats & Hay for their Horses, DO DETERMINE & UNANIMOUSLY AGREE that the Court shall for the next ensuing six months, & longer if not hereafter unanimously agreed on to the Contrary, be held at the Village of Kaskaskia the first Tuesday in every Callender Month.

Despite the fact that the above agreement was said to be unanimous, Jean Baptiste Barbeau vociferously objected to the new arrangement. He complained about going to Kaskaskia and felt the court should continue to meet alternately at the two villages. He was called before the court to answer apparent charges against him for improper behavior. He continued to voice his objections:

> ...when he found the plurality of Voices against him he declar'd he should be frequently Sick if the Court was to be held at Kaskaskias.[29]

Wilkins seems to have disbanded the court shortly after this and held hearings himself. He apparently selected arbitrators in cases of debt, an action which also was followed by his successors, Major Isaac Hamilton and the last British commandant, Captain Hugh Lord. The justices retired to their villages.

The French continued to want civil government. After the disbandment of the court, the villagers decided to request government and laws directly and sent a representative, Daniel Blouin, to

Gen. Gage in New York. The action seems to have been at the initiative of the Kaskaskians, but probably Jean Baptiste Barbeau and Antoine Louvière continued to be involved with the French faction. A counter proposal was sent to the villages by Gage. Major Hamilton held a meeting of the inhabitants. Their response was that they were not interested in hearing from him until they heard from Blouin upon his return. Despite being under a different regime and without civil authority, the villagers continued their independent attitudes.[31]

The channel of the Mississippi River was shifting towards its east bank. In 1771, in spite of efforts of the British to protect the riverbank, it became obvious that the fort was going to be destroyed. The British had found the fort as ruinously expensive as had the French, and it was unhealthy for them. The British soldiers suffered from several epidemics, probably of malaria. The Irish regiment in the Illinois lost a hundred soldiers and camp followers.[32] For these reasons Gage ordered the fort abandoned, and Hamilton determined to destroy the fort by opening the drains so that the next flood would wash it away.[33] Although the wall facing the river tumbled in, the capricious Mississippi swung west again and the remainder of the fort was preserved. Capt. Hugh Lord, who shortly thereafter replaced Hamilton, took some troops to Fort Gage, at Kaskaskia. Fort Gage was the Jesuits' old residence, surrounded by the usual high picket fence—a compound, but not a real fortification. Here Lord installed cannon from Fort de Chartres.

In 1774, at long last, steps were taken by the British parliament to have the Illinois country incorporated in a civil government and the Quebec Act was passed. The entire Northwest—the former French area east of the Mississippi River—was included within the province of Quebec. Plans were drawn up for official positions and for courts, but the outbreak of the American Revolution caused these to be put on the shelf.[34] The planned organization never reached the Illinois. Captain Lord, a fairly popular commandant who had allowed the French to follow their own ways, was recalled to the rebellious eastern colonies with his troops in spring of 1776. He selected Philippe François de Rastel le chevalier de Rocheblave as agent for the British government in Kaskaskia.

The villagers had little respect for Rocheblave. He had left his position in Ste. Geneviève under a cloud of suspicion and became a British subject. As Pease so nicely puts it, he was "available for chance employment."[35] Rocheblave took to himself the duties of commandant and judge, although these were not his official titles.

In his assumed position as judge, Rocheblave referrred a Prairie du Rocher case to Barbeau. In 1776 Marie Anne Dubois, wife of Gerald Langlois, complained to Rocheblave that Louis Pilet La Sonde had beaten her husband so severely that he was unable to work and provide for her and their two children. Rocheblave told Barbeau to hold preliminary hearings, and that if he felt the complaint was justified, Marie Anne should be advanced one hundred francs in goods.[36]

Rocheblave might not have been the best selection to serve as British agent but his position as the representative of the British crown was not to be envied. He had no troops, and he was dependent for defense on the local militia. He was well aware that the English traders and many of the French were sympathetic to the American cause. The sympathizers included some of the most important men in Kaskaskia and in Prairie du Rocher, probably including Jean Baptiste Barbeau.

The amount of sympathy towards the Americans and the knowledge of the inhabitants about the movement for independence remain open questions. Again the lack of letters and diaries is frustrating. The Illinois was not as isolated as it would appear to us now with modern communication. It was located on major trade and transportation routes. Traders from Kaskaskia were still traveling enormous distances—Canada to New Orleans and all areas in between. With the establishment of British control, English traders had seen the advantage of Kaskaskia's location and a number resided there or operated out of the village. Although the relationships between the British and French traders was competitive at times, they also worked together. For example, Charleville supplied Richard Winston and Patrick Kennedy with a bateau for a trading journey, and he also entered into the business as a partner for the trip to New Orleans. Another Charleville was an *engagé* for Thomas Bentley.[37]

The contacts in trade and in community activities gave many

opportunities for interaction between the French and English. Many of the English traders became increasingly involved with the American cause, and through them the French with whom they dealt and socialized learned about the Americans. The traders and voyageurs worked rivers and streams also frequented by American sympathizers. Inevitably, they would have learned about American concepts of liberty and justice, ideals valued by the French, too.

With all of the this interaction, the French must have been aware that the Americans soon would seek to acquire the British territory along the Mississippi. The extent of any actual support for the Americans will never be known. In reality, the French were not so much supporters of the Americans as opposed to the British. Overthrowing the British was a mutual interest.

The colony of Virginia looked on the Northwest as part of Virginia, and wanted to secure the boundaries of Kentucky, a county of Virginia, against incursions by the Indians. They felt that taking the land on the east bank would give them more protection from Indian attacks incited by the British. It would also prevent British attack from the rear on the eastern colonies. George Rogers Clark, under secret orders from Patrick Henry, the governor of Virginia, was sent to take the Illinois villages. Rocheblave had expected an American attack eventually, but thought it would be from the united colonies, not a separate one from Virginia. When he heard rumors of the approach of George Rogers Clark and his "long knives," Rocheblave called out the militia, but then, thinking it was a false alarm, they were allowed to stand down.[38]

Virginian Control

On the evening of July 4, 1778, George Rogers Clark and his men arrived at Kaskaskia, surprising Rocheblave, and immediately took over Rocheblave's fortified residence. The Americans at Kaskaskia welcomed him, but some of the French were apprehensive. Clark's later memoirs concerning the event emphasize the great fears by the French. Such terror as he describes is puzzling, in light of the fact that knowledge about the Americans had been circulating in the community for months. If there had been so much concern, surely the militia, who outnumbered Clark's men, would have responded. Although the militia lacked the military support of the past, they were well trained and experienced; if they had feared for their families and future they were quite capable of fighting for them. Clark's picture of the timorous French is overdrawn, probably to boost his victory.

What the populace most desired was the comfort of the church, connection to their native land, and proper legal courts to manage the succession of property and to handle indebtedness. Clark rapidly realized the real situation—the French were not hostiles. He made his announcements—an assurance of their freedom of religion, the promise to set up courts, and the French alliance with the Americans. These statements were greeted with delight and enthusiasm. The church bell was rung to announce the change in government; this gave the bell its name, the Liberty Bell of the West.[39] When the British had arrived, the inhabitants took a long time in deciding whether or not to take an oath of allegiance, but they wasted no time in joining the Americans.

Captain Bowman, who was supplied with horses by the Kaskaskians, was sent by Clark to the other villages accompanied by members of the Kaskaskia militia. From the accounts it appears that the Kaskaskians went in their best finery to celebrate the end of British rule. Although Bowman implied that the other villages were terrified into submission, this again seems unlikely. The townspeople would have recognized their relatives in the group; the Kaskaskians were armed and under their own militia captain, who was well known by the villagers.[40]

Bowman commented on his taking of what he called "Parraderuski"(Prairie du Rocher).

> Before they had any idea of our arrival, we had possession of the town. They seemed to be a good deal surprised and were willing to come to any terms that would be required of them.[41]

Bowman went on to St. Philippe and Cahokia where American rule was readily accepted. An expedition sent to Vincennes, in present Indiana, also took that village into the American fold.

Interestingly enough, the traditional story related above, about the British takeover of Fort de Chartres, reappeared in 1836 in another version, supposedly about George Rogers Clark's troops.

> When the little band arrived beneath the walls of Fort Chartres, the numbers of the garrison far exceeding those of the besiegers, the latter, as if in despair of success, shortly took up the line of march and disappeared behind the distant bluffs…early one morning a troop of cavalry appeared winding over the bluffs, their arms glittering in the sunlight, and descended from view apparently into the plain beneath. Hour after hour the march continued; troop after troop,…Alarmed and astonished at the countless swarms of the invaders, the garrison hastily evacuated the fortress…[42]

Obviously there are many flaws in this rendition. Clark did not take Fort de Chartres at all. It had been abandoned prior to his arrival and the British garrison long gone. His troops were hardly glittering cavalry; they were ragged and half naked.

A spirit of optimism now infused the villagers; they were rid of the hated British and because of the American alliance with France, their hopes were that they could return to the rule of the French king. They assisted the Virginians with food and clothes and welcomed them socially. Clark went to "Priaria De Rush" to spend the evening at the home of the militia captain, Barbeau. Clark and his officers had dinner there and then attended a ball held in their honor. About midnight however, a messenger came to Clark and said that Lt. Gov. Henry Hamiliton of Detroit and 800 men were near Kaskaskia. Clark, his officers and some men from Prairie du Rocher immediately rode to Kaskaskia, but the information later was found to be incorrect.

However, Governor Hamilton seized Vincennes not long afterwards. Clark was becoming short of men as the enlistment period was up for many of his troops. He convinced some to stay and was able to raise two companies from the French villages. They accompanied his troops to retake Vincennes. This campaign involved a very difficult winter march. The men who went with him showed the quality and courage of the local militia, again indicating that the lack of

resistance to Clark's initial occupation was due more to a predisposi-
tion to supporting those opposing the British rather than to fear. At
least two Prairie du Rocher militiamen are known to have accompanied Clark—Charles Leveille and Pierre de Barria—and probably there
were others.[43]

Clark acted as commandant at Kaskaskia, commissioned the
militia officers, and saw to some legal matters. In December 1778
Virginia created civil government for the Illinois. This was only temporary authority, passed for one year, that would have to be renewed
annually. The governor, Patrick Henry, commissioned John Todd as
county lieutenant. In May 1779 Clark assembled the villagers at the
Kaskaskia church to expound on the formation of the civil government and to assure the French of its benefits.

> In a short time you will know the American system which you
> will find, perhaps, in the beginning a little strange; but in the course of
> time you will find so much peace and tranquillity in it, that you will
> bless the day that you espoused the cause of the Americans.[44]

Todd created three judicial districts—Cahokia, Vincennes and
Kaskaskia. The last included Prairie du Rocher, Chartres, and St.
Philippe. A nine-man court was to have jurisdiction over civil and
criminal matters, and four justices would constitute a quorum. In this
new court all the judges were French, and the law to be followed was
the *Coutume de Paris*. In May six justices were elected from
Kaskaskia, two from Prairie du Rocher and one, Pierre Girardot, from
St. Philippe.[45]

In the selection for Prairie du Rocher, fifteen *habitants* voted
for the justices and attested to the election of Barbeau and Antoine
Louvière, the lieutenant of militia. Louvière was a young man, thirty-
five, but well-to-do, the son of Pierre Louvière, the previous militia
captain. The inhabitants who made their mark on the document—an
X as they could not write—were Joseph Tangue, Joesph Cochon,
François Thibault, Louis Buart, Louis Vasseur, Nicolas Turjon,
François Camus, Joseph Blay, and Louis Pillet. The signatories were
Barbeau, Aymé Comte, Gabriel Decochy, and an Italian who signed

Giovani Baptista Jacomini, but was known to the French as Jean Baptiste Jacquemin. Those who voted were all married men, heads of family. There are two illegible names on the document, probably Gerald Langlois and Antoine Cotineau, also heads of households.[46] Although there were three or four other single adult male residents (in their 30s and 40s), apparently they were not eligible to vote. The franchise restriction may have been to owners of property in the commonfield, but it is difficult to obtain an accurate list of owners in the period. This does throw into question statements concerning the wide franchise under the French regime, since it is doubtful that the Americans would have forced a change at this point.

The election was not held after mass at the church, as usually had been done. Perhaps this was because mass was held irregularly, due to the lack of priests. The election was done by an assembly of the inhabitants in the "audience chamber" of Barbeau, which suggests a room in the house that he used for official actions. Barbeau's titles were given as captain of the militia and commandant of the village. In the French period, the commandant at the fort, who was called the "major commanding," had occasionally appointed a commandant for the village of Kaskaskia. Prairie du Rocher, being near the fort, had not needed one. Apparently Clark made Barbeau the "commanding officer at Prairie du Rocher."[47] Gov. Patrick Henry stated in a letter to Clark that a commandant was a civil officer.[48]

Although no records mention the office of *syndic* in Prairie du Rocher at this time, it probably continued there, as *syndics* were involved in activities concerning the commonfield fence up into the nineteenth century. In Kaskaskia the office appeared in connection with the common fence and a *syndic* represented Fr. Gibault, the churchwardens and the parish in a court case.[49] The documents show that *syndics* were appointed by the court too for duties dealing with estates. Although called in the records a "*syndic* and attorney," the *syndic* was not a lawyer, but an agent. After 1782 the title disappears in court cases and individuals were represented by attorneys.[50]

The enthusiasm for the Americans soon was tempered by the actions of the poorly supplied Virginian troops, who had inadequate food, and no money for purchases, and so obtained items through seizure. Almost immediately the court began to complain about the soldiers killing the *habitants'* animals for food. The paper money that came into the colony from Virginia was devalued and so often counterfeited that the French lost all faith in it.

During Clark's tenure he kept order and the populace had confidence in him, but when he returned to Kentucky his deputies were not as satisfactory. Todd carried on well for a few months, but his successors, Richard Winston and Colonel Montgomery, confiscated goods to support the troops. Montgomery even threated the inhabitants with force if they did not willingly supply what he wanted. This arbitrary military oppression discouraged many of the citizens of Kaskaskia, who had hoped for a better life under the Americans. Emigration to the Spanish side became a steady stream, and it included many of the more important and prosperous of the inhabitants. Most of the loss of personnel and the complaints of the period stem from Kaskaskia; that village took the brunt of the occupation of the soldiers and the requisitions made by Colonel Montgomery. The Kaskaskia inhabitants protested to magistrates to put a stop to "the brigandage and tyranny from the military," ironically looking back to Clark's speech "that you may show us a glimpse of that liberty which has been so many times promised to us..."

Indeed, the Kaskaskians complained that they were assuming all of the burden of supporting the military, and the other villages were not contributing.[51] Someone was sent then to Cahokia to collect; there is no record of whether Prairie du Rocher was impressed for supplies, although it would seem likely. Troops had been quartered at Cahokia before. Perhaps Prairie du Rocher, being so small, was not suitable for this.

Most of the documents from the Virginian period that have survived from the notaries' records or the courts, relate to Kaskaskia or Cahokia. Barbeau would have handled most of the civil actions, such as marriage contracts and land sales, but whatever records he kept are not extant. Only a few court cases from Prairie du Rocher survive, including one that was sent on to the Kaskaskia court. In February 1779 Raymond Labrière petitioned the captains of militia at Kaskaskia to delay the inventory of his mother-in-law, Mme. Cotineau.

He reported that Lionnais, who acted as a scribe for Barbeau, had gone to Mme. Cotineau after the death of her husband to tell her that she should present a petition to Clark to have an inventory made and a guardian chosen for the children, a standard French procedure under the *Coutume*. Labrière claimed that the widow didn't understand and thought Lionnais or Barbeau was going to get something out of this.

Labrière said that he didn't want to bring the cattle together for inventory because of fear of the Indians. He requested permission to start up Cotineau's tannery to pay his debts. He also demanded that Barbeau be prevented from troubling the widow in the peaceable possession of her goods. The petition was approved by Clark. Labrière had gone over Barbeau's head. Barbeau, as village militia captain and commandant, could have forced the inventory to be done.

What part of this is true is difficult to say. Six months later Madame Cotineau petitioned to request an inventory, the election of guardians, and an accounting from Labrière. She alleged that her son-in-law illegally prevented her from doing the inventory and had tried to get control of the estate for his benefit. As detailed in the inventory, the Cotineaus' had a two-story stone house (forty by twenty-two feet), a number of outbuildings, a tannery, and an old mill. It was a well supplied and prosperous household. The inventory took up many pages; a few items are listed below:

> two copper cauldrons, an eleven pot stewpan, one doughbox and two sifters; six faience plates, two silver tumblers, seven pewter candlemolds, seven pewter spoons and ten forks; one fitted sideboard, three bottles, two flasks, nine chairs, one saddle, one cow named Beauty, one cow named Blackie.[52]

Troubles with the British continued. In 1780 a large force of British soldiers and Indians from Detroit and Mackinac approached to try to seize the Illinois villages and St. Louis in order to prevent Spanish assistance to the Americans. Some inhabitants of Cahokia and St. Louis became aware of the impeding attack. Word was sent to Clark, who was hastily recalled from Kentucky. With Montgomery, the Virginian troops, and French militia, probably including Prairie du Rocher militiamen, the attack was successfully repelled. The Spanish in St. Louis also were effective in repulsing the invaders.[53]

The French then became involved with a rather unusual leader. A French officer Augustin Mottin de la Balme had been sent west in 1780, with the blessing of Washington and Lafayette, to try to raise support for the revolution from the French. Their hope was to have forces from the Illinois villages seize the fort at Detroit and march on to Canada, where they could be joined by Canadians to defeat the British. The dissatisfaction of the French with the Virginian soldiers and the lack of governmental order caused them to welcome de la Balme as a representative of France. Without doubt de la Balme over-emphasized the involvement of the king of France and encouraged the villagers to think that royal troops would return, but the area was ripe for change and the hope of restoring a stable French government was a strong incentive.

De la Balme led a small group of Frenchmen and Indians north towards Detroit, but the group was waylaid by Miami Indians. De la Balme and others were killed, thus ending the revolt. De la Balme's appearance and actions were minor in the overall picture, but he had a decided impact on attitudes in Illinois. The villagers expected French intervention and they felt confident in their hostility to the Virginians. Indeed, the villagers wrote the Virginian government that they would not tolerate any more troops in their villages except French troops.[54]

American Territory

In 1783 the final treaty ending the Revolutionary War ceded the land west to the Mississippi River to the new United States; Virginia gave up its claims to the Illinois area in 1784. As the treaty had been expected for some time, the Virginia legislature did not renew the annual authorization for Illinois government in 1782, anticipating that the Congress shortly would take control of the territory. This meant that in January 1782 even the tenuous official rule provided by Virginia ended. But Congress did not provide civil government for the area it called the Old Northwest for another eight years.[55]

In Illinois the courts were the only continuity for civil activity. Jean Baptiste Barbeau was president of the Kaskaskia court in early 1782. By that time he and Louvière had served on the court for three years. In June 1782 another election was held in Prairie du Rocher and nine *habitants* selected two new magistrates, Aymé Comte and Jean Baptiste Jacquemin, the Italian with the Indian wife, a non-Frenchman who obviously was well integrated into the society.[56] They took office

> ...after having taken the oath of allegiance and office upon the Evangelists of the Almighty God, took their places in the Court in the quality of justices of the peace and magistrates of the District of Kaskaskia.[57]

Comte became the president of the court. Possibly both Barbeau and Comte in his turn were selected for this post by virtue of being separate from Kaskaskia and its controversies. This preference of persons from villages other than Kaskaskia for major posts occurred again later.

Soon after their election Aymé Comte and Jacquemin petitioned the court to request that one magistrate instead of two could act on estate inventories; this would lower costs. The documents resulting from any such action would be brought to the Kaskaskia court for confirmation.[58] Costs for the magistrates' time were not given here, but at Cahokia the cost of the justice of the week for each judgment was five *livres*—for each writ two *livres* fifteen *sous*. The clerk received five *livres* for each writ or judgment.[59]

Most of the records preserved relate to estate actions that required confirmation by the court. Some estates were complicated by a second marriage. Joseph Blay of Prairie du Rocher requested the division of the estate of his deceased wife, Thérèse Gilbert, and her first husband, Jacque Boutilliet, for the support of her children. The assembly of friends and relatives recommended that the personal property be sold at auction and the real estate at Prairie du Rocher and Prairie Chassin be leased to provide funds for the children. Blay does not appear to have agreed in his marriage contract to care for the children. A cousin, Joseph Cochon, was to take the two girls. The assembly recommended that the children be maintained in an appropriate manner even if sufficient funds from the estate were lacking.[60]

The court was used for enforcement on the rare occasions when local pressures were inadequate to provide a solution. Aymé Comte, not as a magistrate but in his position as churchwarden of St. Joseph's, had to petition the court to order Louvière to fence his portion of the vestry property. All the other villagers involved had complied. The fencing probably was to keep the animals out since it was said to be necessary for the conservation of the rectory and orchard.[61]

The court was not stable though. Two of the Kaskaskia magistrates, St. Gemme Beauvais and François Corset, resigned sometime during 1782.[62] The court was active throughout the year despite the loss of the Kaskaskia members, then disappeared. But it was revived at the end of 1783. Shortly after that it evidently was suppressed by Timothé Montbrun, county lieutenant. In 1784 he took over the role as judge and magistrate.

The French villages followed very different paths. In Cahokia the local court was well established and able to continue. This meant that the village was under the customary laws, the *Coutume*, and people moved there because of that security. Joseph Labuxière, formerly a notary and royal attorney at Chartres, wrote

> The misunderstanding of the magistrates of Kaskaskia and the extreme disorder of the business of the individuals, occasioned by persons greedy for money, which compelled me to withdraw with my family to Cahokia, where I have found the inhabitants filled with unity of peace and fidelity to the states, and a court of justice which they are careful to administer with equity to those who ask its help.[63]

Cahokia was growing in size. In 1787 it had a population of 400, very few of them Americans. Prairie du Rocher had twenty-two male heads of family. Their male children plus one widow made a total of seventy-nine.[64] Women and female children were not tallied. Ages of the heads of family can be determined for only twelve; there was a preponderance of older men, with the average age being forty-eight—a fairly long lived and healthy population. The number of heads of families was down only two (counting the widow) from 1768, not a significant decline, and definitely not like the loss of inhabitants at Kaskaskia where the decrease in its French population continued. In 1787 Kaskaskia had 191 male heads of household, but by 1790 only 44 heads of family were listed, a loss of seventy-seven percent.[65]

Among the various disruptions and problems suffered by Kaskaskia, the tyranny of John Dodge, lasting from 1784 to 1786, was a major one. Dodge took over the old fort on the bluffs above the Kaskaskia River. From here he ruled Kaskaskia, even threatening the town with cannon. Monbrun did little to stop him. Prairie du Rocher, however, maintained its quiet existence under the continuing leadership of Barbeau.

Numerous petitions were sent to Congress over the next few years with complaints and asking for civil government. The Kaskaskians sent many, but in June 1784 Prairie du Rocher residents were signatories also. After several of these petitions had been received Congress decided in March 1785 to appoint commissioners for land claims and civil government, but this failed to result in any action. In 1786 another petition was sent, and Gabriel Cerré of Kaskaskia was questioned by Congress concerning the events in Illinois.[66]

In August 1786 Congress informed the people of Illinois that they had under consideration a plan for civil government. This raised the hopes of the people sufficiently so that there was a revolt of the French inhabitants in Kaskaskia. Dodge's power was broken and the court was reinstated. Mathurin Bouvet of St. Philippe was appointed judge. Monbrun, who had supported Dodge, departed from the Illinois after naming Barbeau as deputy county lieutenant in his stead. This appointment of non-Kaskaskians to leadership positions was significant. Appointment of a Kaskaskian would have favored one of the many factions that had been vying for power.[67]

When a letter came from Congress for the county lieutenant in January 1787, the villagers were very hopeful. They sent for Barbeau to come and open the official communication; apparently this had to be done at Kaskaskia, the seat of local government. Barbeau sent back a letter to the notary Langlois:

The circumstances of the time and my illness prevent me from going myself to Kaskaskia. As the inhabitants may be expecting us to open the papers and it is a thing very interesting for the citizens, I ask them to have them read, as though I were there. I beg you to be kind enough to tell me the news in a short letter which I shall expect with much pleasure.[68]

Alas, the letter merely said that the civil government was still in the future.

The Americans, who were increasing in number, were dissatisfied with the French court, as they did not speak French. As early as 1782 the American settlers at Belle Fontaine petitioned for a magistrate; they were given permission and elected one. He did not appear on the court. In 1787 three American magistrates were elected and, with three French magistrates, were commissioned by Barbeau in his role as county lieutenant. Henry Smith, obviously an American, was elected president of the court.

Although the last authorization for government from Virginia had been in 1782 and Illinois had been given up to the new United States in 1784, the area continued nominally under Virginia. Timothé Monbrun, appointed county lieutenant through Virginia, had designated Barbeau to succeed him, and Barbeau viewed his authority as proceeding from Virginia. This can be seen from his commissioning of the magistrates. The document is in English of a sort. Probably it was written by Lionnais, his secretary. There is no evidence one way or the other as to whether Barbeau knew English.

The Commonwealth of Virginia to Henry Smith Thomas Hughes, Michal Duff antony Saint geme Beauvais francis Corset John Baptiste saint geme Beauvais Esquires.
From the great confidence in your Judgement & Integrité by the good people of KasKasKias and its Dependencies and agreeably to an act of the General assembly of Virginia you [are] hereby constituted & appointed Justices of the peace for the District of KasKasKias and judges of the Court of the said District in cases both civil and criminal. any four or more of you are authorized to constitute a Court before

whom shall [MS. torn] all actions and cases of which the Court [MS. torn] ties of this Commonwealth, Respectively [MS. torn] your Judgements must have the Concu [MS. torn] at least a majorité and be entered with [MS. torn] previous & subbsequent, and fairly recorded in Books provided for that purpose Witness John Baptiste Barbau Deputy County Lieutenant or Commandant in Chief of the County of Illinois the 18th. day of May in the ten year of the commonwealth anno que Domini 1787   Barbau Liet de conte[69]

The French magistrates wanted nothing to do with the American ones and were not cooperative. Mathurin Bouvet, described as a former mayor of Kaskaskia, now captain of militia at St. Philippe and previously a judge, protested that he had been presented with a writ of habeus corpus on June 3, 1787, issued by Smith, as president of the court. Bouvet retorted that he had no knowledge of the establishment of such a court and when he appeared in Kaskaskia on the appointed day he found no courtroom, no court, and no president.[70]

The French magistrates protested that it was impossible to communicate with the Americans on the litigations brought before them, and that there was no one capable of doing all the translation required. Therefore, the Kaskaskians decided that there would be only French magistrates, and the other Frenchmen who had received votes in the election Barbeau had held would be the magistrates.[71] This rather illegal procedure left the Americans adrift until fall of 1787, when they were incorporated into the Cahokia district.

The Ordinance of 1787, passed in July, created a paper government for the Northwest Territory, but it did not become a reality for another three years. This did, however, create a vacuum, since all other jurisdictions were immediately annulled.[72]

A major concern for both the French and the Americans was titles for their land; the French wanting to confirm the grants they had received from the French government, and the Americans the grants from various commandants, or their rights as squatters on open lands. A report of Congress in 1788 addressed this concern:

That measures be immediately taken for confirming in their pos-

session and titles, the French and Canadian inhabitants, and other settlers on those lands, who on or before the year 1783 had professed
themselves citizens of the United States...[73]

As with most governmental directives, "immediately" took a
while; it was not until 1807 that information on land began to be
assembled; then Land Commissioners were appointed to validate
claims.

Life at the End of the Eighteenth Century

The best source of information about the French villages in
the last quarter of the eighteenth century is to be found in the reports
of the land commissioners. Between 1807 and 1814 the commissioners reviewed documents and interrogated local citizens. The information they took down from the citizenry produced an unintentional
form of oral history. The depositions drew upon the memories of local men concerning people and events twenty to thirty years in the
past. The data is biased towards the restricted topic under discussion—land; but fragmentary as it is, it is all the oral history that we
have.

Towards the end of the eighteenth century some expansion
of land use around Prairie du Rocher occurred. New areas were brought
under cultivation on top of the bluffs, probably in portions of the
upper common. In 1785 Joseph Cochon and Louis Doré farmed about
five acres on the hills about two miles distant from the village. Another man, Charles Aimé, was said to farm one *arpent* on the hills.[74]
These improvements on the bluffs were surrounded by fences.

The Prairie du Rocher commonfield continued to have a common fence. Even in Kaskaskia, although it was more disrupted by the
emigration of the *habitants*, the commonfield fence remained. A document from there related that a few pigs got through a break in the
common fence and were killed, as authorized by the rules. The informants also reported that by the gate in the commonfield fence at
Kaskaskia was a cabin, where a man lived in order to guard the gate.[75]

By this time the commonfield system of Chartres must have

broken down. With very few of the original residents remaining in the area, large portions had been abandoned and were vacant. Many tracts were claimed by Americans, particularly John Edgar, and others were occupied by squatters. The commonfield system could not be perpetuated under those circumstances. In St. Philippe the majority of the lands had come into the hands of the captain of militia, Charles Cadron, who, in the 1780s, sold it to Michel Soumande, who, in turn sold it to American speculators, Moses and Franks.[76]

Although most of the lands occupied by the French had been conceded formally by representatives of the king, some informal usages also existed. Areas designated as sugar camps do not appear to be part of the granted lands, but had been appropriated by various families whose rights to those were recognized by the other inhabitants. Here syrup and sugar were made not only from maple trees, but from other trees as well. The sugar camps were a lumber source too. Both sugar and lumber traditionally belonged to the sugar camp users.

Despite frequent references to sugar camps in other records of this period, little is known about them. The depositions however, actually describe a sugar camp cabin, one that certainly did not resemble a label for Vermont maple sugar! The cabin was a lean-to; the back wall was formed by a very large fallen tree. The front was supported by two posts, and the entire structure enclosed with planks. The two owners of this sugar camp hired four men, and all six resided there from fall to February or March. The four hired helpers were "employed in making troughs, cutting wood and carrying water for the purpose of making sugar."[77] Sugar camps existed near the prairie of the Apacois, the Belle Fontaine area.

By the 1780s the Americans had moved into the bottomlands. Although most took up land outside the French claims, a few purchased land in areas of the Fort de Chartres and St. Phillippe commonfields and settled there. Two of these families were the Drurys and McNabbs. They married other American settlers, but also married into the French families as well. They appear in the Prairie du Rocher records.

Up on the bluffs where the Americans settled, each homestead was widely separated from the next family. Some of the Americans' claims were said to be in very small clearings and not easy to discern. According to the informants, the woods were burned off yearly in the fall, apparently creating natural open areas that were hard to distinguish from these small farming plots.[78]

Statements made by informants indicated that the Americans constructed traditional log cabins. Several referred to the cutting of house logs and the building up of cabins. From the usage in the depositions, the term "cabin" appears to have had a distinctly different connotation than house. A house was a permanent dwelling place and a cabin was less substantial. The French built cabins in outlying fields as temporary dwellings during field work or as places where hired help or slaves stayed during such work. The French *habitants* lived in solid houses of wood or stone. Most Americans however, resided in "cabins." The exceptions were noted as "a good residence" or "lived in a house."

Some of the cultural divergences between the French and Americans are expressed in these differing terms. These sometimes lead to misunderstandings at the time and later by historians of the American pioneer expansion. The historians lauded the individualistic, ambitious American settlers on their farmsteads, but their dispersed settlement left them far more exposed to depredations by Indians than the French villagers. The *habitants* lived in their compact villages, went out to farm on the commonfield, and returned at night to the village. The Kaskaskia land depositions speak often of death by Indian attacks, but it was mainly American settlers who were killed.

Although the French system definitely was not the American way of life, for a time many Americans found this to be the only hope for survival. Several "stations" existed; fenced enclosures with a building in which to retreat for defense. The Blockhouse Station, obviously named for its defensive structure, was one of those where the French pattern was temporarily adopted. The farmland at the station was enclosed in a common fence, and each inhabitant was required to construct his share of the fence. The people who fled there because of Indian threats were allotted land according to the size of the family. A single man was allotted two to three acres.[79]

Although the inhabitants of Prairie du Rocher farmed and raised poultry and stock, the hunting of wild game for personal use, and for meat and hides for trade, continued. The areas utilized in the late eighteenth century for game are detailed in a few of the depositions. Louis Pilet and Baptiste Allary of Prairie du Rocher described themselves as "hunters in the country…from 1775 to this day" (1807). The informants stated that they were well acquainted with the lands about Richland, Silver, and Cahokia Creeks, Wood and Kaskaskia Rivers and the Prairie Tamaroa.[80] This statement defines a hunting region in western and central southern Illinois and indicates that the game sought there would have been deer, bear, and fur-bearing animals.

Buffalo were found only west of the Mississippi River at this period and hunting parties are mentioned for the west bank. The consistent usage of the term "hunting parties" for the west bank and "hunters" for the east, suggests a different composition for the groups, perhaps due to greater danger from hostile Indians on the west bank and/or to different hunting practices.

Hunting practices were described as part of the explanation for geographical names. The Petite Pass and Grande Pass in the bluffs near Prairie du Rocher are mentioned in many early land records. The passes were "so-called on account of the narrowness of the Marais [swamp] at these two places and of their being two positions where hunters sat to shoot the fowls that flew over." The bottoms are part of the Mississippi flyway and had abundant waterfowl. Another interesting note is that nearby Horse Creek was called this because "at this place there was formerly a great number of wild horses which we used to go take." Perhaps some of the horses in the inventories came from here.[81]

In the American period the status of blacks began to decline. At the request of some inhabitants, Clark promulgated rules for black and Indian slaves that forbade the selling of liquor to them and the holding of night dances or feasts. Daytime dances were allowed with permission from their owners and only with permits could they be out "after the tatto is beaten." Slaves were not allowed to buy or sell without a permit. These rules were posted on all church doors although they probably were aimed mainly at Kaskaskia. The repetition of the buying and selling restrictions again a year later suggests that they had not been very well observed.[82]

The land holdings and rights of the French blacks were recognized in the American period. In 1775 Antoine Renau wrote his will giving his land, house, and livestock at Kaskaskia to Françoise Tonton, a black woman, whom he termed his benefactress. In the depositions several witnesses testified about Elizabeth La Buche, a black woman, who was considered the widow of the French hunter François La Buche. She was confirmed in her land ownership.[83]

Few of the Americans were Catholic. In fact, many were strongly opposed to the Catholic church, but the French Catholics had other problems besides intolerance. The shortage of priests in the country continued. Fr. Meurin died February 23, 1777, at age 70. He was born in Charleville, France. Fr. Gibault buried him in the church at Prairie du Rocher "on the gospel side."[84] Fr. Gibault was then left alone to serve all of the Illinois parishes. In a letter he described what caring for the various parishes was like:

> ...a trip by canoe, one on foot, one or several on horseback; sometimes living well, sometimes fasting several days; sometimes passing several nights without sleeping, at other times not being able to sleep on account of gnats and other more malignant creatures, such as lice, fleas, bedbugs, etc.; sometimes too tired to be able to eat or sleep; sometimes trembling with fear through a whole pitch-black night at the foot of a tree or in a dense thicket, at other times running away from the Indians at the full speed of my horse...sometimes with the rain on my body, sometimes hiding in the trunk of a tree; in the morning freezing with cold, and at noon scorched by the heat of the sun;...such is my life at Illinois. Pity me, or rather my soul; pray for it.[85]

Since there was no permanent pastor at St. Joseph's, Aymé Comte in his role as first churchwarden, and later other churchwardens, made the appropriate entries for burials and infant baptisms in the church register. Fr. Gibault verified these on one of his visits.

When possible, the assembly after mass continued. In 1776,

on the last day of January,

> Jean Barbeau, captain of the militia and judge of Prairie du Rocher, Jean Pierre Allard, churchwarden in charge, Jean Baptiste Jacquemin, Aime Le Comte, Joseph Blais, Joseph Tanguis, Nicolas Turjeon, Louis Vasseur and other inhabitants assembled at the home of the reverend father for an assembly of the parish to establish the cost for the rental of a pew of the church of St. Joseph of Prairie du Rocher.[86]

The cost decided was 10 *livres* for the first row of pews and five for the others. In 1788 an election of *marguilliers*, churchwardens for the church of St. Joseph, was held at an assembly convened after mass. Pierre Chevallier was selected as first warden and Jean Baptiste Janis as second.[87]

Fr. Gibault continued as the only priest in the Illinois until 1785 when the German Fr. Paul de St. Pierre, a Carmelite, arrived and took over Cahokia. The vicar general, Pierre Huet de la Valienière, made a brief stay in the area and caused problems because of his overbearing personality and self importance. A report stated that he said

> to Mr. Barbeau, County-Lieutenant of this District & inhabitant of Prairie du rocher, that he wou'd interdict the church of that parish, because Mr. De St. Pierre said Mass there as he went by.[88]

Officially the supervision of the parishes ceased to be from Canada in 1784 when Fr. John Carroll of Baltimore, Maryland, was appointed by the pope to be the superior of the missions in the United States. Fr. Carroll considered Illinois to be under his jurisdiction. Although Quebec did not relinquish control immediately after the vicar general's visit, for practical reasons Illinois was inevitably going to be part of the new missionary region, since Canada was in British territory.[89] But the area continued to lack for pastoral care. In 1789 Fr. St. Pierre moved to Ste. Geneviève and in 1792 Fr. Gibault left for New Madrid. Various priests held occasional services. Fr. Gabriel Richard evidently came to the area a year or so later. Fr. Richard is said to have started a school. Pupils from the area came and roomed with widows who needed money.[90]

Even with all of the difficult political situations and monetary problems, the Prairie du Rocher farmers prospered by supplying products for trade. Antoine Louvière had an inventory done of his property after the death of his wife, Marie Goder, in 1775. Louvière was one of the more prominent citizens who served on the intermittent courts. He was not an average farmer. He had a house on sills, forty-five by twenty feet, constructed *pièce en pièce*, a solid structure. The roof was shingled; the house had a floored loft and porches on the two long faces. The windows were glassed. He had two mills, and both had all needed machinery. His three large stables were roofed with thatch. A slave cabin thirty by twenty feet housed four adult male slaves, three adult females and three children. His barns were large–sixty by thirty and forty by twenty-four feet. He owned eleven *arpents* of farmland.

Among the more elaborate and expensive furnishings of the home were a bed furnished with two large new covers of four points (the points signified a size), five salt dishes of crystal, three silver tumblers, and fifteen place settings of silver. Personal goods included two parasols and a pair of gold earrings of his late wife's and three pairs of silver buckles (his).[91]

Louvière's inventory indicates the quality of life for a person of higher status. In such a small community it is significant that there were persons as well to do as Louvière and Barbeau; not all the prosperous citizens were in Kaskaskia. Later American comments about the village tend to make the homes and their furnishings sound very primitive. Either there is some prejudice being expressed or perhaps the natives had learned it was best not to reveal wealth.

Inventories for persons more comparable in status with Heneaux and Brunet/Loisel in Chapter 3 were Cotineau, who has been mentioned already, and Louis Vasseur. Vasseur was a son of Louis Levasseur *dit* D'Espagne, a convict shipped over from France. With the eighteenth century lack of standardization in names and spelling, Vasseur Jr. had dropped the Le; he did not go by his father's nickname. In 1783 Vasseur had a house on sills with a fenced lot, an orchard, four separate pieces of farmland, two yokes of oxen, sixteen various other cattle, eight horses including one called Beautiful Star, and sundry pigs and chickens. He had ample household goods—a walnut cupboard with its metal work, a feather bed and covers, and many kitchen utensils, but all were of lesser quality than Louvière's. Rather than silver he had pewter spoons, plates, platters, and iron forks.[92]

Another glimpse of the life of the time comes from a list of cloth and other items purchased for the three Tanguis children. Jean Baptiste Barbeau was the guardian for the minor children of Joseph Tanguis, who died in 1781, and Barbeau's report on his purchases indicated the standard children's clothing of the period. Children's clothing in the eighteenth century was a miniature version of the adult dress.

Catherine, the eldest, received over two years:
> 1½ *aunes* of linen for a blouse
> 1¼ *aunes* for a skirt
> 6 *aunes* of linen for two blouses and one skirt
> 4 *aunes* of cotton fabric for a skirt
> 4 pairs of shoes
> 2¾ *aunes* of ratteen for a skirt and short cape
> 2½ *aunes* of calico for skirt and short cape

Joseph, eleven to twelve years old, received:
> 4¼ *aunes* of linen for 2 shirts
> 1½ *aunes* cloth for a greatcoat
> ¾ cloth for one pair breeches
> 1 pair of shoes
> cotton fabric for one shirt
> ¼ of fabric for a codpiece
> 6½ *aunes* of linen for shirt and breeches
> 1 *aune* ratteen for a greatcoat

The youngest, François, received:
> 4¼ *aunes* of linen for two shirts
> 1 *aune* of cloth for a greatcoat

¾ cloth for one pair breeches
2 pairs of shoes
cotton fabric for two shirts
¼ of cloth for a codpiece
4¾ *aunes* linen for shirt and breeches
1 *aune* ratteen for a greatcoat
4 *aunes* of gingham for making two shirts and one pair breeches[93]

The adult male dress of the period is described in a quote from the early 1800s:

> The white blanket-coat, known as the capot, was the universal and eternal coat for the winter…A cape was made to it, that could be raised over the head in cold weather…Dressed deer-skin and blue cloth were worn commonly in winter for pantaloons. The blue handkerchief, and the deer-skin moccasins, covered the head and feet…In 1800, scarcely a man thought himself clothed, unless he had a belt tied around his blanket coat; and it was hung on one side with the dressed skin of a polecat, filled with tobacco, pipe, flint, and steel. On the other side was fastened, under the belt the butcher-knife…Check calico-shirts were then common; but in winter, flannel was frequently worn by the voyagers and others. In the summer, the laboring-men and the voyageurs often took their shirts off in hard work and hot weather, and turned out the naked back to the air and sun.[94]

Despite all the changes in governments, no laws had replaced the *Coutume de Paris*. The French inhabitants continued to draw up marriage contracts following the *Coutume*. In 1775 Antoine d'Amour de Louvière and Jeanne Felecite Saucier, daughter of the deceased engineer of the fort, François Saucier, made a contract of marriage before Jean Baptiste Barbeau. The contract followed the standard format and cited the *Coutume de Paris* as its authority. It was drawn up at the house of Saucier in St. Philippe.[95] The marriage contract of Louis Pilet and Marie Barbeau made during the British occupation was given in detail in Chapter 4.

Marriage in the church was considered permanent and unbreakable, but human nature being what it is and was, there were some unsuccessful marriages and separations mentioned in the land depositions. Marie Grude married Paul Labrosse sometime after the arrival of the Americans. She and her husband moved to the west bank but then separated. She returned to Prairie du Rocher to live with her sister.

Marie Aubuchon married Jean Cleary but she left him and "took up" with an Indian slave of Barbeau's. The informants said she lived with the Indian in a cabin in the vicinity of Prairie du Rocher until the Indian's death in 1790.[96]

Many of the early settlers had Indian ancestry, although by the late eighteenth century marriage to Indian women was no longer common. The métis children of the early French and Indian marriages married into many of the other local families. No indication exists that there was any prejudice or social discrimination with the métis. Among the families in Prairie du Rocher married to métis was Joseph Lavoie. He married the daughter of an Indian woman and a Frenchman, Denaud, an interpreter of the Indian languages. After Denaud's death his Indian widow, Marie Jeanne, married Nicolas Marechal of St. Philippe.[97]

Throughout the years of French regime the *habitants* traveled widely, but in later years travel to Canada and Louisiana was reduced, due to the differences in governments and to hostile Indians. Voyaging to France became out of the question after 1765. In the early eighteenth century the Illinois area had been quite cosmopolitan for such a small isolated settlement. Various nationalities were present, and there were contacts with major European countries. Even the latest Parisan fashions reached the villages. But in the late eighteenth century the communities became more isolated. During the changing rules of the British, Virginian, and American periods, Prairie du Rocher found being peripheral to the major center of Kaskaskia actually was a benefit, allowing the village to keep quietly out of the way of the vagaries of the military governments.

The desire for stable government and law continued. Finally, in March 1790, the long looked-for government from Congress became a reality; Arthur St. Clair, designated governor of the North-west Territory, arrived in Kaskaskia. After twenty-five years the Illinois again had a civil government.

Notes

1. Donnelly 1971, 25.
2. Palm 1931, 88.
3. Rothensteiner 1928, 72.
4. Brown and Dean 1977, D420.
5. Alvord and Carter 1915, 477, 478.
6. Alvord and Carter 1916, 91. Trans. of the French with additions from the English version.
7. Houck 1908, 17 lists these men.
8. Keefe 1992.
9. Interviews with Clyde Franklin 1998 and Nora Bies 1981.
10. Gales & Seaton 1834, 209.
11. Alvord and Carter 1915, 395.
12. Alvord 1922, 251ff.
13. Carter 1908, 217.
14. Alvord and Carter 1915, 124; Dean and Brown 1981, 66:6:14:1; 66:12:6:1; 67:1:20:1.
15. Dean and Brown 1981, 63:1:18:1; St. Joseph Ch. Rec. May 24, 1768.
16. Alvord and Carter 1916, 569.
17. Alvord and Carter 1916, 524-526.
18. St. Joseph Ch. Rec. May 24, 1768.
19. Alvord and Carter 1916, 469.
20. Alvord and Carter 1921, 550.
21. Woodstock Papers Vol. Vll, 1878.
22. Mereness 1916, 476.
23. Alvord and Carter 1921, 496.
24. Alvord and Carter 1916, 191.
25. Alvord and Carter 1921, 307. The Spanish *piastres* continued to be used for exchange, but there was still little coinage in the colony.
26. St. Joseph Ch. Rec. Sept. 29, 1770.
27. Pease 1975, 27, 28; Alvord and Carter 1921, 455; 464; 497; Alvord 1965, 267.
28. Dean and Brown 1981, 70:5:29:; 70:6:2:1; 73:5:20:1.
29. Alvord and Carter 1921, 468, 473.

30. Dean and Brown 1981, 71:9:6:1; 72:6:5:2; 73:6:28:2.
31. Carter 1910, 146ff.
32. Donnelly 1971, 49.
33. Alvord 1965, 297.
34. Carter 1908, 162.
35. Pease and Jenison 1940, 36; Pease 1975, 36.
36. Dean and Brown 1981, 76:7:16:1.
37. Dean and Brown 1981, 75:2:16:1; 75:5:12:1.
38. Donnelly 1971, 68.
39. The Kaskaskia church bell is preserved on the island of Kaskaskia. The inscription on the bell reads: *Pour leglise des Illinois par les soins du R. P. doutreleau.* [For the church of the Illinois, by care of Rev. Fr. D'outreleau.] The inscription is frequently mistranslated as "from the king across the water." This is a nineteenth century romantic version; that was the phrase used by Jacobites. The Rev. Fr. D'outreleau was the superior of the Jesuit missions in the Illinois. I hope this ends the use of that romance.
40. Donnelly 1971, 71.
41. James 1912, 615.
42. Thwaites 1906, 89.
43. Probate Rec. Reel 33, 1832-43.
44. Alvord 1909, 81.
45. Alvord 1907, lvii-ixi.
46. Dean and Brown 1981, 79:5:19:1.
47. Dean and Brown 1981, 83:6:25:1.
48. Alvord 1909, 64.
49. Dean and Brown 1981, 82:4:27:1; 82:4:30:2.
50. Dean and Brown 1981, 75:2:9:1; 82:1:9:1; 82:1:22:1.
51. Alvord 1907, 137, 139.
52. Dean and Brown 1981, 79:2:18:1; 79:8:19:1; 79:9:12:1.
53. Alvord 1907, lxxxviii.
54. Alvord 1907, xciii; xciv.
55. Alvord 1907, cxix.
56. Dean and Brown 1981, 82:2:23:1; 82:6:16:1.
57. Alvord 1909, 308.
58. Dean and Brown 1981, 82:6:20:3.
59. Alvord 1907, 201.
60. Dean and Brown 1981, 82:6:11:1.
61. Dean and Brown 1981, 82:6:19:1.

62. Dean and Brown 1981, 87:7:7:1.
63. Alvord 1909, 513.
64. Alvord 1909, 419-420.
65. Alvord 1965, 373.
66. Alvord 1909, 371; 383.
67. Alvord 1909, 390-393.
68. Alvord 1909, 396-7.
69. Alvord 1909, 402.
70. Dean and Brown 1981, 87:7:5:1.
71. Alvord 1909, 406; 408.
72. Alvord 1909, cxli.
73. Alvord 1909, 481.
74. Kas. Land. Depos. A36; A26, A35.
75. Dean and Brown 1981, 81:11:24:2; Kas. Land. Depos. A27.
76. Dean and Brown 1981, 87:-:-:1; Monroe Co. Bk. B, C260, 1772.
77. Kas. Land Depos. A95.
78. Kas. Land Depos. A87.
79. Kas. Land Depos. A69.
80. Kas. Land Depos. B41.
81. Kas. Land Depos. B70, B55.
82. Alvord 1909, 64; 118.
83. Dean and Brown 1981, 75:5:6:1; Kas. Land Depos. A16; Al01; C16.
84. In 1849, though, Father Meurin's remains were transferred to the cemetery of St. Stanislaus Novitiate in Florissant, Missouri. Palm 1931, 93.
85. Alvord 1965, 272.
86. St. Jo. Ch. Rec. 1/31/1776.
87. St. Joseph Ch. Rec. Mar. 31, 1788.
88. Alvord 1909, 580.
89. Donnelly 1971, 109.
90. Interview, Clyde Franklin, 1998.
91. Dean and Brown 1981, 75:-:-:1.
92. Dean and Brown 1981, 83:7:23:2.
93. Dean and Brown 1981, 84:5:29:1.
94. Reynolds 1968, 39.
95. Dean and Brown 1981, 75:9:4:2.
96. Kas. Land Depos. A62; A25.
97. Kas. Land Depos. A54.

6

Old and New

For nearly a generation the small population in the Illinois wilder-ness had been stranded without a stable civil government, in fact being virtually abandoned by all governments. That loss had a psy-chological impact on the inhabitants. The insufficiency of legal pro-tection for their goods and property, the shifting power structures, the general uncertainty and insecurity took their toll on the villagers. The effects of those years were different for each village. At the northern end of the colony, Cahokia retained its courts and maintained order and control by the French citizens throughout the period. Kaskaskia, being the most exposed to the influxes of Anglo traders, adventurers, and the military, was totally disrupted. Prairie du Rocher, a sufficient distance from Kaskaskia that entrepreneurs and opportunists found residence there inconvenient for their trading and politicking, remained peaceful but very wary of outside interference.

Although the Illinois country settled down, thankful for a more stable government, many of the laws, regulations, and customs were different from those that the inhabitants had known before. These differences caused misunderstandings not only at the time but in later historical studies. Nineteenth century writers of the United States' pioneer history tended to overemphasize the non-participatory aspects of the government during the French regime. The French were looked upon as passive, content to let others decide their fate. But the French *habitants* had not been passive. Although fortunately lacking the violent leaders of the French revolution, the spirit of the Jacquerie was revealed in the *habitants'* persistent and stubborn resistance to military and despotic governments. Their determination to have their rights at law and to uphold their dignity was manifested numerous times under the various political rules as they sought redress, and by their insistence upon the courts.

The assemblies after mass had been their equivalent of town meetings and if the paternalistic rule of the commandant was accepted, it was due more to internal necessity for family and community well-being, rather than any great deference to authority. Also the commandant represented the royal authority, a government against which the Illinois citizens were not interested in rebelling, perhaps because they were not experiencing the injustices prevalent in the home country. The *habitants* in the Illinois did not suffer from lack of bread as did the peasants in France. Nor was the commandant in the Illinois the same as the governmental officials in France. Rather than a repressive authority with taxation and demands of work and products, he represented to them the positive qualities of government—stability, assurance of rights, and protection. These qualities were what they had sought throughout the British, Virginian, and now territorial governments.

The older Frenchmen, having endured the long hiatus in government, had learned to deal with the chaotic world around them by retreating to their village and maintaining the integrity of their homes, farms, families, and customs. The younger people could not recall the comforts of the paternalistic French regime, nor were they as cosmopolitan as their parents. Throughout the French regime widespread travel had lead to a degree of sophistication from extensive contacts with France and Canada. The subsequent political regimes caused for one reason or another a more restrictive set of contacts. Thrown thus on their own resources, they had developed internal mechanisms to deal with strife. Now faced with another new system, although they welcomed the stability, there was an understandable hesitation to become involved. Always a familial society, the external pressures increased the cohesiveness of the extended family and the village organization where the leaders were interrelated.

Old Northwest Territory

The ordinance for the Northwest Territory passed by the Continental Congress in 1787 had provisions allowing the French to keep their traditions and customs for the conveyance of property, *la Coutume de Paris* in essence. The ordinance guaranteed religious liberty and prohibited the further introduction of slavery. The interpretation of this last ruling was that the French were allowed to keep the slaves they had, but others were not to be brought in. The question of whether the children of these slaves were slave or free remained unanswered for quite some time.[1]

When Governor Arthur St. Clair arrived in March 1790 he found the court system in disrepair. He divided Illinois into three judicial districts—Cahokia, Kaskaskia, and Prairie du Rocher. He established courts—the Court of Common Pleas, General Quarter Sessions, Justices of the Peace, and Probate Court. Common Pleas handled civil cases; St. Clair appointed Jean Baptiste Barbeau, Antoine Girardin, John Edgar, Philippe Engel, and Jean Dumoulin to the court. The Quarter Sessions that dealt with criminal cases and general administration included John Edgar, Philippe Engel, Antoine Girardin, and Antoine Louvière. The judge was Barthélemi Tardiveau.

The Northwest Territory stretched from the Ohio River to the Canadian border. In 1790 St. Clair County was detached from this vast region. The new county still encompassed a large area. On the west it extended to the Mississippi River. On the east, to a line drawn from the mouth of the Mackinaw River to the mouth of the creek above Fort Massac (Metropolis, Illinois). Indian warfare continued as the Indians opposed the encroachment of the Americans. Two American attempts to defeat the Indians, one led by St. Clair, ended in ignominious defeat. It was not until 1794 and the battle of Fallen

Timbers that the Indian forces were decisively dispersed. This victory was followed by the Treaty of Grenville, in which the Indians ceded land in Ohio and portions of Illinois.[2]

In 1795 a portion of St. Clair County was split off and called Randolph County. The villages of Prairie du Rocher and Kaskaskia were in the new Randolph County; Cahokia remained in St. Clair. Further changes occurred in 1800, when the Indiana Territory was created. Its boundary ran west of a line starting opposite the Kentucky River and north to the Canadian boundary. Vincennes was the capital. Randolph County was incorporated into Indiana territory. The distance from the Mississippi communities to the capital at Vincennes gave rise to a petition to Congress in 1809 for the formation of a separate Illinois Territory, and this was accomplished.[3] Illinois Territory encompassed more than the present state and included Wisconsin, parts of Michigan, and Minnesota. Kaskaskia was the territorial capital.

With the arrival of St. Clair, Barbeau's position as deputy county lieutenant ceased. St. Clair appointed him a judge, however. It is in this capacity that he performed a civil marriage.

> I, Jean Baptiste Barbeau, do hereby certify to have joined together as husband and wife after having published the Banns agreeable to the Laws of this Territory, George Vitmere and Catherine Doree, relict of the late Louis Doree which marriage was had and solemnized at the Village of Prairie du Rocher the — day of June 1790 and the 14th year of the Independence of the United States. Barbau, Judge of Pleas.[4]

The church marriage took place in the following August.

Barbeau's family was prominent in the county and had created ties with important families in the other French towns binding the communities together. Jean Baptiste's daughter, Reiné, married Jean Baptiste Janis, son of Nicolas Janis, the captain of the Kaskaskia militia and a magistrate. Barbeau's daughter, Marie Jeanne, married Jean Baptiste Vallé, son of the captain of the Ste. Geneviève militia. Marie Louise, another daughter, married Nicolas Jarrot, a new emigrant from France, who was rapidly becoming a major entrepreneur in Cahokia. The relationship to the Le Comtes continued, too.[5] His daughter, Susanne, married Pierre Le Compte, brother to Aimé, who was married to the widow of Barbeau's older brother, Jean Baptiste.[6]

It is not certain when Barbeau died, possibly in 1797. If so within a short span of time the major political figures from the "interregnum" disappeared. Antoine Louvière died in 1801, about fifty-seven years old, and Aimé Le Comte in 1802 at age seventy-nine.[7]

Some of the younger generation became involved in political and military activities. Barbeau's son, also named Jean Baptiste, was an officer in the militia by the 1770s. When he died in 1810 he was referred to as judge and former militia captain; apparently he had followed in his father's footsteps. In 1809 André (Andrew) Barbeau was made captain of the Prairie du Rocher militia; he was the third generation of Barbeaus in the Illinois. Aimé Le Compte's younger brother Pierre was appointed as militia lieutenant, and in 1814 he was elected judge in Randolph county.[8] Clement Drury, an American in his fifties, married a Frenchwoman. Their several children all married French settlers. Drury was made captain of militia in 1811. Antoine Louvière, son of the previous Antoine, was made lieutenant.

The militia was important during this period, as there were again threats of Indian attack during the War of 1812. Although there was an alarm given that 600-700 Indians were gathered at Peoria and an attack on Kaskaskia was feared, nothing came of this. The Prairie du Rocher militia probably took part in the two campaigns to Peoria and elsewhere during the war.

Militia involvement, some disruption in trade, and raids on outlying American farms, were the only effects of the war on Prairie du Rocher. The major fighting was all in the northern part of the territory.

Land Titles

When St. Clair arrived probably the most important item needing to be tackled by the government was the confirmation of land titles. The Land Act of 1785 had directed that all public domain must be surveyed and existing claims settled before the sale of public lands could begin. An unknown quantity of unassigned land existed that the developing country was anxious to parcel out to new settlers.[9] Many individuals and land companies were poised to take up land with the completion of the survey.

The Land Commissioners appointed by Congress were to review the claims for land, but settling claims was no easy task. All the claims were based on grants, and frequently the terms of those were vague. The "ancient grants" of the French were at the beginning of the chain of claims; they were hard to untangle and many records had vanished. In the words of the commissioners

> With respect to the French grants, from the wanton outrage which has been committed on their records by the British officers and others, it has been rendered impossible for the present claimants generally, either to produce the concessions to the conceders under whom they claim or a regular chain of conveyances from them. Of course in default of those proofs we have been obliged to receive oral testimony, going to prove the existence of such grants or allotments, or long and quiet possession of the tracts claimed.[10]

These oral testimonies were the depositions used in the previous chapter to depict the late eighteenth-century life in the Illinois.

The destruction of records was stressed by the Land Commissioners. A review of the Kaskaskia Manuscripts, the preserved records of the royal notaries' offices, suggests that approximately sixty-one percent of all documents that appear on the existing notarial inventories are still extant. The most significant loss is the inventory of the notary, Barrois, that listed documents from 1757 to 1765. This was said to have been turned over to Captain Stirling.[11] Some documents from Barrois' work, mainly those pertaining to land, are preserved. The commissioners apparently did have access to documents that are no longer in existence. Indeed, some records may have vanished after the copying by their clerks; a few pages of original documents are interleaved within the books and records of the Land Commissioners at the Illinois State Archives.

The supposed lack of documentation was helpful to certain persons and it can be suspected that rumors of loss were used in order to justify claims. For example, the claim for the Alary sugar camp was said to have been affected by the destruction of records, but there had never been a grant for this because it was one of the early appropriated tracts. In support of this claim, however, the informant De La Route asserted that "in ancient times the government was at Fort de Chartres and he had heard from the ancients that office papers of the country were burnt there."[12] Other attempts to provide verification for this claim were by false documentation. The commissioners located a book from the recorder's office entitled "Répertoire Général du Greffe des Illinois 1721-1771" (General list from the clerk's office of the Illinois), and reported on their findings with great disgust.

> But, (horrible to relate,) on examining the book from which the aforesaid extract was taken, it seems evident that the same is an interpolation, at a very recent period; for the hand-writing and the ink are evidentally different from the rest of the writing in the same book; but to whom to attribute this black transaction the commissioners are unable to say.[13]

False claims were made too. John Edgar said he had received land from Louis Pilet of Prairie du Rocher, and produced a document signed by the now deceased Pilet. The problem with this was that Pilet's neighbors attested to the fact Pilet had not been able to write.[14]

To verify land rights, multiple depositions were necessary for each claim in order to uncover discrepancies because not all informants were honest. One informant, Simon Toiton, made many depositions. The commissioners reported

> This is a Frenchman, without property, fond of liquor, and who has been clerk of the Roman Catholic parish of Prairie du Rocher; after having given perhaps two hundred depositions in favor of John Edgar, William and Robert Morrison, and some others, he was induced, either

by compensation, by fear, or by the impossiblity of obtaining absolu-
tion on any other terms, to come forward before the Board of Commissioners, and declare on his oath that the said depositions were false,
and that, in giving them in, he had regard to something beyond the
truth.

Toiton himself stated the problem.

I, Simon Toiton, being in my sober senses, having taken no drink, and
after mature reflection...that I was drunk when I gave them, [the depo-
sitions] a failing to which I am unfortunately addicted, and that, when
I am in that state, any one, by complying with my demands, may do
what they please with me.[15]

Toiton's depositions had to be discounted; there were other
false statements that added to the confusion of the commissioners.

The depositions on land provide very few details about the
farms of the French settlers in Prairie du Rocher, as the land had
descended from father to son. Only when the property had been sold
to latecomers were questions raised or when improvements had been
made outside the village and its commonfield.

The communal village lands continued to be under the rule
of the inhabitants. In 1791 an "An Act Regulating the Enclosures of
Grounds" was approved by Governor St. Clair that allowed the proprietors of the commonfield to fence their lands in common in accordance with their custom. In December 1799 an "Act to regulate the
enclosing and cultivating of Common Fields" provided that the proprietors of lands in the commonfield should meet annually (the first
Monday in March was suggested) in order to make rules and regulations

for the well ordering of the affairs of such field, with respect to fencing
and cultivation, and all other things necessary for the well managing of
the same, for the common interest of such proprietors...

They were allowed to select a chairman, treasurer and a clerk to keep a record of all "acts, votes and resolutions." Elections were to be held annually. A committee of three persons, styled the field committee, was to be formed; this body could call a meeting of the proprietors when needed. The proprietors, the owners of land within the commonfield, were empowered to levy taxes on themselves to defray costs for altering fences, making gates or bridges, or for other expenses for the common good. They could appoint assessors and a collector for this tax; the collector would have the same authority as the county tax assessor.

The dates for opening and closing the commonfields were established by the law with the opportunity for modification by the villagers.

> That the said common field shall be enclosed with a good and sufficient fence, according to law, on or before the first day of May in each and every year, or such other day as the said proprietors may appoint; and that no cattle, horses, or other animals shall be suffered to be put into such fields, for the purpose of depasturing therein, between the first day of May and the fifteenth day of November...[16]

The field committee was given the right to designate the place and amount of fence that each landowner was required to build and maintain. The committee had similar functions to the office of *syndic*. In Cahokia, in fact, the term *syndic* persisted. In 1808 six *syndics* were charged with making agreements on the fencing there.[17] In Prairie du Rocher the field committee name seems to have changed to "fence viewers" later. In 1827, for example, Andréw Barbeau, Alanson Brown, and Michel Duclos were appointed fence viewers. The last official mention of fence viewers found in the records was in 1834.[18]

Both the 1791 and 1799 laws about enclosures also specifically stated that an individual had the right to enclose "the whole, or any part of the land" in a separate fence. This provision doomed the commonfields of Cahokia, Kaskaskia, and the other French towns in Illinois. The Americans could not understand nor accept the ideas of communal usage and control; these were alien to their concept of individual rights.

Increasing numbers of Americans moved into the French area, settling on farmsteads located outside the villages. The commonfields and the common were viewed by them as large open areas ripe for settlement, and as soon as it became available, land there was purchased. By the early part of the nineteenth century the common and commonfields had vanished from most of the French villages.[19]

A visitor in 1839 described "farms" in the Prairie du Rocher and Fort de Chartres commonfields, but it is not clear if any fencing is involved; these farms may have been cultivated strips as distinguished from prairie and woods.

> We came from Kaska in a gig. There are a number of very fine farms along the road to Du Rocher particularly the Barbeaus. At one of these farms we saw corn about 5 ft. high. In the Common field of Fort Chartres there is much fine prairie land with some lakes...which can be drained with facility at small expense. The McNabbs have beautiful farms in the Common field...Prairies abound with grass 3 to 4 feet high. The people of the village & neighborhood resort to this prairie to make Hay. A good quantity of wood is in & near the prairie.[20]

Prairie du Rocher was not strongly affected by these changes. Americans did move in. Land in the Fort de Chartres commonfield and at St. Philippe was available. Land at Prairie du Rocher was acquired by Americans mainly through marriage into the French families, and the communal restrictions apparently were accepted. With the abandonment of the villages of Chartres and St. Philippe the settlers in the old commonfields became part of the larger community of Prairie du Rocher, interacting economically and socially with the villagers.

Although the village owned the upper common, it does not seem that extensive use was made of it at all times, probably because it was more exposed to depredations by the Indians. Cattle and hogs were pastured on islands in the Mississippi, and some cattle and horses were in compounds within the village. As mentioned in the discussion on land claims, a few Frenchmen had made individual farms in the upper common, with fences separating the crops from the domestic animals. The common had extensive woods utilized by the villagers for cutting firewood.

After Statehood

The French were prominent in the original courts in 1790, but by the time statehood was being considered for Illinois the French were politically in decline; none were involved in the constitutional convention.[21] When Illinois became a state in 1818, Kaskaskia became the state capital. However, soon afterwards the capital was removed to Vandalia. The "native" French were no longer prominent in politics, although Pierre Menard, a fairly recent emigrant from Canada, was made lieutenant governor of the new state.

The change from territory to statehood probably had little effect on Prairie du Rocher. A few Americans married into the French families, but the town was increasingly becoming a French island in a sea of Americans. The state constitution allowed the French to maintain their slaves and also provided for indentured servants, which perpetuated a form of slavery.

By an act of the state legislature in 1821, the settlement actually became an official village. In that same act, the other communities were called towns. Trustees were appointed for the village—André Barbeau, Antoine Louvier, Henry Barbeau, Henry Kerr, and William Drury. Village organization apparently was not a high priority of the *habitants*, and it was said to have been abandoned shortly. One reason for the seeming indifference to the incorporation may be because there was also the legislated commonfield entity. The proprietors of the commonfield and the franchised voters were synonymous. Such a small village did not need two layers of government. The commonfield organization was closer to what the French *habitants* had been accustomed, and met psychological as well as legal needs.

The village organization was renewed in 1837, the previous incorporation having lapsed. The village "was incorporated under the General State Law, Aug. 19, 1837 and trustees named."[22] The trustees were listed: Joseph Godaire, Jr., Michael Duclos, Jean Marie

Gaudaire, and Joseph Blais; Alexander Pitre was selected as president.

Many of the old spatial features from the French regime remained. The common and the commonfields have been discussed. The old king's highway still ran from Prairie du Rocher to Kaskaskia. Parts of the Big Woods outside the town had been cleared for farming, but the marshes had not been drained. The village of Prairie du Rocher still was spread out by the church and cemetery, with houses situated on one *arpent* square lots. Meandering through the village was Prairie du Rocher Creek. It flooded frequently, with water from the Mississippi River backing it up.

Because of the flooding problem the decision was made in the 1830s to move the village closer to the bluffs. Although movement may have begun earlier, the official grants for new lots commenced in 1835. This land was part of the old lower common granted in 1734, and as such was corporately owned by the village. For this reason the grants were made by the inhabitants to an individual.

The requests and responses for grants in the old lower common were made in the French language. Auguste Derousse addressed himself to "Messieurs les habitans du Village de la Prairie du Rocher." He requested one *arpent* in the common—to the north of the lot was Isadore Goder and to the south, a street across from Jean Marie Godier. Among other requests were those of Jean Baptiste Lessor, the widow Dejarlais, and William Henry, who wanted to establish a cord or rope-making business on the St. Louis road.[23] The grantees agreed to conform to the uses, customs, and laws of the village.

The church continued to have French speaking priests—Fr. Gabriel Richard, Fr. Donatien Olivier, Fr. Jean Timon, Fr. Van Cloostere, and others. Changes in diocesan status occurred. Again this probably had little effect on the local church. In 1808 the Illinois country became part of the diocese of Bardstown, Kentucky. In 1827 the diocese of St. Louis was extended to the western half of Illinois.[24] Church records continued to be written in French. In addition to clerical Latin, most of the priests were acquainted with the English language as well. The first entry in English is in 1827 by Fr. Timon, who registered the baptism of Adeline, the daughter of Ichabod Sargent and

Asstes Brown. Obviously they were English speakers.

Fr. Van Cloostere made two censuses of the parish, one in 1839 and the other ten years later. Both were written in Latin. He enumerated his congregation, listing each household, the head of the family, his father's name, the wife under her maiden name, her father's name, the ages of the couple, their children with their ages, and all other members of the household.

These censuses provide very accurate figures for composition of the parish of St. Joseph. The total number of households in 1839 tallied was eighty-six; this included six free black households. The total population was 526 persons, 475 white and fifty-one black. No Indians were mentioned. The size of the households varied from one to twenty persons with an average of a little over six persons per household, including resident blacks, slave and free. Sixty-five households were headed by males and fifteen by women (widows). For the blacks there were two male heads and four female.

The households were evenly divided between those made up only of the nuclear family and those with extended families. The extended families had a variety of additional members, almost all of whom were related to the household couple. The figure below shows the age distribution of the French population based on the church census.

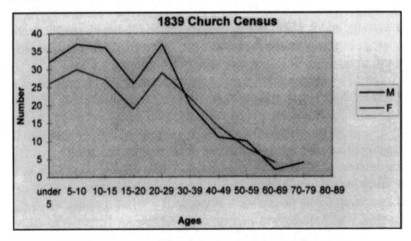

The familial structure of the community meant that care was extended to the elderly, orphaned, or indigent members. Poverty was therefore not a social problem in the community. Attached to the family groups were nineteen slaves; there were eighteen free blacks and fourteen blacks of unknown status, mostly children. As the blacks were looked on as part of the extended family, their social needs were take care of as well. This, then, was the parish that Fr. Van Cloostere pastored.

Slave and Free

The position of the black slaves of the French was an ambiguous one. St. Clair had interpreted the Ordinance of 1787 as preventing the introduction of new slaves, but not freeing of the existing ones.[25] The French were allowed to keep their slaves under the state constitution. The status of children born to the slaves was not resolved; the French populace seems to have assumed that these were slaves, although by the 1830s this was less assured.

Slavery continued in Illinois into the 1840s. In 1830 the Federal census listed eighty-five slaves and nineteen free blacks in the village and surrounding area. In 1839, although several former slave families were free, they were still living with their former owners and probably employed by them.

Indenture was used as a mechanism to continue servitude; children of indentured servants were freed at age twenty-one for males and eighteen for females. In 1830 Catherine Louvière McNabb, widow of Archibald McNabb, made an agreement with Baptiste, who had been freed the previous year. A boy, Jean Baptiste, had been born that year to Françoise, a slave of Catherine; he was indentured to Baptiste, "the reputed father." Jean Baptiste was bound as an apprentice

> to learn such art or trade or occupation of life in business as he himself the said Baptiste shall deem proper and especially the occupation of farming during which time he the said Jean Baptiste is to be under control and full management of the said Baptiste...

Baptiste was to furnish the usual boarding, washing, lodging, and clothing "together with all other such needful comforts and conveniences." At twenty-one Jean Baptiste was to be furnished with "at least 2 good suits of comfortable clothes and at 21 he shall be entirely free of claims of services of Catherine McNabb or his reputed father." By this indenture the widow McNabb maintained control over the family, insuring the presence of Baptiste and his son, who was to be brought up to help with the farming.

Bequeathing slaves by will was not supposed to continue, but in 1819 the will of Marie Louise Bienvenu, the widow of Jean Baptiste Barbeau Jr., gave slaves to her children. To André was given Jean Noel, about ten years old. To Antoine, Pascal, about eighteen; to Henri, Louis, about nineteen; to Jean Baptiste Jr., a young male fifteen to sixteen years; to Marie Louise, a woman and her infant Jeannette; to Lucille, a girl Marguerite, thirteen to fourteen years old; and to Aspagnie, a boy, Charles, and a girl, Julie, six to seven years old.[27]

Twenty years later, in the 1839 church census, the Jean Noel above was listed as free, married, and had a child, but still resided with André. Pascal, who had been given to Antoine, had been freed and he had his own household of a wife and four children listed in the church census. It is possible that Louis, slave to Henri, is the free forty-year-old Louis, who lived in the household of Guillaume Henry in 1839. With the widow of Jean Baptiste Barbeau Jr. was Jacque, thirty-eight years old, probably to be identified as the male of fifteen or sixteen years willed to Jean Baptiste. Jacque was free and married with five children, and had remained with the Barbeau family.

The black women seemed to have fared less well. Marie Louise Barbeau married Antoine Blais, and on his death in 1831 a Jeannette and child are listed in the inventory; this may be the infant Jeannette mentioned in the will. They were sold to Elias Kent Kane.[28] Lucille Barbeau married Pierre Goder and in 1839 she had listed a slave, Marie Anne, eighteen years old, possibly a daughter of Marguerite. Julie and Charles disappeared from the records.

Manumission upon an owner's death continued. Auguste

Allard had a slave twenty-six years old in 1829, born well after the Ordinance of 1787, whom Allard

> lawfully claimed…as such according to the laws of the land, having heretofore faithfully served him in the capacity of a slave, and being desirous of manifesting towards him the said Baptiste proper feeling of humanity for his good disposition and conduct... and now becoming aged myself... if the said Baptiste shall continue to serve me as a dutiful servant or slave during my lifetime that at my death I declare and desire that he be entirely manumitted and released from all further claims of service.[29]

The slaves must have continued to have the ability to earn money. François Tangue in 1831 manumitted Philippe, about forty-nine years old, for 300 dollars.[30]

When the lower common land was platted and divided for the expansion of the village, a number of free black families received grants and constructed houses. In 1837 Philippe George, probably the man freed above by Tangue, made a request in French for a grant of land in the village where he had already constructed a house and made other improvements. He was granted an *arpent* square lot called Lot 1 in Block 41. In 1838 a lot was granted to Antoine Charlotte; in 1838 Paul Auguste (Allard) and Antoine Santy (Sainte Tête) purchased lots from other owners in the village; all these were free blacks.[31]

In the 1830s a visitor claimed that "nowhere in the West have I seen a sleeker, fleshier, happier-looking set of mortals than the blacks of these old villages."[32] The slaves probably were treated well. The attitude towards them was paternalistic. Although this might mean they were treated as children or second class citizens, they were part of the family and as such the family was responsible for all their care and well being. In the eighteenth century this attitude benefitted the slaves; this can be seen from the formation of families and the number of children produced. Unlike what was found in a study of slaves in Maryland, the African-born in the Illinois did reproduce themselves. The family formation also may have been influenced by the fact that the population of blacks was in close contact with each other, not isolated on plantations, and that French rapidly became the language of all, replacing the various African dialects.[33]

Culture and Customs

During the period of govermental instablity, Prairie du Rocher survived by keeping a low profile. Like Cahokia, its peacefulness and order attracted new settlers. In 1767 there were twenty-five families; in 1783 sixty-four heads of families.[34] But by the early nineteenth century the French were becoming an ethnic minority in the region.

The local village officials—election judges, justice of the peace, fence viewers, overseers of the poor, and other minor positions—might be held by local Frenchmen, but the county and state governments were dominated by Americans. Henry Conner, an Irish immigrant who lived in Prairie du Rocher, became the sheriff of Randolph County. The only politically powerful Frenchman was Pierre Menard; a highly respected person who held a number of positions in the governments. Significantly, Pierre Menard was bilingual and he was frequently called on by the courts to translate for the French citizens.

Toussaint La Chapelle and Joseph Melquer were sworn to give evidence to the Grand Jury and Pierre Menard Esquire was sworn to interpret the French language into English to the Grand Jury.

By the 1830s language was beginning to be a stumbling block for participation in government beyond the village level. Three Prairie du Rocher citizens who encountered this problem were Baptiste Roy, Antoine Barbeau, and Antoine Louvière. Summoned as grand jurors, they were discharged by the court from further attendance "by reason...of not being able to understand the English language sufficiently."[35]

By the 1830s literacy was severely in decline in the town. In the church records of the 1780s and 1790s the majority of the witnesses were able to sign; in the grants made in the 1830s more than eighty percent made their mark. The younger generation of Louvières in the 1830s could not write; many of the other families who had moved into the area also were illiterate. The change to English may have made the value of literacy in French, which was all most people knew, seem irrelevant. A few families always had literate members. The Barbeaus continued to be literate; even their daughters were all able to sign their names.

Instruction in English was available early in Prairie du Rocher; there were also schools that taught French. Subscription schools seem to have been held intermittently. Benjamin Sturgess advertised in the *Western Intelligencer* in 1816

> That he has opened a school at Prairie du Rocher, where he will teach the usual branches of English education, viz: Writing, Reading and common Arithmetic, also English Grammar, Geography, Surveying, Astronomy, Latin and Greek languages.

He also advertised that a "commodious and comfortable house has been procured...good board can be obtained at moderate terms and so forth."[36] Boarders from other communities were expected. How many Latin and Greek scholars he obtained in Prairie du Rocher is a good question. The *Western Intelligencer* newspaper itself reached Prairie du Rocher and was read at least by the Conner family. One of the papers in the collections at the Mercantile Library in St. Louis has H. Conner written on it.

Biographies in a county atlas noted that prominent citizens in town attended subscription schools in the early part of the century. Attendance at the schools frequently was only for a rather minimal time; for one farmer—three months. On the other hand, Henry Kerr Jr. attended a French school for two years and an English one for nineteen months. Education was probably important in his family, as his father was a physician educated in London.[37] In addition to formal schooling some children probably were taught at home.

After the mid-1830s when a school district was established for Prairie du Rocher, the literacy rate began to climb again.[38] The Federal censuses did not note literacy as a category in the census until 1850. However, at that time still forty-one percent of the males were listed as unable to read. Nine nuns from the convent of the Visitation in Georgetown, D.C., came to Kaskaskia in 1833 with the encouragement of Pierre Menard and began a school for young women, possibly including girls from Prairie du Rocher.

Within the community the French language continued to prevail; many of the Americans who took up residence in the area learned the language and customs of the natives. This apparently was also true in Kaskaskia, even although it was dominated by English speakers.[40]

Along with the language went songs and stories. Most stories from the area are now lost, but a translation of one appeared in print in the 1840s. Probably typical of many told around the fire in the evenings, it may date from an earlier time, but in the 1840s people of Canadian origin, voyageurs, hunters, and buckskin breeches, were familiar enough that the hearers could relate to them. Here's the story:

Pierre Morceau, a Canadian voyageur, married and settled in Prairie du Rocher. He was a hunter, a good fiddler and dancer, and very popular. Pierre was in partnership with a Kaskaskia Indian, Motty. Pierre would take the furs and hides that the two collected to the traders who occasionally visited the village.

At the end of one hunting season Pierre went to dispose of their stock. Pierre had purchsed the necessary supplies for himself and his partner and was about to go when his eyes fell on a new pair of buckskin breeches. He looked disparagingly at his old breeches and decided to trade for them. That meant that he had to return a large portion of the supplies purchased for Motty and himself.

Motty was astonished at the small amount of goods Pierre brought, but Pierre lamented the low price of furs. However, a few days later, when they were starting off on a hunt, Pierre appeared in the new breeches and Motty realized at once what had happened. They climbed the hill and saw a fine buck, but Motty started shouting out that Pierre had cheated him, that he was a thief, and leveled his rifle at him.

Pierre ran at once through the woods and then reached the

edge of one of the cliffs a hundred and fifty feet above the ground below. He paused, but saw Motty taking aim so he leaped. A broken branch of a large oak tree below caught the posterior part of Pierre's new breeches and there he hung. Pierre yelled and kicked until most of the breeches gave way. He fell to earth unhurt and with "the loss of the nether portion of his breeches which remained on the limb, flaunting in the wind, like a tattered banner."

Pierre went home and his wife mended the breeches with the old, but the patch always reminded his acquaintances of the adventure and gave him the nickname of "Broken Breeches." Dispirited, he finally moved away.[41] This tale also shows how nicknames sometimes were formed from some event in a person's life.

French legal practices persisted for a time as allowed by the Ordinance of 1787. Marie Louise Bienvenu, widow of Jean Baptiste, made a request to the court "that the said estate should be distributed according to the usual customs and laws of the ancient French and Canadian inhabitants as secured to them by the ordinance of Congress."[42] François Langlois wrote his will in 1837, obviously with the *Coutume* in mind. His first wife had died and he had remarried to an American woman; apparently they separated. Under his will, his wife, Suzanne, was given standard marriage contract goods—the bed with the furnishings for it and two cows of her choice. Langlois also stated that she should keep all that she had taken to St. Louis. A sale was to be held of his goods after his death and the proceeds were to be divided equally between his surviving two sons and two married daughters. Under Illinois common law though, his wife should have received a third of his estate.

The donation of lands and goods in return for care continued. In 1830 George Witmer and Catherine Tangue of Prairie du Rocher made a donation to her younger brother, François, of all their goods, the house where they lived, the barn, two *arpents* in the Cul de Sac prairie, and all their cattle "by reason of our age and infirmities which prevent us from the ordinary work of the country." As in the earlier donations François agreed to care for them and provide food, firewood and labor.[43]

Families in the community continued to take care of their own—the ill, orphaned, or those unable to care for themselves. This included the slaves and freed laborers. But new people were coming into the community, and when these were indigent, other arrangements had to be made for their care. The county government stepped in and provided for the poor. An auction was held and the care of the poor was farmed out to the lowest bidder. The fees agreed on were listed in an official Poor Book.

Henry Petit of Prairie du Rocher was allowed thirty-eight dollars for keeping Pierre Richard "an poor old man." Perhaps Pierre was a former voyageur. Pierre died in 1823 and Michel Danis was given one dollar and fifty cents for digging the grave and burying him, presumably in the Prairie du Rocher cemetery. Another person who appears several times in the Poor Book was Reguste Thibot. Although there were a number of Thibots (spelled in a wide variety of ways) he does not seem to be a relative of the Frances Thibout, who agreed to keep him and furnish him with bed, board, and clothing for $500 a year, a fairly tidy sum in those days.

The proper clothing for the keep of the poor was specified—summer clothes included one summer coat or hunting shirt, two pairs of pantaloons, one vest, two shirts, two coarse handkerchiefs, and one pair of shoes. The winter supplies were one blanket capot, one vest, two pairs of yarn stockings, two pairs of linsey pantaloons, two shirts, one pair of shoes, and eight pounds of chewing tobacco.[44] The clothing was similiar to traditional garments in the area.

Orphans belonging to Americans did not have the familial or godparent relationship that the French did; orphans also had to be farmed out to various homes for care. John Marie Godier received five dollars for two months' support of the orphan child of Josiah Horsey.[45] This child continued to appear in records with that family; he must have learned to adjust to French ways and language.

Agriculture was the mainstay of the community. Spring wheat was raised and a hard flinty corn used for hominy. During the French regime the inhabitants used imported cloth rather than to spin and weave for themselves. The crops of flax and cotton raised in the nineteenth century may have been for trade as Reynolds, who was there in the early part of the century, commented that "they neither spun nor wove any of their clothing, but purchased it from the merchants."[46] However, spinning wheels and carding tools do appear in a couple of inventories by the 1830s. A spinning wheel was in Antoine Louvière's inventory in 1831, and two were in Antoine Blais' in the same year, along with ten pounds of raw cotton and two pairs of cotton cards. A carding and spinning mill for wool was advertised in Cahokia, and a wool carding machine operated in 1818 in Harrisonville, a town near the area.[47]

Inns or taverns must have persisted in Prairie du Rocher, although there is no mention in the records of one between Pierre Derousse's in the 1740s and those in the early 1800s, licensed by the county. By 1809 an official license was given to Pierre LeCompte to keep a public tavern. In 1810 Antoine Blais also had one and a few years later Joseph Vasseur was licensed "to keep a public house or tavern." He was allowed the same tavern rates as LeCompte. Tavern rates listed for Kaskaskia in 1815 would have been used in Prairie du Rocher, too. Liquors were sold by the half pint.

French brandy .50
whiskey per .25
taffia .37½
rum .50
peach brandy .18¾
cherry bounce .25[48]

Pierre LeCompte continued in business until his death in 1818. The tavern was continued by his wife Suzanne (Barbeau) LeCompte. An announcement in the *Western Intelligencer* in April 1818 stated that "The tavern heretofore kept in Prairie du Rocher by Major Pierre La compte, deceased, will be continued by Mrs. La Compte." Nor was Suzanne the only woman bartender in the area. Armstice Brown had a tavern at her father's home on the road between Kaskaskia and Prairie du Rocher.[49]

Le Compte's business was also a store. Other commercial enterprises were licensed shortly afterwards. Andrew Barbeau, to "vend, sell and retail any goods, wares, and merchandise belonging to him," and Antoine Blais and William Henry to sell at public auction or private sale. Antoine Blais is said to have opened a store in 1839 and a couple of years later Eli C. Hansborough opened one.[50] The area was fairly prosperous and the inhabitants had access to a wide variety of materials. A visitor to the area, Edmund Flagg, commented that the traders within the village were the wealthier persons who "kept a heterogeneous stock of goods in the largest room of their dwelling-houses..." There was also an interesting announcement in the newspaper:

> Private Entertainment Archibald McNabb, has opened a house of private entertainment in the town of Prairie du Rocher, on the road leading from Kaskaskia to St. Louis, and about twelve miles above Kaskaskia. He assures those who may think proper to call upon him that no pains shall be spared to render their stay agreeable. His stables shall at all times be furnished with the best forage the county affords. He will also take in boarders on reasonable terms.

Flagg also spoke of the "avocations of the villagers" that there were few craftsmen or artisans; most of the people were farmers, but the young men still sought occupations as boatmen, traders, or hunters and trappers.[51] Change had come to the river, though, with the advent of steam, and also to the land. In earlier days property had little monetary value because of its ready availability, but now it was no longer free and available. A gap was widening between the well-to-do and the poor.

The villagers seem to have been law abiding and few cases reached the county courts. Whether this meant that there were no incidents or that misconduct was handled within the village can be debated, but the internal peer pressures to maintain equilibrium probably continued to function. This lack of conflict continued as a characteristic of the local society. The few cases that appear in the courts are related to inheritance or, as in the past, to domestic quarrels.

For example the case of Pélagie Derousse vs. Thérèse Beauvais for slander (given as spelled by the clerk).

> ...the plantiff is a just honest and virtuous inhabitant of this territory and hath never been suspected of the crime of fornication or such like offense...defendant...craftily and maliciously intending to deprive and rob the sd Pélagie of her good name, fame and expectation said on the 5th of July 1807...in the hearing of divers good citizens of the said Country speak utter pronouse and publish in a loud voice in the French language the following malicious scandlius and defamatory words to wit: you, meaning the said Pélagie, are a hore and a strumpet...meaning the plantiff was seen in the bushes with Alix Buias then by meaning that the said Pélagie has been caught in the act of fornication with one Alexis Bavis...Pélagie says she is greatly affected in the esteem of her neighbors.

The suit was apparently not pressed and the judges, Pierre Menard, George Fisher, and James Finny, ordered Pélagie to pay the defendant, Thérèse Beauvais, twelve dollars for her costs. Pélagie also had a slander case against Alexis Beauvais that was dropped, and he was awarded nine dollars and eighty cents for his costs.

Pélagie, a vigorous woman, went on to marry Antoine Cotineau Jr. of Prairie du Rocher, and had four children by him. He died in 1820 and she subsequently had three illegitimate children, said to have been fathered by Andrew Barbeau. She married Bartolomew Oliver in 1830 and had three more children.[52]

John Reynolds, who wrote his reminiscences many years after his visit to the area, said that "Chastity with the Creoles was a sine qua non, and a spurious offspring was almost unknown among them.[53] He must have been idealizing the people, as Pélagie and others showed. In the early French censuses there is even a tally for illegitimate children. No prejudice or stigma seems to have been attached to illegitimate birth; the children married well in the community. The Derousses, descended from Pélagie's children, were not embarassed by their progenitor and one son was prominent in village activities.

Status of Women

Married women in the French community continued to have a higher status than the American ones around them, as Edmund Flagg observed in the mid-1830s, although with some implied disapproval.

> ...the women make affectionate wives, though by no means prone to consider themselves in the light of goods and chattels of their liege-lords, as is not infrequently the case in more enlightened communities.

As another person put it,

> The wife was not the slave but the partner of the husband, and was so considered by law; she was consulted and usually decided all affairs relating to the common welfare.[54]

Unmarried or widowed women continued carry on businesses, as indicated by Susanne LeCompte and Armstice Brown, who operated taverns or inns, as had Reneé Drouin in the past. Business opportunities at the time were not great for either sex as the inhabitants were largely self sufficient or bartered for goods.

Marriage did tend to absorb a woman's identity in the eyes of men. Informants in the land depositions often could not recall a widow's Christian name. Details would be recalled "the same witness knew the widow Miott does not recollect her Christian name, she was the grandmother of witness's wife...she died at her brother's house in Prairie du Rocher where she went to get medical assistance for the disorder from which she died." A deponent knew the widow Cochon, but again did not know her Christian name. An informant could recall the nickname of the widow Perrier, Cattin, but did not know her real name.[55]

As the deponents were all male, the husbands, their names and actions obviously were of greater importance. This probably indicates a gradual decrease in the status of women in a society that was becoming more exposed to American standards. In the family the woman's status was maintained, but their roles in the larger society were more curtailed than in earlier years. The widow Chassin would not have accepted having her identity as Agnes Philippe forgotten, and it likely would not have happened at that time.

Visitors commented that the French women were fashionable. Being in an isolated settlement did not prevent them from obtaining the most recent fashions from New Orleans, their Paris. The 1820s and 1830s were the time of the Empire style, and it is obvious from the descriptions of the dresses worn for balls that this fashion reached the Illinois country.

> ...their dresses, with very few exceptions, were of fine material, colored, figured and showy, cut very décolleté, with short and narrow skirts, extremely short-waisted, and only apologies for sleeves, or none at all.[56]

No doubt these were the types of dresses that were worn to a very important ball, the one held in Kaskaskia at William Morrison's for the Marquis de Lafayette, on his trip through the United States in 1825. The more prominent families of Prairie du Rocher probably attended—the Barbeaus, the Louvières, the Blais, and others. Lafayette's visit was a memorable one for the area, significant for its connection to what was still visualized by the older citizens as their homeland.

The men at the ball would have been dressed in the latest American style of clothing, although elderly people of both sexes might cling to the older styles. In 1836 "some of the very aged villagers may still be seen in their ancient habiliments[sic], the capote, moccasins, blue handkerchief on the head and an endless queue lengthened out behind."[57]

News and Views

The late eighteenth to early nineteenth century had other memorable events in addition to Lafayette's visit. The New Madrid earthquake struck December 16, 1811. The effects in the region are described:

The ground would shake and then rock and roll in long waves.

After a short quiet spell, there would be another shock and roll...the steeple of the church [at Kaskaskia] bending like a reed, here and there stone and brick chimneys fell down; cattle themselves, filled with fear, were running to and fro, furious, wild, filling the air with bellowing.

The shocks lasted until March of the following year. The houses in Prairie du Rocher themselves were not damaged. In 1815 a wind that is described as a hurricane struck the area, mainly affecting Kaskaskia, and another major flood occurred in 1826. Not disastrous but memorable was the night in November of 1833 "when the stars fell"—a meteor shower.[58] These events marked out the succession of years for the community. In the 1790s Victor Collet complained that the inhabitants were so dull that they had forgotten the divisions of time.

If they are asked at what time such an event took place, they answer, "in the time of the great waters, of the strawberries, of the maize, of the potatoes."[59]

The pattern of their agricultural life was significant for them. This consciousness of seasonal change also was noted in Canada where the farm schedule, the rhythm of the fur trade and the coming and going of ships influenced their concepts of time.[60]

Assignments of years to specific events is not an uncommon folk time referent; in recent days, locally, the "year of the flood" is 1993.

The persons interviewed about land claims freely gave out accurate dates, but often the informants' recollections also were pinned to certain events. Things were said to occur before or after a certain year. For example 1784 was *le gros hiver* (the hard winter) when three feet of snow fell and cattle starved. It was a bad year for an agricultural people, and even more so since this was followed when the snow melted by a flood "the year of the high water" (1785). The important arrivals of General Clark and Governor St. Clair were noted in the depositions "the year after the Americans took possession of this country" or "When General Clark took possession of this country" and "before Governor St. Clair first came to this country."

The "year of the smallpox" was 1797. The St. Joseph records are scanty for that year, so it cannot be determined what effect this epidemic had in Prairie du Rocher. Kaskaskia was affected; the disease was said to have been brought there by a colonizing group from Virginia.[61] The St. Joseph records do note in 1792 the deaths from smallpox of two local inhabitants who were in Pittsburgh, perhaps on duty at Fort Duquesne. Auguste Giard, twenty years old, and Louis Vasseur, thirty-six, were buried in the common cemetery at Pittsburgh.[62]

In the early nineteenth century the village became reconnected to the world beyond. With the Louisiana Purchase in 1803, the Mississippi was reopened as a major thoroughfare for the French; Spanish controls had imposed restrictions before. By 1814 a twice-weekly mail route ran from Kaskaskia through Prairie du Rocher, St. Phillipe, Harrisonville, Herculaneum, Cahokia, and St. Louis to St. Charles, Missouri.[63] Postage costs in 1816 were: not over thirty miles, .06; from thirty to eighty miles, .10; up to a hundred and fifty miles, 12½ cents; up to four hundred miles, 18½ cents; over that, .25.[64] Transportation to St. Louis by the mail stage was available. The mail carrier ran an advertisement in the *Western Intelligencer* for passengers.

> Stage to St. Louis, can accomodate four passengers each trip he makes with the mail, to St. Louis he starts from Kaskaskia every Sunday morning and arrives at St. Louis the next day at two o'clock pm.
> Returning he leaves St. Louis every Tuesday morning and arrives at Kaskaskia the ensuing evening. $4 each passenger payable in advance. James Watson.[65]

The weekly newspaper also gave news from around the world—news of Spain, Britain, and France, and a great deal about Napoleon Bonaparte. Proclamations by President James Madison, appeared in it, along with acts of the United States government, and in 1818 the full text of the Illinois Constitution. So information was available to the community.

From 1800 to the mid-1830s travelers' accounts are abundant concerning the area. Many Americans were passing through the American Bottom. Kaskaskia was a major community and Cahokia was the seat of St. Clair County. The trails between them ran through Prairie du Rocher. Because of the slow travel and poor roads, frequently people had to spend a night enroute, and this might be in Prairie du Rocher. Travelers often lodged in one of the larger private homes in the community; Antoine Barbeau, son of Jean Baptiste, was one of those who opened his home to guests.

The villagers were still definitely French in their language and customs, and the visitors generally viewed them as curiosities, although they found them very friendly and kind.

> The Barbeaus, our host and hostess, were unalloyed specimens of the non-progressive exotic Creole race…dark-complexioned, black-haired, slow-motioned, contented, sociable, very kind and hospitable.[66]

The ambitious, get-ahead Americans either felt patronizingly about the "unambitious" natives, or slightly jealous of their seeming contentment. Flagg's remarks are rather contemptuous:

> Content to live where his father lived; content to cultivate the spot he tilled; to tread in the steps which he trod; to speak the language he spake, and revere the faith he observed, the French villager is a stranger to the restless cravings of ambition, and acknowledges no inclination to change.

The life they lived was rewarding; crops grew bountifully, cattle produced well, wild game was abundant. The older generation could still recall the years of insecurity but found reassurance in their traditional language and faith.

Reynolds, looking back at his impressions of the area from many years later, sounds more approving.

> In a century before 1800, they were enabled to solve the problem: that neither wealth, nor splendid possessions, nor an extraordi-

nary degree of ambition, nor energy, ever made a people happy.[67]

The local attitudes had been fostered during the long period of various governments and military personnel, who commandeered provisions and needed funds. The inhabitants realized if they were seen to have money, or large amounts of cattle or possessions, they likely would be assessed. This did not encourage ostentation nor ambition to increase production. This problem was recognized by the visitor Flagg.

> The virtues of these people are said to be many: punctuality and honesty in their dealing; politeness and hospitality to strangers; though, it must be confessed, the manifold impositions...of late years has tended to substitute for the latter virtue not a little of coolness and distrust.[68]

One of the most consistent normative traits that comes through the accounts is politeness and manners. Obviously social manners were highly valued. From the visitors' remarks, the balls and dances held that were a source of entertainment for the populace also were a place where the children absorbed these norms of behavior. "No people ever conducted the ballroom with more propriety than they did. Decorum and punctilious manners were enforced by public opinion." "...the ball, which was by no means a place of frivolity, but rather a school of manners."

The training in these values was expressed in polite behavior, hospitality, and in a certain physical grace and assurance.

> And it is a remarkable fact, that the roughest hunter and boatman amongst them could at anytime appear in a ballroom, or other polite and gay assembly, with the carriage and behavior of a well-bred gentleman. The French women were remarkable for the sprightliness of their conversation and the grace and elegance of their manners.[69]

Morris Birbeck, who had founded an English settlement in Edwards County, also was impressed with the French citizens and their deportment.

It is a phenomenon in national character I cannot explain; but the fact will not be disputed, that the urbanity of manners which distinguished that nation from all others, is never entirely lost; but that French politeness remains until every trace of French origin is obliterated.[70]

Despite these favorable comments from some persons, there was an increasing tendancy to look at the French *habitants* as quaint, peculiar, and belonging to the past. Descriptions of the village in the travelers' accounts accent the differences from what the Americans were accustomed to. Prairie du Rocher still presented physically a traditional appearance, "The narrow lanes, the steep-roofed houses, the picketed enclosures, the piazza,…all point back to a former age."[71] The comments of Flagg in 1836 about the houses indicates that the construction continued to be in the old styles; this implied to him a lack of keeping up with modern trends. The houses were

constructed, some of rough limestone, some of timber, framed in every variety of position—horizontal, perpendicular, oblique or all united…interstices stuffed with fragments of stone and the external surface stuccoed with mortar; others—a few only—are framed, boarded, etc., in modern style. Nearly all have galleries in front, some of them spacious, running around the whole building, and all have garden-plats enclosed by stone walls or stoccades.

Even the barns were different. Reynolds described the continuing usage of *pièce-en-pièce*, actually a better quality, more solid construction than the American-style log structures.[72] But these old styles were not appreciated by the new people pouring into the Illinois. Change and improvement were what they desired.

Customs and behavior also seemed strange or irreligious to the Americans. Everyone commented on the love of the French for dances; some with Calvinistic disapproval—if they weren't having so much fun they could do more work. Their observation, or lack thereof, of the Sabbath did not please American religious moralists either. However, in the opinion of the French inhabitants they

…observed a strict morality against hunting or fishing on the Sabbath;

but they played cards for amusement ...this they considered one of the innocent pastimes that was not prohibited to a Christian.

Carnival, or Mardi Gras, was celebrated by the French. At this time it was not a festival in which Americans took part. Although descriptions of Mardi Gras are lacking in the records, there is a brief earlier mention of the "three last days of Carnival."[73] This is one indication of activities that were carried on but not recorded in the early records; others are the *charivari* and *La Guiannée.*

The *charivari* was a custom that the Americans found unusual and so commented about. Originally, a *charivari* was held when a widower married in what was considered too short a time after the death of a spouse, but later it became customary when any widower remarried. Traditionally, on the evening of the marriage a group went to the house of the couple late at night.

They enlisted into their service all sorts of things which could by any means be forced to make a noise. They used bells, horns, drums, pans, tin kettles, whistles, and all such articles as would make loud, harsh sounds...[74]

This din was supposed to call forth the newly married who were obliged to invite the crowd in for food and drink. If they did this that was the end of it, but if not they were regaled by the noise for successive nights until "they yielded to custom."

A custom preserved to the present, *La Guiannée,* is never mentioned in the eighteenth century records. It undoubtedly existed, but the legal documents were unlikely to mention it and there are no personal records. Even with all the visitors to the area in the early nineteenth century, only one brief mention of this New Year's Eve custom occurred. Possibly this was due to the time of year and the hazards of travel in the winter; visitors may have tended to come in the more clement months. John Reynolds, who resided in the area for some time, spoke of it:

The ancient custom was for the young men about the last of the year to disguise themselves in old cloths, as beggars, and go around the village in the several houses, where they knew they would be well received. They enter the house dancing what they call the Gionie, which is a friendly request for them to meet and have a ball to dance away the old year.[75]

Reynold's account mentioned also the traditional King's Ball that associated with *La Guiannée*. The ball was held on the last day of the Christmas season, Epiphany, January 6.

La Guiannée revelers were photographed in the 1950s.

About the 6th of January, in each year, which is called Le Jour de Rais [sic] a party is given, and four beans are baked in a large cake; this cake is distributed among the gentlemen, and each one who receives a bean, is proclaimed king. These four kings are to give the next ball.[76]

This, too, was an ancient tradition going back to their home-land.

The language, architecture, customs, and adherence to ancient agricultural practices, such as the commonfield, marked the Prairie du Rocher villagers as distinctively different from the neighboring American communities. Although their courtesy, manners and hospitality were noted, the nineteenth century American attitude tended to be condescending and prejudicial. Flagg rather sums this up in his really delightful comments (from the present perspective) on the village of Prairie du Rocher.

> Its site is low, and, buried as it is in such enormous vegetation, the spot must be unhealthy; yet, year after year, and generation after generation, have its present inhabitants continued to dwell where death almost inevitable must have awaited an American. But where will you search for a fleshier, sleeker, swarthier-looking race than these French villagers? Some attribute this phenomenon to diet; some to natural idiosyncrasy; and some do not attribute at all, but merely stand amazed. The truth of the matter is—and the fact is one well ascertained—that, give a Frenchman a fiddle, a pipe, a glass of claret, and room enough to shake his heels, and, like a mushroom, he'll vegetate on any soil![77]

Notes

1. Pease 1975, xiv.
2. Davis 1998, 102.
3. Boggess 1968, 82.
4. Illinois State Archives, trans. by Rose Josephine Boylan of Cahokia Rec. Bk. A; St. Jo. Ch. Rec. 8/28/1790.
5. The name is given variously as Le Compte, Compte, Comte, Lecompte, Le Conte and Conte.
6. The Jean Baptistes are confusing. The first Jean Baptiste lived and died in New Orleans. His son, Jean Baptiste (I) born about 1721 was known in the Illinois as *l'aine* (the elder). He married Catherine Allard and died in 1760; his widow married Aimé Compte.
   His second son, Jean Baptiste *le jeune* (the younger) (II) was born in 1727 and married Jeanne Le Gras. They had Reine, Susanne, Marie Jeanne, Jean Baptiste and others. He was the captain of the militia, the commandant of the village and the president of the Kaskaskia court. He may have died in 1798. Jean Baptiste (III) son of (II) was known as *fils*, son. He married first Catherine Le

Jeunesse, who died in 1791. He then married Marie Louise Bienvenu. He was an officer in the militia and died in 1810. Jean Baptiste had, among other children, Jean Baptiste, who died at thirteen years, and another Jean Baptiste, born later, who lived. Aren't you glad there is no quiz on this!

7. St. Jo. Ch. Rec. Nov. 10, 1797; Sept. 12, 1801; Nov. 15, 1802.
8. Circuit Ct. Rec A; Reel 5, 1, 307.
9. Hammes 1984.
10. Amer. State Papers 1834, 124.
11. Dean and Brown 1981, 68:11:3:1.
12. Depos...Kas. A 108.
13. Amer. State Papers 1834, 213.
14. Depos...Kas. B64; Amer. State Papers 1834, 128.
15. Amer. State Papers 1834, 126; 137.
16. Pease 1975, 498-50.
17. McDermott 1949, 178.
18. Co. Comm. Ct. Rec. Reel 41, 94; Reel 42, 94.
19. Ekberg 1998, 243ff provides a provocative and in-depth study of these events; Pease 1925, 50.
20. Ind. State Lib., Diary, 11-12.
21. Davis 1998, 163.
22. Laws of Illinois, 1821; Revised Ordinances...1915, I.
23. Deed Record Q, 288; Deed Record P, 40, 42.
24. Burnett 1987, 18,19.
25. Harris 1968.
26. Circuit Ct. Rec. A, 152. 27. Harris 1968, 103; Probate Records 1809-1825, 107.
28. Probate Records 1831-1833:102.
29. Deed Rec. D 1821-1834.
30. Deed Record Q, 101.
31. Deed Rec. R, 26; S, 66; Q, 1837-1839.
32. Thwaites 1906, 56.
33. Menard, Russell 1975.
34. Alvord & Carter 1916, 469; Mason 1890, 66-67.
35. Ct. of Quar. Sessions Bk. A, l; Reel 5, 58, 307.
36. Burnham 1904, 187.
37. Illus. Histl. Atlas...1875.
38. Co. Comm. Ct. Rec. Reel 41, 33.

39. Rothensteiner 1918, 203.
40. Walton 1962, 94.
41. Wild 1948, 96-98.
42. Circuit Ct. Rec. Bk A; Reel 5, Ap. 17, 1810.
43. Circuit Ct.Rec. Bk O, 278.
44. Kas. Township Poor Bk.; Co. Comm. Ct. Rec. Reel 41, 142, 297.
45. Co. Comm. Ct. Rec. Reel 41, 127; 137.
46. Reynolds 1879, 22; 39.
47. Probate Rec. Inv. Sale bills, 1829-1833, 90; 102; *Western Intelligencer* newspaper.
48. Co. Comm. Ct. Rec. Reel 3.
49. Co. Comm. Ct. Rec. Reel 41, 2.
50. Co. Comm. Ct. Rec. Reel 41, 216, 352; History of Randolph, Co... 377.
51. Thwaites 1906, 54, 55; *Western Intelligencer* newspaper.
52. Ct. Common Pleas 1801-1808, 327; St. Jo. Ch. Rec; Menard, Ruth 1997,11.
53. Reynolds 1879, 37.
54. Thwaites 1906, 54; Houck 1908, 272.
55. Depos...Kas. A56; A62; A51; A46; A80.
56. Walton 1962, 96.
57. Thwaites 1906, 55.
58. Berry 1908, 75; Rothensteiner 1918, 203; Reynolds 1879, 114.
59. Collet 1909, 286.
60. Harrison 1995, 96ff indicates "an important distinction between *le temps mesure*, time of the clock, and *le temps vécu*, lived time.
61. Reynolds 1879, 237.
62. St. Jo. Ch. Rec. 9/1792, 11/1792.
63. U.S. Nat'l. Archives, Vol. 16, 428.
64. *Western Intelligencer* newspaper.
65. *Western Intelligencer* newspaper.
66. Walton 1962, 98.
67. Thwaites 1906, 72; Reynolds 1879, 37.
68. Thwaites 1906, 53.
69. Reynolds 1879, 38; Brackenridge 1868, 25; Ford 1968, 36.
70. Birkberk 1968, 101.
71. Thwaites 1906, 72.
72. Thwaites 1906, 29; Reynolds 1879, 56.

73. Reynolds 1879, 39; Alvord 1909, 579.
74. Reynolds 1852, 178.
75. Reynolds 1852, 52.
76. Reynolds 1879, 72.
77. Thwaites 1906, 72, 73.

7

Becoming American

Travelers' accounts about the quaint French ceased to appear by the 1840s. Immigrants from all over Europe were moving into Illinois; many small ethnic communities were forming, both in rural areas and in urban settings. Foreign customs, language, and mannerisms were no longer unusual features confined to southwestern Illinois.

The flight of people to the United States from the old world escalated because of the problems of wars, politics, and famine. European emigration had occurred earlier—Germans fleeing the Revolution of 1830 and Irish affected by demanding landlords and increasing famine—but the flood swelled throughout the 1840s and 1850s. The potato famines worsened in Ireland; crop failures and political upheaval affected the Swiss, driving them to emigrate. Religious problems drove Germans to America, and again later in the 1870s, when Bismarck opposed organized religion. Many Germans arrived in New Orleans on the cotton trade ships and travelled up the Mississippi River. By the mid-1850s German communities had sprung up near Prairie du Rocher—Millstadt, New Hanover, Red Bud, and Waterloo.

When Germany took over Alsace and closed French schools

in the 1870s, French speakers fled to America. They were attracted by the French ties with New Orleans and St. Louis. A few ended up in the Illinois communities where their language still was spoken.

Railroads were beginning to spread across the country. The companies that were building railroads in Illinois recruited construction workers from Germany, Ireland, and from the eastern coast of the United States.[1] The population center was shifting. Now the northern part of Illinis was receiving the largest amount of immigration. Illinois was no longer the western frontier. St. Louis, across the river, provided the jumping-off place for further expansion to the West.

Population

In 1839 Prairie du Rocher was a French village with a few resident American families who had intermarried with the local *habitants*. The 1839 census covered a parish of 526 persons. The parish and the village community were virtually synonymous. In 1849 the church census, written in August of that year, listed 471 persons (the distribution is shown in Figure 3, below). The cause of the decrease

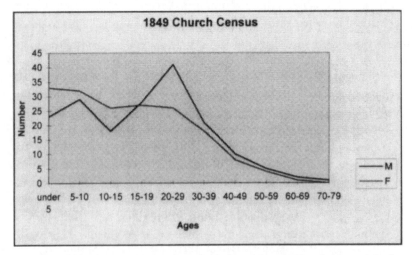

from 1839 may have been the cholera epidemic that had struck the community earlier in the year, killing at least twenty-five persons, including a family of five—Henry Tibout, his wife and children.

The composition of households in the 1849 census was similiar to that of 1839, with two exceptions. All blacks were free, and there were proportionally fewer extended families, thirty-five nuclear family units to twenty-nine extended families. However, the number of persons in those extended families was greater than in the 1839 census. The cholera epidemic may have caused this; persons who had lost providers in the epidemic may have been taken into the homes of relatives.

The congruity of community and parish was beginning to break down. The church census listed several new arrivals from France and from other localities, as well as couples noted as not married by the Catholic Church, but by civil ceremony. A year later the federal census of 1850 listed the birthplaces for the people counted. These give an indication of the demographic changes taking place. Only half of the family heads enumerated were born in the Illinois country. The others had been born in France, Canada, Louisiana, and different regions of the United States. The largest number of new males came from Kentucky, but seven other states and four foreign countries in addition to France were represented.

In 1860 the census indicated that the original settlers were now less than half of the population at least as far as the heads of family were concerned. The majority of the immigrants were from France. People also were tallied from eight states and four other foreign countries, Germany, England, Canada, and Ireland. A similar pattern appears again in the 1870 census. About thirty people were born in France and an almost equal number in Germany. A number of the latter, even though they are listed in the census as being of German birth, may have been French speakers from Alsace-Lorraine. Some families in the village with German surnames were French speakers and considered themselves French, as later interviews indicated.

The number of new immigrants is significant for the population composition and the retention of customs. The proportion of "native" French Illinoisans fell rapidly over the twenty years between 1850-70. The influx of additional French speakers did help to maintain the language, despite the surrounding predominantly English speaking society. The emigrants would have brought new customs and attitudes, though. France had not been static in the hundred years between waves of emigration. This influx of personnel and ideas must have affected the society, but the lack of personal records obscures their influence.

The new people did come with a different mindset towards immigration than had those from the early eighteenth century. They were like their earlier colonial British counterparts, seeking a new country where they could live as they wished, free from oppressive restrictions, and where land was plentiful. The persons who came were true immigrants. They were seeking a better life and were ready to adapt to a new environment. They provided new blood and new vigor to the society. Although for a brief time the records suggest social division (marriages not being done between "old" French and new), this rapidly broke down and the newcomers were integrated into the society.

Common and Commonfields

By the 1850s the full commonfield system was no longer functional, but the fence viewers continued under a new guise. In 1853, legislation that probably was requested by the local families was passed. Leon Vion, Antoine Albert, and Felix Mudd were appointed commissioners to supervise construction of ditches, embankments or roads necessary to drain "the wet lands of the proprietors of the common field." The term "proprietors of the common field" implies that some concept of corporate ownership still existed. Under the law, the lands being drained were to be assessed proportionately and payment was to be enforced by the sheriff if necessary. However, labor on the project would be acceptable payment. No fences are mentioned, but the endeavor affected people in a similar manner as had the construction of a commonfield fence.[2] As far as the personnel were concerned, it is noteworthy that none of the commissioners were of the old Illinois- French families—two were born in France. The implication is that the commonfield lands had changed hands; the new emigrants had acquired farmlands by purchase and marriage.

The common was important for the identity of the village and remained a distinguishing feature. The summary below of legislation through the end of the nineteenth century reveals the changing perceptions and needs of the community.

In 1835, a hundred years after the first common was granted by Ste. Thérèse Langloisière, the usage of the lower common changed from pasture to residential. The land was divided into blocks of lots, with easements for streets between the blocks. As mentioned earlier, because the land was owned in commonage by the people of the village, the grants for lots were made by the inhabitants to individuals. This "un-American" activity seemed to have cast doubts on the validity of these deeds in American eyes. A legislative act was felt to be necessary to insure clear titles.

By an act of the Illinois General Assembly in 1857, the present occupants of the village lots were confirmed in their titles by the commissioners—André Barbeau (fifth generation), Antoine Blais, and John Brewer. They were appointed to resurvey the village and to divide the land still unoccupied into lots. They were to make their survey and plat of the village to conform as closely as possible to the plan that had developed since 1835. The unoccupied lots could be offered for sale, and the proceeds from the sale were to be used for the building of a church.[3] The construction of the 1858 church of St. Joseph was funded partly through the sale of communal lands.

The second, upper common granted in 1743 by Bertet, the commandant of Fort de Chartres, was on the bluffs above the village with a frontage of two leagues and a depth of one league—about five miles long by two and one-half miles deep. Later governments had made no changes; the common remained quietly in the possession of the villagers.

In 1818, Article VI of the Illinois State Constitution guaranteed that commons granted by previous governments would remain the property of the inhabitants of the villages to whom they had been given. The villages were not stated, although exceptions were allowed for Cahokia and Prairie du Pont.

In 1844 the Prairie du Rocher village trustees ordered prosecution of a person who had trespassed on the common. The board found that they did not have the right under state laws to press charges for trespass and apparently requested legislation to do this. In 1845 an Act on Trespass was passed that gave the inhabitants of Prairie du Rocher the right to initiate action for trespass against anyone who cut timber on the common.[4] The act did not specify action by the trustees, but by "one or more of the inhabitants." No other towns are cited in this law, indicating that in the other French communities the land was no longer held in commonage by this time.

The Illinois constitution of 1848 in Article XI reasserted the rights of the inhabitants to the common, but significantly it provided for possible dividing, leasing, or granting of these lands to individuals in the future at the request of a majority of the voters. In 1851, a short three years later, such a request was made and the legislature authorized the town of Prairie du Rocher to lease lands in the common.[5]

The common was no longer needed for communal pasturing. The system that included the common and commonfield had vanished. By now farms in the commonfield had fenced areas for cattle, horses, and hogs; hogs were confined also on some of the small islands in the Mississippi River. Nevertheless the commonfield strips were not fenced individually. Even today the old commonfield is open and unfenced.

In the legislative act, André Barbeau, Leon Vion, Antoine Albert, Joseph Blais, and Ambroise Kerr "constituted a body corporate and politic, by the name and style of "The President and Trustees of the Commons of Prairie du Rocher, and by that name they and their successors shall have perpetual succession and existence,…" The trustees were to be elected every two years, and elections continue to be held. The trustees were authorized to have the common surveyed and divided into lots; these could be leased for any period of time up to ninety-nine years.[6] Lots were to be auctioned individually and to go to the highest bidder with a leasing fee, payable annually. The proceeds from the leases were designated for the education of the children from the town and common. The money could be used for not more than two elementary schools, for teachers' salaries, books, a library, and other educational uses. The Commons Board now was given the right to institute suits for trespass on the common. They were to provide "a good and substantially bound book" in which to keep their records; this book still exists. The board was to organize and meet within ninety days of the passage of the law.

In June 1852 the portion of the 1851 law requiring organizing within ninety days was repealed, apparently the trustees had made no rapid effort to organize. However, the leases that had been made were allowed to be valid anyway. Also under the 1852 law, payment in advance could be required for leases, and the trustees were allowed to loan the money obtained.

The leasing of the lots in the upper common provided space for the new settlers who were moving in and additional land for children of old inhabitants. Leases were confirmed by the president of the trustees.

> This indenture of Lease, made and entered into this first day of October in the year of our Lord One thousand eight hundred and fifty three between André Barbeau President of the Trustees of the Common of Prairie du Rocher,…and Benjamin Louvière…for in consideration of the sum of 67.50/100 dollars, in hand paid…do hereby demise, grant and to Farm let, unto the party of the second part, his heirs and assigns, for the time and period of 99 years…the following described Lot in the Common of Prairie du Rocher,…Lot No. 101 containing forty-five acres.[7]

In 1855, the portion of the 1851 act that empowered the president and trustees to establish not more than two elementary schools was repealed. The proceeds from the common were to be distributed proportionately to the number of white children under twenty years of age attending school and residing in Prairie du Rocher and on the common.

The changes in law about the common over time reflected changes occurring in the society. The small lower common was utilized for expansion of residences. Part of the upper common may have been used as private lots quite early, as suggested by the land commissioners' depositions. The upper common's continuance depended in part on the commonfield system. It remained a communal source of firewood into the mid-nineteenth century, as the Trespass Act shows. Although the landless would not have legal access to the common, anyone with even a small strip of commonfield land would have had rights—the commonfields and the common being an integrated system.

This source of free grazing, free firewood, and probably wild game served to keep the community as a fairly egalitarian society. The poorer inhabitants would be able to utilize these resources helping to equalize economic differences. However, as the need for land increased, the common, no longer being used extensively for pasturage by the commonfield proprietors, became desirable for settlement. Leasing removed the pressure for land but maintained the ownership of the common by the village. The concept of usage by the community still was expressed by designating the lease money for the support of education, so the lands on the commons, although outside the village boundaries of Prairie du Rocher, were identified as educationally, socially, and economically with the village.[8]

Church and Education

The church and its authority were above and beyond the village organization. Although persons belonging to other denominations now lived in the village, St. Joseph's was the only church structure. Roads were too poorly constructed to allow persons to attend religious services in another town, so St. Joseph's remained the moral and social focus of the community, even for non-Catholics.

The church hierarchy now definitely controlled the local parish. In 1849 Bishop Van de Velde from Missouri came to Prairie du Rocher to locate the burial place of Fr. Meurin. He found it "by the help of some old records there and the tradition of the neighborhood." Whether the parishioners were willing or not, Fr. Meurin's remains were removed from the parish where he had spent his last days. The grave was opened, the remains exhumed and taken to the cemetery of St. Stanislaus Novitiate in Florissant, Missouri, and reburied.[9]

Many of the new emigrants were Catholic. Henry Fogel married Elisabeth Walker in 1849; they were said to be "Germans who lived on the hills." Most of the church records continued to be written in French, but there was an occasional English entry, including the marriage of Felix Mudd to Sarah, the daughter of "Henry and Barghart A Hara." Early Irish settlers, the O'Haras lived in Ruma, six miles away. The spelling in this entry seems to be the priest's attempt to deal with the Irish brogue; one feels that Bridget O'Hara herself must have told him her name.

Another record is in a mixture of French and English:

> The nineteenth of Septembre one thousand eight hundred and
> forty one j baptised josephine nee heir du mariage legitme d'Antoine
> Langlois et felecite vasseur.[10]

This mixture probably reflects the pattern of language of the day. As English became more common, English words would have worked their way into conversations resulting in an interesting "franglais."

Fr. Van Cloostere, the priest at St. Joseph's from 1832 to 1854, was greatly respected; later a street in town was named for him. According to an interview with a local person, some thought he was a saint. Tales have been preserved about him; it was said he could go out on a parish visit in the pouring rain and enter a house absolutely dry. Tradition also related that the Virgin Mary appeared to him and predicted the day of his death.[11]

Fr. Van Cloostere wrote the church censuses. His 1849 census included a few families who were not part of, or were peripheral to, the Catholic parish. In 1843, when Nicolas Degagne, fifty-eight years old, died, Fr. Van Cloostere wrote:

> I did not wish to inter him myself because for many years he had
> not been to confession nor did he have me called before his death. I
> have committed him where it is not blessed in the corner of the wall
> and I would not allow sounding of the bell.

One of the few old wooden crosses still preserved in the Prairie du Rocher cemetery

Despite the expressed respect for Fr. Van Cloostere there seems to have been persons in the community who did not share in this attitude. In 1848 he wrote in the church register that "they have interred the body of Josephine Tibout in the cemetery despite my wishes. Nicolas Derouan was at the head of this affair to spite me." Again in 1851 he had a problem with a burial, "they have interred in the cemetery Amenda [Amenda Leone Conner, 11 mos. old] while I was in the presbytery, but they did not ask me to do the interment."[12] He may have been stricter than some of the earlier priests in his requirements for burial in the church cemetery. Degagne had not been to confession and there is no baptismal entry for Amenda.

After the death of Fr. Van Cloostere the parish remained without a permanent pastor for five years. Between 1858 and 1863 baptisms generally took place at Ruma or Kaskaskia. Construction began on a new church building in the cemetery in 1850, but after the foundation was laid a flood came again the next year. Although this was not as serious as the flood of 1844, the cemetery obviously was susceptible to flooding, so construction there was abandoned. In 1858 a new location was selected closer to the bluff, between Middle and Main Streets on the newly resurveyed town plat.

Placement of the cornerstone of the new church was entered in the church records.

> Act of laying the cornerstone of the new catholic church at Prairie du Rocher 19 July 1858 dedicated to St. Joseph. Cornerstone 15" in length, 4 1/2 inches in thickness stamped with cross on every side in

one of the corners a square hole cut in which is deposited the authentic act of blessing of the cornerstone. It was laid with the ceremonies of the Roman rite on the South corner. Nicolas Perrin, parish priest at Kaskaskia.[13]

In 1863 Fr. Froblege came as pastor. The church records then continued in Latin. The church building was enlarged in 1874, and a new sanctuary was built onto the north end of the structure. In 1881 a new front and a tower with two bells were added. By now the majority of the parishioners spoke English, and for an increasing number English was the sole language they knew. Sermons at St. Joseph's ceased to be given in French in 1889.[14]

Changes in the dioceses to which St. Joseph's belonged occurred several times throughout the latter part of the century. In 1843 the Chicago diocese took over the whole state. Later, southern Illinois became the diocese of Alton; in 1887 St. Joseph's became part of the Belleville diocese, where it has remained ever since. These changes did not materially affect the lives of the local people.

The parish of St. Joseph's owned two full blocks in town, one where the church was located and another on which a school was built. The first church school was a small one-room frame building built in 1850, opposite the church. In 1885 a large brick two-story school, with two big rooms on each floor, was constructed for $5000. Both nuns and lay people taught there. The black population received a separate school that lasted into the 1930s.

The censuses from 1850 and later list whether or not people were able to read (see Table 1, p. 244). According to the censuses the majority of the inhabitants were literate now—females about equally as males, but a significant proportion even in the younger population still was illiterate. From the percentages of pupils listed as going to school in the 1850s and 1860s, it would seem that many still received education at home or in subscription schools (see Table 2, p. 245). Education was not a high priority. Most boys were drawn back to the family farm and those who yearned for other occupations and professions moved out.

The concept of separation of church and state did not exist in

Table 1

Those listed as unable to read in the federal censuses
Percentage of total population

White males	1850	1860	1870	1880
10-19	-	-	2%	18%
20-29	17%	15%	2%	24%
30-39	8%	21%	5%	28%
over 40	16%	9%	16%	23%
White females				
10-19	-	-	6%	16%
20-29	8%	13%	6%	30%
30-39	18%	6%	3%	27%
over 40	36%	11%	22%	36%
Black males				
10-19	-	-	55%	57%
20-29	100%	50%	100%	83%
30-39	75%	100%	100%	100%
over 40	100%	62%	100%	100%
Black females				
10-19	-	-	73%	66%
20-29	88%	100%	75%	100%
30-39	83%	-	77%	50%
over 40	100%	38%	100%	33%

- data given only for over 20 years of age

Table 2
Children attending school
Percentage of School Age Group

	1850	1860	1870	1880
White males	2%	13%	67%	51%
White females	5%	17%	60%	48%
Black males	-	-	23%	26%
Black females	-	-	17%	7%

the communal mindset; the Catholic parish and the village commune were still one and the same. In 1863, the 1851 commons law was supplemented by an act authorizing the president and trustees to use a portion of the proceeds from the leases for "religious purposes and support and advancement thereof," upon petition of the majority of the voters.[15]

Black Citizens

Not until the 1840s did slavery finally end in Illinois, with a historic case at Cahokia. Joseph, a descendant of a French slave, was bequeathed in Nicolas Jarrot's will to his wife, Julia Beauvais Jarrot. When Joseph challenged this, the Illinois Supreme Court in 1844 ruled that the descendants of slaves born since the Ordinance of 1787 could not be held in slavery in the state.[16]

There is no report of what happened in Prairie du Rocher after that ruling, but the 1849 church census listed all blacks as free. A number of them were still resident with their former owners. Indentures persisted, continuing a form of slavery. Julia, formerly a slave of Bartholomew Durocher and Antoine Albert, had her son apprenticed to them in 1849 to learn farming until he was twenty-one.

Charles, then ten years old, was to receive

> meat, drink, washing, lodging, suitable apparel for working and holy
> days and at twenty-one years two new sets of clothes and a farm mare
> trained to work with saddle and bridle.[17]

This way his services were basically free for eleven years.

The black population was never very large and it grew entirely by natural increase until the mid-nineteenth century, when blacks moved in from the southern states. Although there was out migration, many of the original French black families remained in the area until the 1930s.

Baptismal records in the nineteenth century frequently give only the mother's name. If the father was not Catholic he would be omitted. Also, many black couples may have had a civil marriage that was not recognized by the church. County records provide some supplemental material to the church registers. The federal censuses list family members and give other data.

Surnames for the blacks had come into general use by the time the nineteenth century rolled around. Frequently the surnames were patronymic; the first name of the "founding" father being maintained throughout the following generations. The use of these cognomens resulted in similar names, Joseph Baptiste and Baptiste Joseph, for example. These similarities sometimes confuse the issue. If a single name is used, which is the Joseph referred to in a document? Some black families maintained the use of the former owner's name, Louvière or Allard, for example, and in records that do not state race it becomes difficult to determine if the Pierre Louvière or the Baptiste Allard in a specific transaction is black or white.

It was possible to trace some of the black families through time. Two family histories are given here as examples. Joseph was a slave of Antoine Louvière's. He was about thirty years old in 1770, when he married Marie Magdelene, twenty years old. In Antoine's 1775 inventory, Joseph and Marie Magdelene had two children; some years later another son, Joseph, was born. By the 1830s Joseph Jr. had been transferred to Antoine's son, Pierre.

Joseph Jr. was bound by contract, an indenture, to Pierre

Louvière and his wife. In 1837 Catherine McNabb, the daughter and heir of Pierre Louvière, freed Joseph in terms indicating this was the end of his contract.

> I Katherine McNabb widow of Archibald McNabb deceased and only heir at law of Madame Pierre d'amour late of Prairie du Rocher, now also deceased, do acknowledge to have acquired full and complete satisfaction for the time and services of Joseph Louvier served Mother and to me since her death as by reference to a contract and note given to Joseph Louvier by my mother in her lifetime Ap. 8, 1831…my approbation and wish that he may be manumitted and forever free.[18]

Joseph Louvier, also referred to as Joseph Joseph since his father was Joseph, married Cecilia George, the daughter of George. One of their children , Pierre Joseph or Pierre Louvier (he was known as both), married Clarissa Barbeau in 1838. The couple was freed at marriage by their owners. A son of Pierre Joseph and Clarissa appears in the records variously as Pierre Joseph or John Pierre, and is probably the Peter Joseph who served in the Civil War. He is listed in the federal censuses of 1860, 1880, and 1900 as Joseph Perry. The Perry name seems to stay with this branch of the family permanently from then on. The permutations of the names can be seen clearly from this sequence; the names even ended up in reverse order.[19]

Marie, a slave of Jean Baptiste Barbeau, had at least fourteen children between 1794 and 1815; no father's name was given with the baptismal records. One of these children born about 1800 was called Pierre Paschal. Possibly his father was an Indian because there was a Pascal *sauvage* (Indian) living nearby at the Louvière's. None of Marie's other children have this surname.

In 1819 Paschal was given to Jean Baptiste Barbeau's son, Antoine, but he was freed sometime before 1839, perhaps in 1829, when he married Lenore Gendron, who was free. Both Paschal and Lenore are described as mulatto. Paschal's family appears in the 1839 church census with four children and in 1849 with eight. One of these children, Jule Henry Paschal, married and had a son, Felix, in 1877. Photographs taken of Felix in the 1930s suggest that the *sauvage* ancestry for the Paschals is likely. Felix was tall, with high cheekbones and a narrow nose. Felix was well respected in the community and was knowledgeable about the local French traditional culture and language. He sang with La Guiannée. His son, Felix, now deceased, lived in St. Louis and continued to visit the community throughout his life.

Table 3, below, gives a summary of the black population and its relative size in relation to the total population through 1880. In the 1850 and 1860 censuses, occupations were given for a few blacks—farmers or laborers. A number had fairly substantial real and/or personal property values listed. In fact at least one black farmer had land and personal property that was equivalent to the more affluent French farmers.

Table 3
Black Population

Year	Slave	Free	Unknown	Total	% of Total Population
1726	59	1	-	60	28%
1732	63	-	-	63	19%
1752	173	-	-	173	23%
1800	60	4	-	64	43%
1810	62	1	-	63	27%
1820	-	-	69	69	27%
1830	85	19	-	104	26%
1839	10	37	16	63	15%
1840	43	16	-	59	10%
1849	-	67	-	67	16%
1850	-	71	-	71	10%
1860	-	71	-	71	12%
1870	-	91	-	91	8%
1880	-	25	-	25	12%
1880	-	47	-	47	5

Village Life

Like other nineteenth-century towns, Prairie du Rocher provided for most of the needs of the citizens. At least two general stores were available in the village—one run by Blais and the other by Hansborough. Blais' store first occupied a building opposite the Mellière house. In 1872 a brick grocery was built for it on Market street; the building is still used for that purpose.[20] Inventories from Blais' and Hansborough's stores in the 1840s showed the wide variety of materials desired and available to the villagers. For example, children's red morocco shoes, padlocks, glass tumblers, white blankets, merino shawls, silk dresses, a keg of ginger, axes, handsaws, files, fur hats, calicos of various colors, shaving soap, and teapots were sold.

From earliest times the community had been tied to the river for shipping. Beginning at least by 1820, steamboats stopped at a landing midway between Prairie du Rocher and Fort de Chartres. Goods for the stores in town came that way; flour from the mills and produce were shipped out on boats.

The steamboats also had a negative effect—the destruction of the bottomland forest along both banks of the Mississippi. The great demand for wood to keep the steamboat boilers fired resulted in complete deforestation along the river.

> Steamboats of the smaller class burned from twelve to twenty-four cords every twenty-four hours, and the larger boats running at mid-century consumed anywhere from fifty to seventy-five cords each day. …one large steamboat consumed enough wood in one day to construct approximately 15 small frame houses.[21]

The clearing of the forests affected the river. The Mississippi had been a fairly narrow and deep river. As the vegetation was removed more and more soil eroded from the banks. The channel began to fill in. This widened the river, because the quantity of water remained the same. The widening of the river resulted in more erosion and more loss of depth.

Between 1821 and 1888 the river became increasingly wider and more shallow. By 1880, the surface area of the river had increased approximately 50% from the area recorded during the [Corps of Engineers] 1821 survey.[22]

The increased shallowness of the river reduced the volume of water that could be removed rapidly in periods of high water, thus exacerbating flooding and drainage problems.

Flooding was something people were used to in the river bottom. When high water threatened, household furnishings would be moved upstairs to the loft; the water came up, went in and out. The floods generally were neither deep nor forceful. The river, uncontained by levees up and down its length, spread gradually as the snow melted or the rains fell. The floods also worked like the Nile floods; they renewed the fields.

...land in the bottoms, when they first moved there with the floods they would get one crop in five years and they did all right.[23]

There were people living out in the bottoms who had two houses: one on the bottom where they lived most of the time, and one on the hills where they could go when it flooded. However, the severity of flooding increased over time as the river widened, as levees were built upstream, and urban areas developed.

The village government as reorganized in 1837 lasted until 1844, when a disastrous flood hit the area in mid-June. As usual, most accounts about the flood come from Kaskaskia, where the entire town was inundated to a depth of about seven feet. The academy taught by the nuns was destroyed, and the nuns moved to St. Louis.[24] For Prairie du Rocher, the only record of the flood is found in the church registers. The burial of Hypolite Mougin was said to have to been near the cemetery, not in it, because the waters of the Mississippi covered part of the cemetery and came up to the door of the church.[25]

The effects of the flood were so severe that the state legislature passed an act for tax relief for the counties of Madison, St. Clair,

Monroe, Randolph, Jackson, Union, and Alexander.

> ...at the time of the late high and unexampled rise in said Mississippi river in June, 1844, have suffered great losses in the destruction of personal property, in the sweeping away of fences, and great depreciation of real estate...General Assembly is impressed with the propriety and justice of their claim to relief from sharing, for a time, a portion of the public burdens...[26]

The legislature also sent a memorial to Congress seeking relief for the people affected by the flood.

> Many of the farms have been stripped of their buildings, fences, the live stock drowned, all the crops entirely destroyed, the land itself covered to the depth of several feet with sand, and vast quantities of flood-wood, and rendered a dreary waste, and the inhabitants left destitute of the necessaries of life, and dependent upon charity for a subsistence.[27]

Illinois State Historical Library

This house in Old Kaskaskia was destroyed by the Mississippi River as it changed its channel in the late 1880s.

The flood led to the abandonment of the village organization. Perhaps the cleanup and repair absorbed the inhabitants' interests and the local government was not seen as helpful or necessary for reconstructing their lives. The last meeting of the village board of trustees was held in September.[28] When the incorporated village structure ceased to exist, its functions were taken over by the commons board—a return to a familiar pattern. As cited above, the right to initiate prosecution for trespass on the common was now in the hands of the commons board—elected officials, but a traditional authority in the communal mindset. The leasing of lots and other activities by the commons board apparently took the place of the village organization during the 1850s and 1860s.

Although the majority of the population were still farmers, other occupations began to appear in the census reports. The farmers had been self-sufficient for most crafts and skills, but specialization increased along with their dependency on market exchange. In the 1850 census, fifteen occupations are listed, ones that could be found in the eighteenth century as well. By the 1860 census the number of occupations had doubled (see Table 4, next page). Some of these were specialists in occupations practiced earlier—shoemaker, tanner, mason, or miller—but were now full-time jobs. Others came directly from the new governmental structure—clerk, justice of the peace, postmaster, and constable.

Prairie du Rocher differed from many Midwestern towns that were growing up in the 1840s and 1850s. Those towns were planned communities laid out with town lots and streets, and were developed deliberately to attract settlers. Although both the old and new villages had fairly standard sized lots laid out along streets in Prairie du Rocher, this came from within the existing communal system. This was not a pioneer community. That time was long past. Landed proprietors made up the village, but land holding was not reserved for an elite group.

Many of the nineteenth-century American communities, hoping to grow and become urban centers, promoted themselves towards this end. Prairie du Rocher was not situated in a prime position for urban growth, although it did have access to the river for shipping. No real attempt to attract other settlers was made. A few Americans, Franklin Brickey particularly, were more entrepreneurial, but they were interested in success on a personal economic level rather than urban prominence for their community.[29]

As can be seen from the population table in Appendix I, the

Table 4

Occupations from federal censuses

1850		1860	
farmer	73	farmer	75
laborer	21	laborer	20
woodchopper	14	cooper	8
carpenter	3	servant	6
physician	3	blacksmith	5
dramseller	2	barkeeper	4
miller	2	merchant	4
merchant	2	clerk	3
cooper	2	carpenter	3
blacksmith	2	engineer	2
bricklayer	1	justice of peace	2
stonemason	1	physician	2
priest	1	teamster	1
lawyer	1	tanner	1
teacher	1	ferryman	1
		merchant/miller	1
		landlady	1
		landlord	1
		wagonmaker	1
		mason	1
		saddler	1
		miller	1
		shoemaker	1
		postmaster	1
		foreman	1
		cabinet maker	1
		constable	1
		millwright	1
		lawyer	1
		auto typist	1

community did not increase greatly in size over the years, but more children were being born than could be absorbed into the local economy, resulting in out-migration. A portion of the population followed the western expansion model. Young men eager to seek other opportunities joined the westward movement, and from this migration the community acquired relatives spread out over the western states.

The village was Union in the Civil War, despite the long history of slavery, although there were southern sympathizers. The official records list only sixteen men enlisted from Prairie du Rocher, but more than this number participated in the war.[30]

A minor skirmish in the Civil War actually occurred at Prairie du Rocher. In 1864 the Chester paper reported that a group of "bushwackers and desperadoes" came to Prairie du Rocher. In search of these, Union soldiers of the Third Cavalry of the Missouri State Militia under the command of Captain H. B. Milks, came over from Ste. Geneviève. The guerillas fled from the town up the bluff, followed by the soldiers who killed two of them and captured a few. The town was searched for others who might be hiding there. The subsequent actions of the soldiers were reported differently by people in town and by the captain. Abraham Lee wrote to the newspaper with complaints that Blais' store had been robbed of goods by the soldiers and three inhabitants had had horses stolen from them. The captain firmly denied this and claimed that Blais was a "copperhead," and that people in town sympathized with the bandits.[31]

Travel from Missouri to Illinois during the war required permission.

A pass was issued by Mr. Palmer to Mr. and Mrs. Brickey on Oct. 11, 1867, by order of J. McNuistry "Major U.S.A. Provost Marshal" in St. Louis, granting them permission "to pass beyond the limits of the City and County of St. Louis, to go to Ills."[32]

At least seven blacks from Prairie du Rocher were in Colored Infantry units, including Frederick Joseph and Peter Joseph, sons of Joseph Joseph. John LaCava, who died in 1929 at age eighty-five, was a Civil War veteran. His mother was a slave, but he was born in Illinois in 1844, and free. His obituary stated:

> Mr. LaCava was held in high esteem by all people of Prairie du Rocher, he was a good citizen who tended to his own business and lived his life in an honorable way and at all times ready to meet his obligation to the community.[33]

This small village came to national notice when an unusual event took place. In Chicago a Mr. Crosby built an elaborate opera house, and then ran out of money. He decided to dispose of the opera house, and the works of art in it by means of a nationwide lottery. This caused great excitement over the state. In 1867, the winner of the opera house was Abraham Lee of Prairie du Rocher. Having no need for an opera house, Lee sold his ticket back to Crosby for $200,000, a very substantial amount in the funds of the day. Lee then built a three-story mansion on Market Street with a mansard roof, stained glass windows, and a beautifully finished interior. He lived only a short time to enjoy it. After his death it was acquired by his partner in the milling business, Franklin W. Brickey.[34] It was subse-

The Lee-Brickey mansion, Maple Hall, shortly before it burned in 1970.

quently known as the Brickey home, or Maple Hall.

The village was re-organized in 1871, and again under new state law in 1873. Villages trustees were elected. According to the village records, fifteen persons voted for the reorganization, and one against. The six candidates for the offices were elected by the twenty men who voted. There were about 300 males in the Prairie du Rocher precinct in the 1870 census. Not all would have been eligible to vote in the village election, but still, this was a rather poor representation. Participation in elections improved in 1874, when there were fifteen candidates for office, and fifty-nine voters. In 1875 sixty-two men decided between nine candidates. Enthusiasm waned after that. There were thirty-six voters in 1876, and forty-nine in 1877. The Board of Trustees elected the village president from within its ranks until 1888, when the position became selected by the people.[35] Unlike the American villages of the period where politics was a vital issue, the Prairie du Rocher villagers remained rather indifferent to it.[36]

The village trustees now proceeded to pass ordinances concerning such things as tavern hours, keeping the town clean, the appointment of a village constable, and other regulations typical of small towns around the state. The commons board continued with its traditional functions, but the village government moved the community into the mainstream of small-town America. The functions of the locally elected and appointed officials were not all that different from those in the eighteenth century. The county courts were similar to the old courts of justice. Some citizen duties remained the same, too, such as the requirement for working on county roads.

...each and every able bodied person within their respective Road District to labor three days on the Public Roads and highways...[37]

Work on roads also was required of all residents within the village. The trustees exempted themselves, though.

That for the purpose of keeping in repair the streets, alleys and sidewalk of the village of Prairie du Rocher all able bodied male residents of the village, except the members of the Board of Trustees, over the age of twenty one years and under the age of fifty years shall be required to labor on said streets alleys or sidewalks not exceeding three days in each year.[38]

The French population in Illinois was involved in American life and laws, willingly or not. The American system of government was accepted now. The citizens appear to have adjusted to the jury system in the courts, and to other foreign elements of government. The French population in St. Louis was more conservative. Of them it was written:

> They resented the procedures of common law that seemed to put power in the hands of lawyers and emphasized an adversarial system...the ideal of reconciliation was lost in such a system; trial by jury was expensive, time-consuming, and needlessly tied up property.[39]

Some of the inhabitants of Prairie du Rocher avoided the adversarial system by resolving problems among themselves, continuing traditional social control. Intermittently, with the incorporation and abandonment of village government, there were officials who took the place of the *syndic* or militia captain in local regulation of minor matters. The local attitudes towards government were strengthened by the new immigrants' wariness of government, due to their experiences in the old world.

The American law was disliked in St. Louis also for its "fragmented notions of property," and for the lack of freedom it gave to wives and widows over the management of the community property of a marriage. Fortunately, the inheritance laws of the state of Illinois were similar to the *Coutume de Paris*, with regard to the division of property. However, legally women did not have as many rights as they had under the *Coutume*. Their status was changing, but in Prairie du Rocher women still held property in their name and controlled it, unlike in some American communities, where women were never listed as legal owners.[40]

By the 1880s most migration from France had ceased. A few who had come from France to Prairie du Rocher were well educated;

Abraham Lee and William Henry were in this group. William Henry, who was bilingual, was appointed as a special commissioner to translate the old records affecting titles to real estate under an act of the State Legislature in 1855. Apparently there was some need for the old land deeds.[41] Most of the Alsatian, Swiss, and French immigrants were literate; there was a much lower literacy rate among the native-born Illinoisans. There were successful Americans, particularly the Brickeys, who with Lee and Henry formed a small elite group in the town.

By the 1880s the French villages of the Illinois had become thoroughly integrated into the American economy and system of law. For all of the French settlements, the latter years of the nineteenth century sounded the knell of their existence as separate cultural entities. The inexhaustible flood of Americans continued to flow in. St. Louis, and its neighboring communities settled by the French, were swamped by the new American settlers, and by the early twentieth century French St. Louis had vanished. Cahokia persisted into the twentieth century with vestiges of its ancient culture and architecture. Excellent examples of eighteenth century French architecture still are preserved in Ste. Geneviève, but urban expansion overtook both Ste. Geneviève and Cahokia. The Mississippi River dealt major blows to the French communities in the late 1880s. By changing its course, it wiped out St. Philippe. Old Kaskaskia now lies beneath the river. In Prairie du Rocher, American culture became predominant, but social control and the integration of the populace remained influenced by many of the old cultural values. These probably helped to keep the village viable.

Notes

1. Burnett 1987, 24; Pooley 1968; Greenleaf 1970, 57; Hansen 1940.
2. Laws of Illinois 1853, 249.
3. Laws of Illinois 1857, 619.
4. Laws of Illinois 1845, 307.
5. Origin and History of State Lands, Vol. 833; Laws of Illinois 1851, 51; Laws of Illinois 1852, 98; Laws of Illinois 1855, 112; Laws of Illinois 1863, 273.
6. The maps produced from the survey are on file in Randolph County courthouse.

7. Deed Record 2, 515, 1857.

8. In the twenty-first century a question arose about the boundary of the school district. Part of the old upper commons area was claimed by the city of Red Bud as part of their school district. Although maps and legislative acts relating to the common were provided for the court, the decision was made to award the disputed piece to Red Bud, the larger community.

9. Woodstock Letters 1878, 134. All the St. Stanislaus graves were relocated to Calvary Cemetery in St. Louis in 2003.

10. St. Joseph Ch. Rec. 1841, 46.

11. Interview, Meredith Connors, 1977; Burnett 1987, 22.

12. St. Jo. Ch. Rec. May 3, 1843; Nov. 10, 1851; Jan. 1, 1848.

13. St. Jo. Ch. Rec.

14. Carrière 1939, 44.

15. Laws of Illinois 1863, 273.

16. Harris 1904, 117.

17. Deed Rec. 10, 499.

18. Circuit Ct. Rec. Bk. A, 152.

19. This was traced through names and ages in the records. The sequence of logical steps is rather long to be given here, but it is correct.

20. *Prairie du Rocher Sun* newspaper (hereafter *PdR Sun*) Nov. 13, 1931.

21. Norris 1997, 145-6.

22. Norris 1997, 149.

23. Ekberg 1998, 203; Interview Tom Roy 1983; Informant B.

24. County Comm. Ct. Rec. 1842-1848, 128.

25. St. Jo. Ch. Rec. June 28, 1844.

26. Laws of Illinois 1845, 353.

27. op. cit., 374.

28. Revised Ordinances...1915, 11.

29. See Doyle 1978; Faragher 1986; Carr 1996 for discussion of models of Midwest American communities.

30. The achives list: Ambrose and Joseph Bequett, Peter Bono, John W. Brewer, Patrick Carr, Cornelius Hicks, Thaddeus Lausance, Charles Oxey, Joseph Palmer, Joseph Roman, Andrew J. James, John B. and John H. Skidmore, and W. H. Strickland. Other records indicate William Horrell and a Mr. Ellner.

31. *Belleville Democrat* newspaper, Ap. 23, 1864; War of the Rebellion

…127-128; 87. My thanks to Dennis Hermann for bringing this to my attention.

32. C. W. Brown 1979, 261.
33. *PdR Sun* Dec. 1916.
34. Johnson 1986.
35. Revised Ordinances…1915, V.
36. Carr 1996.
37. Co. Comm. Ct. Rec. 1841, 90.
38. Revised Ordinances…1915, Ordin. 10, Chap.11.
39. Gitlin 1989, 4.
40. Faragher 1986, 109.
41. Laws of Illinois, 1855.

8

On Into a New Century

The period from the 1880s to the 1920s, the heyday of rural villages, was a prosperous time for Prairie du Rocher also. Like others of the time, Prairie du Rocher had diverse businesses supporting the farm economy: general merchandise stores, farm equipment suppliers, blacksmiths, livery stables, lumberyards, drugstore, bakery, millinery shop, saloons, horse and carriage supplies, and later a garage. Grain from the farm production was handled by St. Luke's Mill, later Schoening Koenigsmark Milling, and the Farmer's Elevator. Meat was processed by Hauck's livestock and meat processing business. Services in town included hotels, a bank, a dentist, and doctors.

Local resources were important. Trips by horse and buggy to nearby towns could take most of the day, even in good weather when the roads were dry. When it rained there was even more of a problem. Arthur Bessen, who delivered mail around Prairie du Rocher for forty-eight years, described one trip on his route:

> We had a creek to go through, there was a bridge at one time and
> the creek washed the bridge away. One day it rained all day, poured,

and when I got to that creek it was high and it was swift…I said, well, I'll try it. When my team got in it pushed them downstream, they had their feet on the ground but the buggy was full of water. It broke one of my wheels. That's when you think—I could have drowned in that creek.[1]

In later years he had a car that he used only when the roads were dry.

Economy and Government

The villagers were interested in the same amenities as were other towns. On the main streets, oil burning street lamps came into use in the 1890s. In 1906 a new hand-cranked motion picture machine was advertised in town, using a carbide lamp for projection.[2] The Strand Theatre was built about 1914, offering the continuing saga of Pearl White, and a film starring Dorothy Gish.

This undated photograph of Market Street in Prairie du Rocher was probably made at the turn of the twentieth century.

The Brickey residence, the house built from the proceeds of the opera house lottery, had its own generator in the basement for lighting in the house. A local tavern made improvements too: "Palmer is putting in electric fans in his saloon powered by gasoline engine, and to pump water for a public horse trough."³ The horses were watered while their owners were cooled by the fans and consumed other drink.

By 1916 the village had its own electric plant, a one cylinder diesel engine with a cowhide belt, but it was only used for a few hours in the evening. Ten years later the town board considered running the electric plant during the day, too. This, the board thought, could provide power for fans, enable women to do the family wash, and furnish power for various motors. In other words, modern conveniences had arrived. A year later there was a petition from citizens for twenty-four-hour service. Electric service was available only in town; the outlying farms were not electrified until the REA arrived in the 1940s. Telephone systems were in early. By 1907 several systems were in operation, including the Commons Mutual Telephone Company, and Harrisonville, the current local telephone company. In 1914 a water plant was built.⁴ Far from being backwards, the town was as modern and up-to-date as many larger communities at the time.

All this was changing the lifestyle of the inhabitants, and other developments modified the old cultural landscape. Railroads were expanding across the state, and in 1902 the Iron Mountain Railroad came through Prairie du Rocher. The railroad right-of-way required a modification in the old road—the King's Highway from Fort de Chartres—as it cut off passage from the cemetery to the bluff road. If the road realignment was an inconvenience, the railroad made up for it by providing ready access to St. Louis; passenger trains ran three or four times a day. Local people were able to ride up to St. Louis in the morning, shop, visit friends or relatives there, and return in the early evening.

Photographs taken about the turn of the century show that the town, although retaining some of its earlier appearance, took on the rural architectural styles of the day. Old French-style homes existed, but additions, window treatments, porches, and fences were built in the American style. Many homes did not have lawns; the ground was bare and actually swept to keep it that way. There were wide dirt or cindered streets used by horses, carriages, and wagons.

Within the bounds of the village were pastures; people kept

Real-photo postcard views of Prairie du Rocher, 1901

cows and chickens in their yards. It was a very bucolic environment. As late as 1921 the local newspaper made the suggestion that corn should not be planted in closely settled sections of the village because it attracted insects and blocked the flow of air; also "it gives a hick appearance to visitors."[5]

The general store orginally started by Blais had become W. L. Connor's store. In the nineteenth century, shipments had come by riverboat, but with the advent of the railroad, rail shipping took over. Competition in business led to a change in the village street pattern. Main Street used to run through town, from Bluff Road to Henry Street (Highway 155). In 1900 a Mr. Kribs built a brick store right where everyone coming along Main or Henry Streets would see it. Connor then decided to build a new house and got permission from the village board to build it smack in the middle of Main Street, where it sits today. Traffic from Bluff Road had to follow Market Street which incidently went by Connor's Store.

Around the turn of the century, the farms were still largely self sufficient for food. Their cash crops also provided funds for clothing, tools, and other manufactured items. But in Prairie du Rocher, as in other small towns throughout the country, the people soon became dependent upon a wider economic framework. The change was gradual. Some purchasing was still done by barter. Connor's took in eggs, butter, lard, and rabbits, in exchange for other goods.[6] But by 1899 canned foods appeared, and by 1910 dry cereals, spaghetti, Jell-O and even caviar are listed.

A study was made of the amount and variety of stock in Connor's Store, which showed how it increased over the years, reflecting the demands of the villagers. For example, in 1890 there were 2,640 items, and by 1910, 3,959 entries in the inventory book. The interest in fine clothes continued. Ready-made clothing was available, as well as fabrics. For the ladies, silk, linen, dotted swiss, and satin were obtainable for dresses, and lace, hats, hat pins, gloves, fans, and parasols completed their outfits. Men's clothes were more prosaic—suits, ties, and celluloid collars. Violins, strings, and bows attested to the popularity of this instrument and its use for dances. The store also carried revolvers, sewing machines, carpets, couches, and other furniture.

Although paralleling the development of other Illinois rural villages in many ways, Prairie du Rocher also was influenced by its background and its geographical location. People today look upon the village as being isolated and distant from urban areas; this is not the reality nor has it ever been. Access to St. Louis by steamboat, then the railroad, and finally roads, always has been relatively easy. This urban contact and convenience created quite a different situation for Prairie du Rocher from many rural villages in the middle and eastern parts of the state, for whom contact with cities was very limited or virtually non-existent.

Therefore, although it did take some time for new inventions (or news of them) to come to Prairie du Rocher, the wait was not nearly as long as that experienced by many other small towns.[7]

There were automobiles in the village by 1911, but the use of the horse and buggy continued, as the roads were poor. In 1919 the road was built from Prairie du Rocher to Fort de Chartres, and in 1929 the "hard road" (macadam rather than gravel), Highway 155, was constructed between Ruma, north of town, and Prairie du Rocher.

World War I brought forth patriotic feelings in the community; many men went off to serve in the armed forces. Two who were bilingual, Lawrence Bies and Welda Laurent, served as interpreters for the French language, even though in the words of one informant, "Lawrence used to say that we in this country didn't always speak the proper French; he found that out when he was in France." Neighboring towns, such as Red Bud and Waterloo, where German had been spoken on a regular basis, faced rapid change under the de-Germanization pressures associated with the war. Prairie du Rocher's background being French, and the hostility of the Alsace-Lorraine people to Germany, made them strongly supportive of the war effort. A Red Cross drive in town was said to have resulted in 100 percent membership, the best in the United States.[8]

The postwar weakening of the economy affected the area somewhat, but the heaviest effects of the Depression were felt between 1930-33. One informant recalled that at the time he had five children in school, "It was rough but we had all we wanted to eat, that's one thing we had." Although the farmers had adequate food, the money to purchase other items was scarce and prices on farm products were down. As in most areas, this was a period of great difficulty.

In 1932 the community's merchants made an effort to help the farmers by what was called "wheat script." The farmers brought their wheat to the mill and for every dollar's worth of wheat they received $1.05 in merchandise.

> The merchants are making a sacrifice to give the farmers a chance to pay their debts, buy their needs and supply their families with clothes. One of them who was sincerely honest, but who owed me a debt brought in script and said it was the chance he had been waiting for to cash in his produce to pay me what he owed me.[10]

For a small and certainly not a politically prominent town, the village produced a surprising number of state legislators. A. L. Brands was a state senator from the 48th District from 1893 to 1896. A. A. Brands was a representative from the 44th District, serving several terms from 1933 to 1950. Charles Kribs, who was elected mayor of Prairie du Rocher in 1911, remained in town for some time in that capacity and then moved to Chester, from where he became a state senator in 1933. Most individuals were not interested in or involved with government beyond the local level; a few held county posts.

The village itself went along its way, maintaining a fairly casual approach to authority. Village government was firmly established, but the newspaper commented in 1925 that Prairie du Rocher had not held a primary for years.

> It cost a lot of money—One year the city officials decided to "forget" to issue a call for the primary and nobody said or done nothing about it and this has become the rule—forget the primary and save the money.[11]

The village managed its internal affairs as it had in the past within a strong community structure. When offenses occurred they generally were handled within the community. In the 1920s and 1930s the newspaper published the following notices that indicated social control was still primarily at the local level.

Notice to the party who last Wednesday night took and carried away my harness. I have a witness who saw you and I want to give you a chance to correct your false step by returning my property, but if you fail to so do, I shall prosecute you fully and you will be greatly surprised.

(tires stolen)...authorities have a pretty good idea who is doing this stealing and will keep their eyes on the youngsters in the future and they may be suddenly called upon to give account of their actions after one of these jobs is pulled.[12]

The general pattern of non-violence persisted; there were thefts, fights, and some domestic upheavals. In an unusual domestic situation a man claimed he was going to shoot his divorced wife. The village marshal was called and the newspaper had the headline, "Sensational Arrest in Church Yard." Sunday morning in the churchyard crowded with churchgoers, the marshal met the man and they both drew guns. A bystander grabbed the man's gun and then the marshal attempted to take him to jail. "When he resisted again the marshal struck him with his billy club."[13]

Some effects from external crime were reported in 1926. The newspaper said the community had been visited by "real yeggmen... Prairie du Rocher Lumber office safe was blown open with nitro glycerin, that a real yeggman was on the job is shown because the job was a clean one."[14]

Prairie du Rocher even had an airport at one time. It was not for transportation, just an emergency landing field. A grass landing strip was prepared in 1932, south of town near the cemetery. In July the newspaper reported that "construction of the emergency landing field will start as soon as the wheat and oats are off."[15] The landing strip with landing lights and a tower with a flashing light, remained there until 1950. Whenever emergency landings were made, a crowd of townspeople came out to see the plane.

Flooding not only from the effects of the steamboats, but also from runoff from the bluffs above the village, continued to be a problem. Prairie du Rocher creek emptied into the swamp (Gossiaux's) and a shallow lake with no adequate outlet to the Mississippi River. The creek followed a serpentine course through the town and could not drain away all the runoff. The water would spread out and flood the town. The newspaper commented,

> As is well known, the creek is, besides General Apathy, the greatest menace and drawback to the town.[16]

Efforts were made to improve the channel of Prairie du Rocher Creek through the village. A new or modified channel was dug, and this was continued through the old Marais Gossiaux and Fish Lake, to an exit into the Mississippi River some distance away. The former creek bed presently is a ditch wandering through town. Levees designed to be higher than the railroad tracks were built around the new creek channel. Flooding did not stop, though. In 1928 water coming down from the bluffs covered the town east of the railroad and all down Market Street. In 1930 the creek levee broke, flooding the town.[17]

The Common

State law in the 1850s had allowed for leasing of the land of the upper common for a period of time not to exceed ninety-nine years. Many of the people taking up the leases were emigrants from Alsace-Lorraine. Although these residents had constructed houses, barns, and sheds, and made other improvements, they did not pay the property tax and they were not the owners. The common was still communally owned. As the newspaper stated, "The improvements which they put on the farm lands will not be theirs to pass on to their children at their death but revert to the village."

In 1932 the newspaper noted that:

A petition for writ of mandamus, which would compel County Assessor and Treasurer…and the county board to assess the Prairie du Rocher Commons land and also the $15,000 in sale of leases therefrom was filed in circuit court at Chester this week…

6000 acres of land are involved in the 146 tracts of land in question. The petition…sets forth that the land is owned by the city of Prairie du Rocher and held by trustees. It is stated that the land is leased by the persons occupying it many of the leases dating back as far as 1852…

It is claimed by the residents of the commons…that the land is owned by the village and that it is leased for profit and therefore should be taxed. No amount of tax is now being assessed by state or county or road districts, they claim and assert it is the duty of the Treasurer and the county board to make an assessment so that it may pay its fair proportion of the tax.[18]

The article also stated correctly that the land could not be sold outright without legislative action. Therefore, in 1933 the state legislature amended their previous act to allow the trustees to sell the lands in the common. In 1937 four persons were appointed to make appraisals of the lands and lots in the common. When the appraisals were made and accepted by the county court the trustees could convey parcels to individuals for "an amount equal to at least 90 percent of the appraised value."[19]

Having to purchase land that they had lived on for years caused resentment. The purchase prices do not seem high now, forty to sixty dollars an acre, generally, but this represented a large investment then, particularly since the area was still in the grip of the Depression.

Although these sales finally ended the communal ownership of the upper common, it did not end the commons board. The Prairie du Rocher Commons Board is the only one that survives in the country; it still meets regularly and elects trustees.[20] The money obtained through the old leases and the sales was invested; the interest is donated annually to the local school. For over a hundred years loans were made to residents from the commons fund. Then in the 1950s the board felt it was better to support the local bank and have it handle loans. There are still people in town who purchased their homes through a loan from the commons fund.

Language and Traditions

Elderly persons now deceased were interviewed in the 1970s; they spoke about the years around the turn of the century. The women—mothers and grandmothers—seem to have been responsible for maintenance of cultural elements. The women's role now followed the American "norm" more closely. Education was not important for them, professions generally were not open to them, and their main concerns were the home and children. This more restricted life led to conservatism in language, foods, and customs, preserving cultural elements.

Many of the informants reminisced fondly about traditional foods—*bouillie* (a hot cereal composed of flour, sugar, and milk); *pain sauvage* (Indian bread or fry bread, a small piece of bread dough pinched off from the rising loaf and fried); and *bouillon* (clear chicken soup). The women also dried and canned produce and always grew herbs for flavoring. Families would get together and slaughter pigs, rendering the lard, smoking meat, and making sausage (*boudin*). Each family had their own recipe for making sausage.[21]

Nicknames were common among the French. Many have been mentioned earlier, such as Vadebonccoeur, La Plume, and Dulongpré. Some nicknames from the eighteenth century became surnames later. The family of Deguire *dit* La Rose had descendants who used Deguire, and another set of descendants used La Rose as a surname. Guillemot *dit* Lalande became only Lalande.

Many people had the same surname, due to the intermarriages, but also frequently even the same Christian name. Nicknames were useful for distinguishing persons with the same name. The use of the father's Christian name as a patronymic was common among the French, as well as what has already been described for the black population. The death record of Jean Baptiste Louvière, in 1905, includes the comment, "commonly known as Baptiste Charles." His father was Charles.

Informants in the 1970s spoke of this also. There was a man known as Peter Robert—his father was Robert—and a woman, Millie George, whose father's name was George. Wives in the Bienvenu family were distinguished in the latter part of the nineteenth century by their husband's names—Mary Henry and Mary Louis.

The French language still could be heard on the streets in town in the early twentieth century but change and loss was occurring rapidly. A man raised in Prairie du Rocher came back in 1906 after a thirty-six-year absence and

> Found a complete change in the inhabitants as well as the town. When he last visited the place, the French language was in almost constant use. Now it is hardly ever heard.[22]

In the mid-1930s Carrière, who researched the French cultural remnants in the old colony commented, "the last grey shades of the twilight of the French survival in Illinois were to be seen in the first years of the twentieth century and not during the period 1810-20, as historians often tell us."[23] Carrière sought out some of the elder citizens to study the old language and reported:

> In Prairie du Rocher several inhabitants between the ages of forty and forty-five, no longer fluent in French, told me they had not spoken a word of English until they began to attend grade school.
>
> Christmas even spent at the home of Captain Noah C. Duclos, who had also invited for the occasion his father, Mr. Michel Duclos, Mr. Frank Louvier, and the two Pascahels, father and son, descendants of slaves brought to the Illinois country in the eighteenth century. We spoke an archaic and picturesque variety of French and sang old folk songs in that language.

A footnote added later stated that:

> Mr. Michel Duclos, Mr. Frank Louvier and Mr. Pascahel, Sr., have all died since 1936. The last survivors of the generation acquainted with the days when the community had a distinctly French flavour are

fast disappearing. In another ten or fifteen years, none will be left.[24]

In school the classes were taught in English, and this was the end of the French language. The loss of French was not a purposeful elimination of foreign speech. In Old Mines, Missouri, when schooling became compulsory, the children were punished for speaking French.[25] There was no coercion at the schools in Prairie du Rocher to speak English, and no punishment for using French. Classes were taught in English, so it became the common speech for the children.

One woman interviewed in the 1970s had known only French before school, but said that after she started classes, "I thought I was smart; I could speak American."[26] None of the informants in the 1970s could recall much French. Their parents did not encourage the use of French at home, often using French as a private language between relatives. So the generation that married in the 1920s and 1930s were English speakers. A few continued a little use of French while their parents were still alive. A number of elderly persons, mainly women, still knew only French in the 1930s and 40s. Because of this, Connor's store kept a French-speaking clerk there until World War II.

Loss of the language probably is the reason why no old French folktales can be recalled in the community. No one remembered poor old "Broken Breeches." In the early part of the century, the parents told stories in French to their young children, but as the children went to school and spoke English, translation of the tales into that language was probably beyond the bilingual capabilities of the parents, particularly the mother. The older women did not know English or were not fluent in it. Some informants mentioned that, although their mother knew English, she was hesitant to speak it, as she could not speak it well. Since the next generation did not speak French, the stories were not passed on. Carrière found many folktales in Old Mines and Ste. Genevieve and published these. There were none from Prairie du Rocher.

About 1946 John Allen, a folk historian, came in search of tales. The only story related to him was a relatively recent one from the 1880s, about a ghostly funeral, all in English. The tale is of two women sitting outside a house in Prairie du Rocher late at night, who suddenly saw a funeral procession coming along the road. In the funeral train were forty wagons and twenty-six horsemen, but there was no sound to this apparition.

> You'd see the horses raise their hoofs and put them down on the ground, but there was not a sound. You could see the wagon wheels as they were turning, and the people in the wagons seemed to be talking. There wasn't a sound made by anything.[27]

The sighting was on Friday, July 4, 1889, between eleven o'clock and midnight; a bright moon was shining. This story has been related in more recent interviews too, some quoting from John Allen, but others had talked to the women who supposedly saw the funeral. There is a tale attached to this that some important person at Fort de Chartres had been killed and had to be secretly buried. This may be related to the story told to Reynolds.

> At the time the British troops came to take possession of Fort Chartres, two young officers, one French and the other British, had a misunderstanding at the Fort. This quarrel was...on the account of a lady. These officers fought with small swords early on a Sunday morning near the fort, and in this combat one was killed. The other left the fort, and descended the river. I was informed of the duel nearly fifty years ago, by a very aged Frenchman. He informed me of the details, and said, he was present and saw the combat.[28]

The story of the funeral is well known outside the area because of Allen's book. Several hundred ghost hunters descended upon Fort de Chartres in 1997 and again in 2003, when the Fourth of July fell on a Friday, in hopes of seeing the apparition. The funeral procession did not appear.

Carrière in his work spoke not only of language, but also of various traditions.

> Some of the older residents, particularly Messrs Frank Louvier, Michel Duclos and Alexis Palmier, have given me some interesting

information on the history of their village. They spoke wistfully about old-time customs, the Christmas révillon, the Guillonée carolling on New Year's Eve, the gay family reunions on New Year's Day, the King's Ball, the Pancake Supper on Shrove Tuesday and the burlesque serenading of the Charivari.[29]

These customs must have been observed in the eighteenth century, though not mentioned in the legal documents. A few have persisted into the twentieth century, especially la Guiannée.

La Guiannée

The origins of la Guiannée are lost in antiquity in Europe. The custom shares many elements with the mumming and misrule celebrations widespread in antiquity on the continent and Britian. The name itself is of doubtful etymology; a number of suggestions have been made but there is no consensus.

Accounts come from other French communities as well as Prairie du Rocher. In mid-century it was reported from St. Louis:

> On New Year's Eve, soon after nightfall, the young men of the town would assemble together at some appointed place, dressed out in the most fantastic masquerade costumes, each one provided with a bucket, sack, basket, or other article suitable for the carrying of provisions, solids or liquid. Thus accoutered and provided, at a given signal proceeded from house to house, without exempting any from their visit, and at each place, in full chorus, sang "La Guignolée.[30]

Although the account does not explain the bucket, sack, and basket, informants in later times have said it was the custom to collect food for the poor during the rounds.

From descriptions and comments in Prairie du Rocher, the basic format was for a group to gather in the early evening and go on a selected route of twenty or more houses, singing at each house and often continuing until early morning. The local custom has been to sing the first two verses of the song outside the house. If invited in, they would sing the whole song for the householder and family. They were served wine and whiskey, sandwiches, and cookies, and then went on to the next house.

The Guiannée singers dressed in various ways—"their clothes had big patches on the seats of the overalls, the oldest clothes you could find," and they would turn their coats inside out. Many blackened their faces with burnt cork and some wore masks. In the 1920s and 1930s, Felix Paschal dressed as an Indian. In the 1920s Indian costumes were popular, and for a time in the 1930s a group of men rented military costumes. In Old Mines, Ward Dorrance reported groups "...dressed as Indians or blackened as negros, shuffling in line with fiddles and singing the old song."[31]

In 1907 the local weekly newspaper, the *Democrat Sun,* reported on the 1906 Guiannée.

La Guiannée celebrants dressed in military costumes in the 1930s. Felix Paschal is in Indian garb.

The guillione made their rounds, New Year's eve. The guillione is another custom handed down to the people of Prairie du Rocher by their French ancestors, who settled the place. The members of the party called the Guillione are masked, and accompanied by string music, go from house to house, first stopping outside near the door and singing the guillione song. When the door is opened they file in, repeating the song. The occupant of the house gives them refreshments and they depart, on their way around. They visit every house, and are seldom refused admittance... The guillione this year was under the management of Raymond Mudd, Andrew Langlois and Louis Tebeau, and tho small, on account of adverse conditions of the weather, was a good one. The masks were well-chosen and presented a mottery [sic] of quaint, ugly and comic people. The conduct of the members was excellent...It is one of the old customs which it would be well to keep.[32]

Early accounts from Missouri included dancing, and most people agreed that in the old days in Prairie du Rocher, at the verse about the eldest daughter, someone would dance with her. "The dance was more jump around, part of the group would go around in a circle and pick out the young girls with the eldest daughter, and there was jigging after the song."[33]

Originally only men were the singers, later some women went with them and women's groups formed. A black Guiannée group existed sometime before the 1930s. On New Year's Eve a number of different Guiannée groups went around singing. They walked on the rural roads, going to every house along the way. Each assembly had an area that they covered.

It was not until the 1930s that the Guiannée began to go around in the village itself; at that time there were four groups, two men's, one composed totally of women, and a troupe of instrumental musicians. The serenading may not have appealed to all non-French. Mr. Brickey, living in the large Lee mansion, is said to have come out one New Year's Eve and inquired, "How many more of these Guiannées are there?"[34]

The traditional King's Ball continued to be held in the early part of the century, but in the 1930s, rather than a king chosen through finding a bean in the cake, there was selection of a queen. This was done by voting. It became more a popularity contest than choice by chance.

Visitors always had reported how the French liked dancing and this did not change. Dances were popular. One informant recalled:

> One year there was twenty-eight days in February and twenty-eight dances. Lots of fiddlers then. They'd load up the kids in the wagon, fill the wagon with straw, not be cold. Had the dance down in the barn in the hollow here—fiddlers, guitars, mandolins, what they called tater bugs, harmonicas, jews harps, accordions."

They would dance the quadrille, waltz, and two-step.[35]

Black Citizens

Local memories of the blacks seemed to be mainly of two extremes, the very well-respected Paschals and the dubious character known generally as Nick Paul. Nick Paul's official name was Enoch Allard; his father, Paul, had been a slave of the Allards. Nick Paul was married and had two sons. His wife worked as laundress for families in town. Nick Paul did various small jobs around town but was arrested at least twice for stealing pigs. The family lived in a shack with a dirt floor along the bluffs and one informant commented, "I guess maybe we'd gone out and stole a pig too if we had to live like that." Although the villagers might complain about Nick Paul's actions, when it was a question of outside law enforcement getting involved, that was another matter. The weekly paper reported in 1921 that:

> Enock [sic] Allard, colored aged about 75 years, was arrested by railroad dectective [sic] last Friday morning and taken to Chester on the local freight train to answer a charge of larceny, it is said.

The article also quoted from the *Chester Herald* newspaper.

> It is alleged that Paul had been for some time stealing coal by the truck load and peddling it about town, selling it as low as $1.00 a load.

The local newspaper continued:

> The *Herald's* article greatly exaggerated the offense, in the opinion of Prairie du Rocher citizens who ought to know. The *Sun* man went around and could find no one who ever saw old Nick with a truck. He was seen with a push cart holding perhaps a couple bushels of coal. Coal stealing in this city is just about the same as in other towns and the rail road detectives have not made a prize catch in Old Nick, is the opinion of most Prairie du Rocherians.[36]

The article suggests that people were aware of what Nick Paul was doing and were turning a blind eye to it. Internal mechanisms for regulating social behavior were preferred to involvement with the authorities. Nick Paul may not have been one of Prairie du Rocher's more upstanding citizens, but he was part of the community and the solidarity of the village structure closed around him.

At the other end of the spectrum were the Paschals. Felix, senior, was a member of La Guiannée society and dressed as an Indian for the New Year's event. Besides singing La Guiannée, Felix knew an old French song, the so-called Slave Song, that he taught to Percy Clerc, who was a later Guiannée leader. When Felix died in 1939 his funeral was held at St. Joseph's with all-white pallbearers. When Felix's three children went to school they were the only ones left in the black school; when they finished grade school, it closed. Felix, junior, related that he went on to three years of high school in Prairie du Rocher, which was all the school was offering then. A close friendship continued to exist between Felix, junior, and a local family, until he died in the late 1980s.

The older residents interviewed in the 1970s uniformly felt that the relationship between blacks and whites in Prairie du Rocher had been harmonious and equitable. However they were looking back from a perspective influenced by the civil rights movement. The anecdotes they related unconsciously reflected the paternalistic attitude of the past and the actual position of the blacks as second class citizens.

Conflicting statements were offered about where the blacks

sat in church. One person said that the blacks always sat in back. If one had sat farther to the front the congregation would have been horrified. Nothing would have been done about it, but each "knew their place." Another said that the widowed Mrs. Paschal always sat in back, but when her folks came from Chicago and sat up front, she stayed in back. Felix, junior, himself, stated that the family always sat three to four seats from the front. One man recalled looking down from the choir loft onto Felix senior's head several seats from the back on the left side of the church.

Mrs. Nick Paul always sat at the back of the church and her sons sat at the rear of the catechism class. In speaking about this catechism class a local person related that one of these boys died of pneumonia. In the next class session his death was announced by the priest and all the heads in the class swivelled to the back. The priest said, "He's not there!"

Ambiguity was expressed about the relationships between blacks and whites. A man related that as a small boy he was close to an elderly black man he called Uncle George; George, born in 1830, had been born a slave.

> When I went to school we were talking about our relatives and I said Uncle George. One of the older boys in the fourth grade, said that black's not your uncle, he's just an old nigger. I was hurt and went home crying and told my mom, they said Uncle George wasn't my uncle. Well, she said, he's really not, but I'll let your daddy explain it.

He also said that "Uncle George gave an entirely different line of thought about slavery than that they have on TV now." However, the proof to this was the response to the question he asked, "Uncle George, do you like your master? He replied, finest white man that ever lived."[37]

One man, a child during the last few years of the life of Felix Paschal, senior, recalled coming home from school and seeing Felix walking along the street and thinking he was such a dignified person. Even at that age he found it difficult to reconcile the local treatment of blacks as second-class citizens with the very strong sense of community that he found within the village.

In earlier days the blacks had belonged to a family through legal ownership. Even after they were freed there was a paternalistic attitude that included them in the close-knit community. In the church burial register it was recorded:

This undated newspaper photo shows that blacks, as well as whites, were employed by the post office in Prairie du Rocher.

George Mischaud oldest colored member of the parish in his 94th year, was verified by the following extract of the baptismal record 1813 viz:[translated from the French]on the twenty-eighth Ste. Therésè has baptized George born the day before, slave of Monsieur La Chance.[38]

The local newpaper reported on the death of

Ethel Pickett 17 years, daughter of Henry, colored barber for many years in Prairie du Rocher, moved to East St. Louis. Mrs. Pickett's a Prairie du Rocheran, Grace Joseph, others of this family sleep in St.

Joseph's cemetery.[39]

However, these family bonds weakened with movement to other towns and especially cultural influences. The distance between the groups increased, leaving only the second-class status. Descendants of the black slaves continued to live in Prairie du Rocher until the 1930s, but with the Depression and the lack of jobs other than farming, they gradually moved to St. Louis and East St. Louis. Some descendants still live there.

Fort de Chartres

From the days of the land commissioners until the 1840s, Fort de Chartres was a government reservation, not open to land sales. Victor Collet in 1796 described the fort and stated that the walls and buildings were still in good preservation. In 1841 Wild drew a picture showing the "remains of exterior wall—the right shows part of one of the bastions, with two port holes complete, and on the left, is the magazine, almost entire." However, when Reynolds visited in 1854, he spoke of it as a "large pile of ruins" and found that "the walls of this fort are torn away almost even with the surface."[40]

A local legend says that the Eads Bridge, opened in 1874 across the Mississippi, has Fort de Chartres stone as part of its fill, but there are no records to substantiate this. The local inhabitants carried off most of the stone from the walls and buildings for construction material, and the old fort was lost to sight. The reserved land was sold in the mid-nineteenth century. A house was built on the foundations of the barracks, and the powder magazine, still largely intact, was used as a root cellar. The parade ground became a farmyard.

In 1913 there was a revival of interest in Fort de Chartres. The state park system in Illinois had been created only a few years earlier. A flyer was put out by Monroe County showing the powder magazine and appealing to the legislators to create a state park. The *Prairie du Rocher Sun* reprinted this and urged its readers to support it.

Fort de Chartres, from John C. Wild's The Valley of the Mississippi Illustrated, *1841*

Gentlemen—We, the undersigned residents of Monroe County, and State of Illinois, respectfully ask your honorable body to appropriate $10,000, or as much as may be necessary, for the purpose of purchasing Old Fort Chartres and converting it into a state park...The old magazine, still standing, is undoubtedly the oldest structure of its kind in the state. Civic and historic pride demand that these ruins be preserved. And to that end we pray to receive the attention of your honorable body.[41]

Local support was forthcoming. Tom Connor, now in charge of Connor's store, was a leader in this movement. The legislature did designate it a state park. The area was cleared, and the old walls rebuilt to the height that most still have today. In 1928, the former royal storehouse was reconstructed as a custodian's quarters and museum. In the 1930s there was interest in restoring the buildings more accurately, but no one was able to find the plans and drawings prepared originally for the fort, and they still have not been located. The guardhouse and chapel were rebuilt in 1936, based on buildings at Fort Niagara in New York.

Various local people were employed in these construction projects, including Felix Paschal, senior, who did concrete and mortar work there. The wood shingles for the buildings were hand split by local workers—Arthur Bienvenu, his father, and his brother. This was done with a frow and a wood mallet. Thick blocks were split to proper thicknesses.

Fort de Chartres Archives

Ruins at Fort de Chartres included an old barn, left,
and the powder magazine, photographed in the 1860s.

The village again became involved with the fort, but on a different level. It was a popular picnicking spot for the locals, not just for individuals, but for large organized picnics. Tourist visitation began, and in July 1923 the paper commented that there had been 500 visitors to Fort de Chartres. Renovation of the fort was part of a minor revival of interest in the French heritage sustained by Tom Connor, his son, Meredith, and the continued popularity of La Guiannée. However, except for a few persons, the fort's history was not of great interest—it was a place to picnic.

Post World War II

The economy began to pick up again after the Depression and federal projects had an impact on the town, including the instal-

The fort's gate was reconstructed in the 1940s and 1970s.

lation of water lines by the WPA in 1940. Nearly a hundred men went from the village into the second World War and possibly another hundred from the surrounding area; some men were given agricultural deferments because of the need for crops. The increased demand for workers in other towns provided employment for the remaining men and even women moved into the job market. No new industries came into Prairie du Rocher.

Many changes occurred in the village after World War II. At first it was a boom time. Large numbers of temporary workers were housed in the village for work on the railroad, a gas line, and the levees. Prompted by floods in 1943 and 1944, the creek channel was deepened and straightened. Agricultural levees were constructed along the Mississippi River and up both sides of the creek bed. During these improvements the highway from the fort to Prairie du Rocher was rerouted and a bridge over the creek was removed. The bridge at that time still was referred to as the King's Highway bridge. The King's Highway also was referenced in 1921 in relation to overflow from the creek.[42] Surprisingly this name had managed to survive for over 200 years from the *Chemin du Roi*.

For several years, while improvements were carried out on the railroad bed, the levee constructed, and a gas pipeline laid out, Prairie du Rocher was a center for workers. Also, a limestone quarry along the bluffs west of town employed many local men. All these people purchased food, goods, and services in town, so the businesses prospered. By the early 1950s the construction projects were completed. The railroad and the gas line employees moved on; the levees were finished. In the spring of 1949 the quarry laid off a third of its employees, leading other employees to strike.[43] A new firm took over the quarry and reduced the hours.

All of these events severely affected the economy of the village. The number of businesses in town declined; people found jobs in nearby towns. With modern transportation systems it was now possible to work outside of town and still reside in the village; as in most places the automobile had taken over. The railroad discontinued the last passenger train, the Dinky, in 1950; the railroad became strictly for freight. Access to St. Louis was by road only.[44]

After the war, housing development took place and the appearance of the town changed. The national attitude of "out with the old, in with the new" meant that old houses were torn down and new ones built. Most of the old French architecture vanished and the customary fences around the town lots began to disappear. One person recalled that all the houses used to have fences. One would describe the fence rather than the house, to someone seeking directions. The Brickeys abandoned the Lee mansion and moved to St. Louis in the 1950s; the house remained unoccupied until it was destroyed by fire in 1970.

St. Joseph's Church remained the focal point of the community religiously and socially, with church picnics and various celebrations. Sometime in mid-century the time for the annual church picnic shifted from Wednesday to Saturday; a recognition that for an increasing number of people in the village, the business work week was the standard rather than the seven days of the farming schedule.

Until the 1950s the Catholic church continued to be the only church in the village, although members of other denominations resided in the community. When the former state senator, A. L. Brands, died in 1910, a Methodist minister officated at his burial in the Prairie du Rocher cemetery. In 1956 a Baptist congregation set up a church in an old building in town. This was a new thing for what one person called "a Catholic ghetto." One comment was that "you'd have thought the town was going to fall apart;" but others saw no problem and felt that the town was tolerant and friendly. A person remarked dryly that thirty Baptists could sing louder than the whole Catholic congregation.

After the council of Vatican II in the early 1960s, with its far-reaching changes in the Catholic Church, the priest made modifications at St. Joseph's. One of the changes was the installation of new pews. Up until then the pews had been rented and small numbered tags marked each leased pew; now rental ceased after 230 years of the custom.

The schools in town included the parochial school, St. Joseph's, that continued to use the brick building built in 1855; a public school in town, Bessen School; and a few small one-room schoolhouses on the upper common and in the old commonfields toward Fort de Chartres. In 1920 a two-year high school was started in the church school; later this was extended to three years. Students wishing to continue for a fourth year could go to nearby towns. Basic education was available for all, but few young people went to college in the early years of the century. In 1911, Edgar Brands was said to be the first university graduate (University of Illinois) since 1887, when F. W. Brickey graduated from St. Louis University.

A new modern school building was built in 1951 by the church. The building was never used as a parochial school, but from the start was leased to the public school district. The parochial school closed. Nevertheless, separation of church and state came late in Prairie du

Louise Brands

St. Joseph's Eighth Grade Class of 1922

Rocher. About 1956, someone then a student in the third grade re-called, "the janitor came in and removed the crucifixes from the walls of the classroom; I guess someone complained." Nuns taught in the public school until the early 1980s, when lack of teaching nuns caused the school to hire only lay teachers. In 1971 a public school was con-structed on the same lot and attached to the building owned by the church. Catechism classes are still taught twice a week in the church building before regular school hours. In the 1970s the old brick school was torn down.

To the End of the Century

Economic resources and services within the town continued to dwindle. The last doctor left in 1948; the town has been without a resident physician since. In 1965 a county planning document listed the existing businesses:

a barber shop, two TV repair shops, auto repair, café, bank, grain elevator, lumberyard, warehouse, confectionery, theatre, apparel store,
four grocery markets, two service stations and a used car lot.[45]

Far fewer exist now. The lumberyard closed and the Western
Auto store burned when the restaurant next to it caught fire; no building and construction materials are available in town now. No clothing
store exists and only one grocery is left. The theater closed in the
1970s. The quarry closed. It reopened later, but the company now
operating it ships gravel out by river barge and few local people are
involved.

Nearby towns, Red Bud and Waterloo, have expanded their
business districts and services and act as secondary centers for the
region. Wal-Mart, fast foods, large chain groceries, service stations,
high schools, lumberyards, a hospital, and nursing homes are there.
Purchasing not done in these towns is carried out in St. Louis, or at a
large shopping mall on the east bank of the river; both sources are
about an hour away by car. All this is similar to what has happened in
many other small rural villages, but despite this, the population has
remained quite stable.

Farming is still a major occupation for the area, but with
modern machinery fewer people are needed for production. Not all
the children can be supported by the farm, so most go elsewhere for
jobs. In a way, it is a reversal of the difficulties the French had been
facing in France in the eighteenth century, that led them to leave the
countryside for the cities. In France the farms had become smaller
and smaller because of the inheritance rules, so that a family could no
longer subsist from its crops. Now farms have to be large in order to
compete in the modern economy but they require fewer workers, so
out-migration is necessary. This trend will probably continue, as more
farming comes under large corporations.

The 1970s saw a revival of interest in the historical background of the area, partly motivated by the general retrospection of
the United States bicentennial. In 1971, the 250th anniversary of Ste.
Anne's parish, St. Joseph's, and the founding of the town was celebrated. Modern gravestones were added to the eighteenth century
ones for Fr. Gagnon and Fr. Collet. To commemorate the anniversary,

a large marble marker and an aluminum cross were placed at the location of the former church of St. Joseph's in the cemetery. Part of the inscription on the marker reads:

> Here lie buried the remains of Michigamea Indians; early French adventurers; black slaves; victims of wars, massacres, floods and plagues; veterans of all wars of the United States and pastors and parishioners of St. Joseph's Church of three centuries. May they rest in peace with God.

In 1976 the village decided to build a new village hall to house offices, fire department, post office, and police. The initial plans were to construct a metal building that would be of moderate cost. However, the board and local citizens decided that this was not what they wanted. Community interest resulted in raising the money to build a building designed in traditional French style with upright rough sawn cypress logs and a split cedar shake roof.

National recognition of the French settlements came in 1974 when the National Register of Historic Places recognized the French Colonial District that extends from Prairie du Rocher to Kaskaskia. In the late 1970s the Creole House, on the site of the old Brickey home, was given to the Randolph County Historical Society for preservation. This home had been constructed and remodeled between 1825 and 1875; its exterior appearance is of the old French style architecture.[46] The Randolph County Historical Society renovated the

Prairie du Rocher's village hall, built in 1976.

house, furnished it with antiques, and operates it as a house museum. Situated on Market Street, it has a visually favorable location but it is open only by appointment. Therefore, it does not add greatly to historical interpretation in the area.

Fort de Chartres State Park—now State Historic Site—began to hold "Rendezvous" in 1970. This rapidly grew to be a very popular annual event, attracting 20,000 or more people to the fort the first weekend in June. A few of the townspeople participate in the Rendezvous with food stands. In the first few years of Rendezvous, Prairie du Rocher held a street fair in town on Saturday night, but the beer stands took business away from the local taverns and there were complaints about the rowdiness of people who came into town. Although local young people actually were involved also in the behavior, the disruptions were perceived as coming from the outside. The street fair was discontinued. Several years later a parade was instituted that usually involves the Boy Scouts, the American Legion color guard, La Guiannée, politicians (particularly in election years), the Prairie du Rocher Fire Department, other nearby fire departments, some tractors, and horses. It is a pleasant non-participatory event,

La Guiannée performers during Rendezvous in the 1980s

particularly enjoyed by the children because candy is thrown to them from the floats.

In 1996 the 275th anniversary of the parish of Ste. Anne (counting from 1721) was celebrated with the dedication of a sign near the first location of the church of Ste. Anne. Special services were held at St. Joseph's throughout the year.

In 1997, the 275th year of the village of Prairie du Rocher was observed with the dedication of a calvary along the road to Fort de Chartres. The calvary is a wayside shrine with three crosses. In the eighteenth century another was located somewhere along the road-

A cannon is demonstrated by reenactors at Fort de Chartres in the 1970s.

side. In former times, on the Feast of the Holy Cross, a procession would have come from Ste. Anne's to the old calvary. The tradition of an annual procession has been renewed.

Many of the family names from the eighteenth century are no longer represented in town today, but the local telephone book still has, for example, Barbeau, DuClos, DeRousses, Bienvenus, Roys, and Godiers. The later arrivals from France and Alsace-Lorraine are represented by Albert, Bachelier, Laurent, Bise, Mudd, Mellière, DuFrenne, Kerr, and others.

La Guiannée continues to be the main element identified with the French heritage. Prairie du Rocher is the only one of the French communities to have kept La Guiannée going continuously from the beginning of the French settlements. The Ste. Genevieve group ceased for a while and has been revived. Old Mines' was revived in the 1970s but does not travel around on New Year's Eve. Cahokia's group ceased, but a few members go with the Prairie du Rocher group. The other communities have lost it entirely.

The local term used for La Guiannée is pronounced "Gi-oh-ni." No one knows the origin of this. It must have been in use for many years. Reynold's account, based on his experiences in the early 1800s, spells it, "Gionie."[47]

In 1948 the local Guiannée took part in the National Folk Festival held in St. Louis. It was reported that Charles Clerc sang the solo at the end of the song. Charles Bise, eighty-one years old, danced "one of the graceful pioneer dances" and Frank Coleno did an "old time jig."[48] In the 1950s the newspaper reported that these three participants, all past "three score and ten," still walked and sang with the group. Bise was ninety years old when he died and had played the fiddle for the Guiannée for forty years.[49]

Charles Clerc was the leader of the group for many years, and after him his son, Percy, became the leader. Percy often wore a costume covered with corn husks; his grandmother told him it was a traditional costume in France for La Guiannée. Another son of Charles Clerc, William, played the fiddle with the group for seventy-three years, beginning when he was fourteen, and continuing until his death in 1998.

The group has always had fiddlers, and later other stringed instruments were added. Currently there are two fiddlers and a guitar player. Now on New Year's Eve the assembly goes only to private homes in the village and surrounding countryside where they have been invited. They travel by bus. Public performances are given at the fort, the Creole House, restaurants, and bars in town. The song also is performed at Rendezvous, as a demonstration of the heritage of the area. The group tends to be formed of persons over forty, but including the young children of the members. The youth usually drop out when they get old enough to attend New Year's Eve parties. The hopes of the group are that they will return when they are older, perpetuating the tradition.

Attired in his cornhusk costume, Percy Clerc joins other entertainers for La Guiannée.

La Guiannée is probably what is visualized most often in the community as the historical identity of the town. When in 1981, Percy Clerc the elderly leader of the group, died tragically in a fire, there were fears that the Guiannée would not survive. Several men gathered at the Legion hall to "try out" as the next leader. One of the younger men, Dan Franklin, took over the lead. The next performance was in June at Rendezvous; large numbers of townspeople who did not usually attend Rendezvous turned out to hear it.

La Guiannée continues to have a strong identification for the community, but interest in the French background is largely nostalgic. As for other traditions, they mainly have vanished. The charivari continued throughout the 1940s and 1950s. The last occurrence was in 1966, when a couple, both widowed, were married and were entertained by loud noises and music until they let the group in and provided food and drink.

The King's Ball was held throughout the 1930s, but ceased during World War II. It was revived as a bicentennial event in 1976, and has continued since. Celebrated on the Saturday closest to the traditional January 6th date (Epiphany), it has become a popular event with the local people and particularly with historic reenactors. Many of the dancers wear period costumes, and a band with fiddlers plays and calls old dances. Again, it is a nostalgic event with little real connection to the past.

Prairie du Rocher's most recent claim to fame is one that the village would rather not repeat, the flood of 1993. The year was one of devastating floods all over the midwest. Prairie du Rocher's fight to maintain the creek levees was news not only all over the country, but internationally as well.

The old attitude of self-determination and ignoring officials showed up during the battle to save the Mississippi levee. When the Corps of Engineers felt the levee near Fort de Chartres was going to break and wanted to abandon it because of the danger, the local farmers refused and continued working to keep the levee stable. That levee held, but further upriver the levee was breached. This made flooding of the homes in the community outside the creek levee inevitable. The village was still protected by the creek levees, but those were not designed to hold back the Mississippi River.

The town also made the news because the Corps of Engineers made an unprecedented decision—to cut an opening in the Mississippi levee to give an exit for the water, hoping to prevent overtopping the creek levees and to preserve the village. The cut was made; however the opening could not be enlarged quickly enough to discharge the volume of water coming down.

A local construction firm took the initiative, deciding that the only hope for the town lay in blowing out a section of the levee with dynamite, to allow more rapid egress of the water. The governor of Illinois was called out of bed about 2 A.M. for permission to do this. At 4 A.M. the first charge was blown. There were fears the saturated earth in the levees might fail from the reverberation of the blast, but they held. At 5 A.M. another section was blown; this relieved the pressure sufficiently so that the river did not overtop the creek levee.

The town was saved, but the homes located outside the north creek levee were inundated over the rooftops. Many were destroyed beyond repair. Help in the cleanup not only came from within the community but from outside as well. A group of Mennonites did a tremendous amount of work. For many local people this was the first contact they had had with this religious body, and it was an eye-opener. Their generosity and faith impressed the local people. In 1994 the village received the Governor's Home Town award for their efforts during the flood.

The school population was impacted by the flood; previously the enrollment had been 220-225 children, and immediately afterwards it dropped to 137. However, it has been climbing back since and now is about 180, including pre-school children.

This local school provides education only through the eighth grade. Prairie du Rocher is the only school district in the state that is classified as a non-high school district. Other small towns with only a grade school are part of a larger district that contains a high school within it. Prairie du Rocher students can attend high school in other local communities and state funds will be paid into that district for them; most attend high school in Red Bud or Waterloo. The educational opportunities are quite good. The Red Bud high school has consistently won high placements in the state and national TEAMS (Test of Engineering and Mathematics and Science) which promotes academic competition and achievement. The program is now called WISE (World Wide Use in Science and Engineering), and is even more competitive and demanding. Students from Prairie du Rocher have participated in both programs. About half of the local students continue to college.[50]

The flood had substantial impacts on the area. Where there had been many houses on the other side of the creek associated with the community, now there are only a few. Most people who lost homes moved to neighboring towns. About ninety-five percent of the town of Prairie du Rocher was classified by FEMA (Federal Emergency Management Agency) as floodplain. This means that new homes could not be built unless they were a foot above the hundred-year flood elevation, equivalent to twelve to fourteen feet above ground level. As houses on stilts do not appeal to most people, atheistically or economically, this has prevented new construction in town. In May 2004 this restriction was lifted, as the village was reclassified as out of the floodplain.

At the end of the twentieth century Prairie du Rocher faced problems of most small rural villages—declining businesses, lack of employment, and a more unusual difficulty, the inability to build homes (though this has now changed). The village is not on a major highway leading to any larger town. There is no industry. Problems such as these have lead to the decline and extinction of many small rural towns. Such communities can be glimpsed from any highway—streets with only a few houses, empty lots, and empty businesses. Towns either go up—get bigger—or down and vanish. Prairie du Rocher has done neither. Why? Some thoughts on this follow in the final chapter.

Notes

1. The buggy that he used from 1917 to 1945 is now in the Museum of Transportation in St. Louis.
2. *Prairie du Rocher Sun* June 2, 1905; Sept. 8, 1906.
3. *PdR Sun* June 2, 1905.
4. Revised Ordinances…1915.
5. *PdR Sun* Dec. 1921.
6. Annual inventory books from Connor's Store, 1890 to 1939, donated to the State Historical Library, Springfield, by Meredith Connor. Brennan & Durkin 1974.
7. Brennan and Durkin 1974, 1.
8. Percy Clerc, interview 1978. Generally, names are given only if the informants are deceased. Other referenced interviews are on file, but for privacy the names are not included.
9. Tom Roy 1983.
10. *PdR Sun* Feb. 5, 1932.
11. *PdR Sun* March 1925.
12. *PdR Sun* Oct. 1923; Aug. 1932.
13. *PdR Sun* Sept. 1932.
14. *PdR Sun* June 1926.

15. *PdR Sun* July 1932.
16. *PdR Sun* Jan. 8, 1910.
17. *PdR Sun* April 18, 1910; June 1928; Jan. 17, 1930.
18. *PdR Sun* May 27, 1932.
19. Warranty Deed Lot 146.
20. In 2001, twenty-two persons voted for the trustee positions.
21. Interviews with Leona Ellner, Nora Bies, and others.
22. *Prairie du Rocher Democrat* newspaper May 12, 1906.
23. Carrière 1937, 47.
24. Carrière 1939, 44, 45.
25. Thomas 1979, 4.
26. Leona Ellner 1981.
27. Allen 1963, 54; interviews with Nora Bies, Louise Brands.
28. Reynolds 1852, 81.
29. Carrière 1939, 45.
30. Primm 1900 (my thanks to Ray Bassieur for this reference)
31. Dorrance 1935, 122; Thomas 1978.
32. *Prairie du Rocher Democrat* newspaper Jan. 5, 1907.
33. Interviews with Arthur Bienvenu and Meredith Connors 1977.
34. Interviews with Percy Clerc 1978; Mary Bienvenu 1977; Meredith Connor 1977.
35. Mr. and Mrs. Arthur Bienvenu 1977.
36. *PdR Sun* Jan. 20, 1921.
37. Meredith Connor 1977.
38. St. Jo. Ch. Rec. May, 13, 1906.
39. *PdR Sun* Feb. 1925.
40. Collet 1909, 289; Wild, 1841; Reynolds 1879, 32.
41. Fort de Chartres Archives; 1913 folder.
42. *PdR Sun* Nov. 1921.
43. *PdR Sun* April 1, 1949 35:13; Aug. 26, 1949 35:34.
44. *PdR Sun* March 10, 1950.
45. General Planning and Resources Consultants, Inc.
46. Brown, W.C. 1979.
47. Reynolds 1852, 52.
48. Connor's Store letter 4/28/1948.
49. *PdR Sun* Jan 6, 1950.
50. Thanks to Kathy Franklin and article in *North County News* by Amy Barbeau June 20, 2002.

9

Present and Future

The village of Prairie du Rocher still exists in the bottomlands, having survived for nearly 300 years. It is the only one of the former French villages that remains as a small rural village. In the eyes of the local inhabitants, the present and future are naturally more important than the past. However, as for every community, the past has contributed significantly to the configuration of the present.

This chapter tries to round out the social history of the community. In no way does it pretend to have produced the final analysis of the village, instead, it presents ideas for reflection. This chapter is not based on documents, as the preceding chapters have been, but on observation, and particularly with interviews with local citizens. Their opinions and perceptions about the present and future of the village define the local views of the community.

In the introduction the following questions were asked: Does the French ethnic heritage still influence the community? Do the values of the local population, expressed verbally or through community interaction, reflect the past?

The answer to the first question is simple—consciously no. Prairie du Rocher is not a French village. The language, culture ,and customs have vanished. La Guiannée still is sung on New Year's Eve, but it is now a curiosity, with little meaning to most of the townspeople, although they maintain a certain pride in it.

A community awareness of the existence of the French heritage remains. Occasionally programs are given at the grade school about La Guiannée or on other French-related topics. Suggestions have been made to include French in the school curriculum, but no real demand for it exists. An adult class in the French language was held many years ago, but it did not persist for long. An annual eighth grade essay contest was established by the La Guiannée Society in memory of Percy Clerc, the former leader of the group. The purpose of the essay contest is to promote appreciation of the cultural heritage of the community. Each year the students' essays are reviewed by a committee and awards are given for the best three essays. Through this contest the children derive some knowledge of the history of the village.

The local informants mentioned the historical background as an attraction for new people to move into town. Although this also was cited by some newer residents, the historical aspect the newcomers visualize is the architecture of the Victorian-era homes. Only a few of these exist in town; none of the French architectural heritage homes are available for purchase, and restoration and their significance is not recognized.

The only real value of the French heritage perceived by people is its draw for tourism. The community views tourism from at least two perspectives. The local businesses feel exploitation of the historical aspects of the town would be useful for them in obtaining more trade and in improving the economic situation. Some individuals, however, don't want tourism. They don't want tour buses through the area, and just wish to be left alone.

Those persons who feel tourism would be of economic benefit recognize that the village needs to coordinate activities with Fort de Chartres Historic Site, the major nearby tourist attraction. The fort, operated by the Illinois Historic Preservation Agency, is only four miles away and is accessed by Highway 155, which runs through the town. Throughout the year the fort attracts tour buses and school groups, and on weekends holds special events and activities culminating on the first weekend in June with the Rendezvous, which attracts an estimated 20,000 people. Some of these tourists eat in town or shop for snack supplies and food for weekend re-enactment camping. Other historical attractions in the National Register French Colonial District are Fort Kaskaskia and the Pierre Menard Home. The road that leads to these sites from Prairie du Rocher is Market Street, where the Creole House still stands. The ferry crossing the Mississippi River to Ste. Genevieve, Missouri, can be accessed off this road also.

Most persons feel that the community has not exploited its potential for attracting tourists interested in history, but there is a notable lack of ideas on how to do this promotion. Problems in obtaining funding for any possible projects play a strong part in the lack of initiative.

Although the fort personnel are well liked, "the state" is a negative concept. Fears always seem to exist that "the state" will take over anything historic and prevent the locals from doing what they want. On the other hand, the lack of financing for tourism-related activities also leads to hope for assistance from the government.

The question about the continuity of values may be answered more affirmatively. Family and church orientation are two values that have always been of importance, and they continue to be expressed today as such, both verbally and in action. These values reflect the community's perception of how life should be organized.

In Canada the survival of cultural features from the French period to the modern day was felt to be:

> (i) the religiosity of the French-Canadian family; (ii) its familism as an integrated value system; (iii) the operative significance of the "family" in the sense of a wider kin group; (iv) economic and aspirational limitations arising from the cold facts of economic dominance by those of English origin.[1]

Much of this is operative also in Prairie du Rocher. The structure of the community still rests strongly on the family. One needs only to listen to a conversation discussing local people to be aware of this. The relationships among all the participants are detailed meticulously—she used to be a —; married a cousin of —; or, he is the son of my uncle's boy.

The politeness mentioned in earlier years continues to be manifested in their interaction with strangers, but the family predominates. One lady who lived in the community for a while and then moved said, "Everyone is very friendly and warm, but they don't drop in or visit around, only within their family."

One informant related that in the 1930s his family did not fit in. One parent was neither Catholic nor French. He and his brothers were picked last when a group of boys formed a team, since the boys selected their relatives first. Although the local people were "great party people, our folks were not asked." He did not find people unfriendly, just that their family was a little on the outside. He hastened to add that things were not that way now. In the more recent past one man said that his brother had married a first cousin of his wife, and a second brother married another first cousin, "you get related real quickly that way."

Intricate and multiple family relationships exist between many of the inhabitants, particularly those of long entrenched French families. Outlanders are integrated more readily now than in the past, but single individuals are less readily accepted than couples or families. This assimilation, though, is made into institutions—government, church, civic organizations—but the basic interaction remains at the familial level.

The Catholic Church is still the centralizing institution. It is the focus not only for church services, but for many other activities in town as well. The church hall, in the lower part of the church-owned school building, is used for senior citizen meetings, luncheons, quilting, and numerous other events. The congregation of St. Joseph's currently numbers about 170 households or individuals—an estimated 500 souls. The small Baptist church continues. Some Protestants go to church in neighboring communities, and others do not attend at all.

Additional values appear that might reflect the community's heritage. Prairie du Rocher has maintained an attitude of indepen-

View of today's Prairie du Rocher, taken from the creek levee. Fallow fields lie in the foreground and the steeple of St. Joseph's rises in the center.

dence from its beginning, and has distanced itself from from governmental activity since the days of British rule. Nowadays, of course, projects for improvements and development tend to involve government agencies at various levels. Needs often conflict with the desire for independence. This ambivalent attitude was evident after the flood of 1993, when governmental assistance was available in many areas. According to some residents, not all the possible grants and funding for projects were sought energetically by the village board. Government continues to be a negative concept "People like government just to stay away." Involvement in local politics is not strong. Often it is difficult to get persons to run for the village board and president. A comment was that "anybody new could move in and run for mayor; they'd get elected right away."[2] The idea is that no local person would want the job.

Certain attitudes appear to be consistent through time. The quote given earlier, "the creek is, besides General Apathy, the greatest menace and drawback to the town"[3] seems to hold true today. The creek does continue to be a major factor in the town. The levees along its banks were all that held back the river in 1993. Most villagers came and made tremendous efforts that year to fight the Mississippi River. There were a few who just came and watched.

The only volunteer organization that has consistent vitality is the Volunteer Fire Department, with a team of about twenty-five men. People in the village are proud of the firemen, their abilities and responsiveness to calls. Volunteerism in other areas is sporadic. Over the years there have been a chamber of commerce, an improvement association, and a beautification committee for upgrading town appearance and development purposes. These organizations seem to come and go, although the small group of people involved in them generally accomplishes projects. The present one has been successful in planning, raising money, and developing a much needed park.

Several organizations from within the village participate in the Rendezvous, with food stands at the fort and in town, but the general, town response to Rendezvous is to bring out lawn chairs for the parade, watch it, then go back in the house. This seems to be a pattern; there have been periods of organizational effort in the past, then everything was left to tick along.

The village still acts as an integrated community, not overtly in volunteerism, but in readiness to assist when need arises. One man spoke of an incident in his childhood when he fell off his bike, scraped his knee, and a woman in a nearby house bandaged it. He said the woman was not unique in helping—anyone would have. Women bring in food for funeral lunches, elderly citizens are driven to medical appointments, and people from the community residing in the nursing home in Red Bud are visited regularly. On a wider scale, there are donations for assistance for families experiencing major medical expenses, and support for dinner or dances held to raise money to benefit someone in need, such as a man badly injured in a farm accident. This friendliness and the readiness to assist when needed was mentioned by several people as one of the features that they saw and valued in the town. These activities are not unique to Prairie du Rocher but the concerned involvement shows that it is still a community, and still a network of relationships.

One reflection of the past appears in the fact that social control remains largely at the village level. Crime is infrequent and the more violent crimes virtually non-existent. This has been the pattern from the initial settlement. The idea that people in the village "pretty well take care of themselves," expressed by one person, is seen as positive by many. Another informant recognized the existence of internal social control and cited as a indication of this the fact that there is no non-emergency telephone number for the police.

The same types of problems that occurred in the past continue—bar fights, disturbance of the peace, petty thefts, and domestic problems. Few incidents ever get beyond local resolution, even to the county level. There are few thefts and when these occur, recognition of the identity of the perpetrators may lead to reproof and restitution, but not criminal charges. The resistance to outside government and the imposition of external control continues. The village is connected to the wider world; it is known that illegal drugs are present. Action to remedy this problem would require a higher level of authority, but there does not seem to be enough pressure for it.

The local governing body continues to be the president and board of trustees.[4] Although the president is generally referred to as the mayor, as the position is called in other towns, his title is still properly the president of the board of trustees. People sometimes speak disparagingly of the board and its work and feel they haven't done enough for the town. Political involvement is, as it was in the past, moderate.

The ongoing focus of village life on family, church, and local interaction, does not imply lack of knowledge or involvement in a larger world. The villagers in the past traveled far and wide, and they still do. Out-migration has occurred over the years. Relatives are widespread and visits to them extend over the whole country. Vacations are taken in other parts of the United States and abroad, although few have gone to explore their ancestry in France or Alsace-Lorraine.

Television—local and cable—satellite dishes, and computers are everywhere. Farmers' discussions over coffee include the Internet now, and the town has a web site.

But what about the future? Will the village continue to survive under the modern pressures of centralizing government and urban development? Most sociologists do not give a favorable prognosis for the future of small communities in the twenty-first century. Small rural towns throughout the country are struggling for survival. The problems they face are the ever expanding demands for public services—water, sewer, roads, and schools—that cannot be supported by a restricted tax base.[5]

Major improvements in public utilities would be impossible for Prairie du Rocher if based on local taxes alone. Since the village has maintained a grocery store, school, bank, and church, it is eligible for assistance in government grants as an ongoing viable community. The Volunteer Fire Department obtains its equipment partly through grants and partly through fund-raisers. Some funding comes through the fire dues requested of each inhabitant, but these are minimal charges that do not provide a large income.

New water service recently was developed. Again, funding came through grants and loans. Sewers and a sewage treatment facility were installed in 1970. Recent improvements to the sewage lagoons came through a grant received because of the flood of 1993. The protective berms around the tanks were raised to meet the requirement for greater holding in case of high water again.

Despite the small tax base, Prairie du Rocher has been able to maintain its infrastructure successfully. The need for grants to achieve this restricts its freedom in decision making. Like most small governing bodies, the board is severely limited in what it can do. There has been a constant loss of autonomy, and the actions of the board are hemmed in by an increasing number of federal and state laws and regulations. This is a problem seen by sociologists who observe that small towns have to "adjust their actions to either the regulations and laws defined by state and federal agencies...or to the fact that outside agencies have the power to withhold subsidies to local political institutions."[6] No longer can Prairie du Rocher casually dispense with primaries or other formalities. State rules governing municipalities have to be observed.

Continuing trends in the wider society are to consolidate schools, to develop corporations from individual farmsteads, and to decrease the authority of small town governments through the growing involvement of state and federal agencies. Cities and suburbs, consolidated and regional units, and agribusiness are more viable today. These trends have been reflected in Prairie du Rocher. Starting as early as the 1930s, the small one-room schools, the parochial school, and the high school underwent consolidation. However, as mentioned earlier, the village has been able to maintain the elementary school and its unique position as a non-high district.

Agriculture always has been the mainstay of the economy of the area and remains so today, but it is a very different kind of farming than in the old days. Agricultural college training provides information on new strains of crops and new methods, including computerized analysis of soils—skills needed in a competitive market today. Some men are full-time farmers, but more are part-time with second jobs, and many farm wives work outside the home.

The increasing tendency in agriculture is towards corporate farms. Some local farms now are family corporations, but the next step (foreseen by informants) is the shift to non-family corporations, as has occurred in other areas. Nationwide, major corporations control most of the dairy, poultry, and hog markets, and grain cartels monopolize the corn, soybean, and wheat production. One man said that his son wants to continue the family farm, but he advised him against it, as he feels there is no future for small farms.

The nationwide trends to malls and large chain stores affect small communities. In the 1930s Prairie du Rocher had thirty-five businesses, now there are fewer than a dozen. Where formerly five or six stores sold groceries, now there is only one, the former Connor's store, presently Huntley's. The "business district" contains a bank, a barbershop, two taverns, a flower shop, and two restaurants. Two former gas stations in town still do repair work on cars, trucks, and tractors, but no longer dispense gas. New government regulations requiring replacement of underground gas tanks, and the major oil companies' desire to have "mini-marts," represented too great an investment for the amount of usage in the rural area. The "mill," Farm Service, has installed gas and diesel pumps—a boon to the town, as otherwise fuel would be about twelve miles away.

The town never has had an industry. In one sense that has been to its advantage, for it never had an economy built around one factory, only to have that later fail, as has occurred elsewhere. Sporadic attempts have been made to attract industry, mainly through the county government economic development office. The quarry outside town does not provide much employment for townspeople. Although attracting industry often is seen as the panacea for the lack of jobs in a rural area, this is not as simple as it sounds.

> At least a partial myth exists among the planners for non-metropolitan communities that "industry" will bring general economic and social betterment regardless of the circumstances...anticipation that the economic benefits of the industry will remain largely in the community. This frequently does not happen.[7]

This indeed is recognized by the locals. A few years ago a limestone industry was proposed on the bluffs, but the feeling was that hiring would not be from the town. The industry did not materialize.

The lack of jobs forces many people, particularly the younger ones, to look elsewhere for work, but this has been true throughout the village's history. There has been constant out-migration. Many women work outside the home, but women who want careers generally have to move to the city. The society is strongly family oriented, and marriage is still the expected goal for a woman. Numerous people work in nearby towns or commute to St. Louis, which is about an hour or more distant, depending on the destination. Commuting this distance or for that amount of time is not unusual these days. Residents of suburbs outside large cities often have a similar commute. But the lack of jobs causes many to feel pessimistic about the village's future.

Small towns all over the country have been losing population. Prairie du Rocher has not. Its population has stayed fairly consistent in numbers, and also in demographic balance. In 1965 a preliminary development plan for the village done by a county planning project commented on the population.

The present population contains a relatively high proportion of persons over retirement age, and a large proportion of workers whose jobs are in other places; it is expected that Prairie du Rocher will become even more a location for retired persons and commuting workers. (See chart below.)

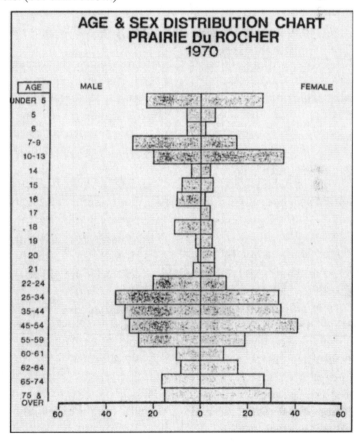

Although there continues to be many widows and retired persons, the present population profile of the community shows a strong representation of families with school-age children. The population has been relatively stable since 1960, between 600 and 700, except when the flood caused a temporary decline.

All of the local hopes for future residential development hinged on the planned improvements to the levees. Now that the village is classified officially as being out of the floodplain, new housing construction can take place. Growth in housing in the future is needed to stabilize existing numbers and to allow for increase in the population. The last housing development was built about thirty-five years ago. Without new housing it is unlikely that there will be any increase in local businesses either.

After the flood, the water system was upgraded by running a line from Ruma along State Highway 155, and this may lead to expansion of housing on the hills. Some see this as beneficial to the town. Others think that it will not lead to any increase in business in town, feeling that people living up there will be oriented away from the village towards their jobs in other communities, and will do their shopping there, also.

Those who were inclined to be pessimistic when asked about Prairie du Rocher's future cited many of the problems mentioned above. "Town's not going anywhere, its going backwards, it can't expand." Restrictions on the construction of farm sheds and fences in the bottomland outside the village are resented; there is the feeling that the farmlands are seen as merely open space for diversion of flood waters. "The Corps wants to make us a swamp."

For most small towns the lack of industry and employment is one of the more severely damaging elements, but some residents feel this disadvantage may be offset by other factors, particularly the exodus from the cities by people seeking safe and quiet homes. Many local people view this as the salvation of the village. Urban dwellers tiring of the fast pace of the city, the dangers on the streets, and the high price of real estate, are looking towards rural settings. The attitude of some urban residents is shifting from seeing the cities desirable for their many social activities, to an interest in a more tranquil life in a smaller circle of friends. Even within cities there is the tendency to focus on "neighborhoods," as a way to integrate the inhabitants. Rural towns provide this type of interaction.[9] Locally most people feel that the pleasant rural area, the slower pace, safety, and security, are factors to draw new residents. Children can ride their bicycles all over town, people can go for a walk in the evening in safety and the car can be left unlocked in the grocery parking lot—these are factors that have become important in society today.

Many informants stated that the most important positive elements for them and the reasons why they felt new people would come were the friendly, concerned attitude of the people and the lack of pressures. The townspeople were seen as "laid back," not driven by ambition, and life in town is safe, secure, and tranquil. A negative view of this attitude was expressed too, in terms of "staying in their shell where it is safe."

People inside and outside the village saw the inhabitants as friendly, polite, tolerant, and always helpful, attitudes of course not confined to Prairie du Rocher. But several persons felt there were differences in these attitudes between Prairie du Rocher and other nearby communities. One person said she felt an outsider in another nearby town, and that here there were roots. The sense of roots in the community may be due to the familial social structure. Although values might be the same in another town, the loss of the integrative supporting social group could make the other community seem less desirable.

Like the nineteenth century historians, a few informants observed that the people were neither aggressive nor highly ambitious. That is not to say that they do not desire comfortable homes, good education for their children, a new car or truck, vacation travel, and a secure retirement. Most homes are well cared for and equipped with all modern conveniences, but they are for family living, not show. Conspicuous consumption is not a value now, anymore than when Reynolds commented earlier on wealth and ambition. The people who want to live here have found that "wealth alone does not make a good life." They are not ambitious, at least for wealth, important jobs, social standing, and keeping up with the Joneses. The people in the community prefer the safety, security, and tranquillity of the familial community to the impersonal, frequently dangerous life of the city. Those who are ambitious for financial success and social prominence move out, going where more opportunities for such are available.

Sociologists recognize this pattern in studies of small communities.

> The men and women who choose a rural residence and a rural-based occupation today, or in the immediate future, also accept a slower rate of upward social mobility. Along with this, however, they also may enjoy a greater stability in their occupational career and style of life.[10]

The values expressed by the present day inhabitants echo the values cited by the early nineteenth-century observers—friendly, not aggressive, unambitious, content. It can be questioned whether this attitude has come from the past, or whether people with like temperaments to those already residing in the village were attracted there. As noted earlier, by 1850 less than half of the residents were descendants of the original French settlers. The society has either made the emigrants over into the image of the town, or people came because the town had the cultural values they preferred. The question whether or not these are cultural values from the past, or associative values gained by temperamentally adapted newcomers through social interaction, cannot be fully resolved. Such a predominance of continuity of values does suggest strongly that certain behavioral elements of the earlier culture may exist despite the loss of more observable cultural elements.

The feeling expressed in an editorial in the local paper in 1932 still seems to sum up the feelings most often expressed by residents about living in Prairie du Rocher and their hopes for its future.

> There are advantages to living in the small town that wealth, position, and all the goods the gods may bestow cannot compensate. The wail of the man who has left the small town and made a place for

himself, all the money he needs, fame as well as fortune, in the big city, is that all is as dross compared with the friendliness of the small town.

There is a feeling of stability in living in a town where most everybody owns his home, where you are greeted on a walk down the street by your first name…

It is a social privilege to see your friends easily and frequently without having to make a date a week ahead as one must do in meeting the exactions of social life in a city.

If sorrow enters the home, there are many to render the little services that are nothing in themselves, but speak volumes in tender solicitude when extended in behalf of a neighbor. In the big city you are just one of thousand pegging away…

In the small town there may be frequent or infrequent gossip you would rather had not been spread; lack of fine concerts, and one thing or another you would have different, but when a balance has been struck if you are wise you will be grateful you live in a small town where you can share your joys as well as your sorrow with friends, who are friends in stormy weather as well as in fair.[11]

Downtown Prairie du Rocher

Notes

1. Ishwaran 1976, 27.
2. Interviews on file.
3. *PdR Sun* Jan. 8, 1918.
4. In 2001 no one filed for president, but there were three names for write-in votes. The instructions for the ballots included the fact that it was necessary to write Village President as the title; if mayor was written the vote wouldn't count. The new Village President was elected by 129 votes out of 160 voting residents.
5. Ford 1978, 127.
6. Vidick and Bensman 1966, 204.
7. Ford 1978, 83-84.
8. General Planning…1965, 22.
9. Ford 1978, 123.
10. Ford 1978, 219.
11. *PdR Sun* June 10, 1932.

APPENDIX

Population Summary

One difficulty in obtaining accurate numerical data for the community of Prairie du Rocher is the spacial definition of the community. The village boundaries are not coterminous with the community; this community is formed from a wider geographical area with people whose focus is on the village. Family ties, economic interaction, church attendance, and schools integrate a larger area than the corporate limits. The total geographical area of community activity can only be estimated. Surnames were used as an indication of social groupings that extended beyond the legal boundary. Despite the boundary problems and the subjective method used for some aspects, the information below can be used in comparative studies of other small communities as it is felt that it does represent demographic change over time.

Census Data: Summary and Sources

Year	Pop.	Source
1723	126	Fort de Chartres area and Meramec (ANC C13A 8:226 in Norton 1935:xxi); including Kaskaskia and Cahokia 334.
1726	208	Fort de Chartres area (ANC G1 A1:464 1/1/1726); Kaskaskia and additional persons (not Cahokia), estimated 600.
1732	317	Fort de Chartres, St. Philippe, Prairie du Rocher and military (ANC G1 A1:464, 1/1/1732); the whole Illinois country estimated 729.
1752	101	Prairie du Rocher 13 households
	539	Prairie du Rocher, Fort de Chartres, St. Philippe (not including military)(Vaudreuil Papers, Kathrine Seineke); all villages 1621.

1767	(25)	families (Alvord and Carter, 1916:469)
1769	(24)	*habitants* (Alvord and Carter 1921:550)
1783	(64)	heads of family Prairie du Rocher, St. Philippe (Mason, 1890, 66-67)
1787	(79)	heads of family and male children only, Prairie du Rocher (Alvord, 1909, 419-420); estimated additional women, 160.
1800	212	Prairie du Rocher township (Fed. Census, Norton 1935:xxviii)
1807	(43)	estimated over 21 years (Indiana Historical Society, 1980)
1810	293	Illinois census (Norton 1935:14) (based on names)

For the federal censuses from 1820-1850, where areas within Randolph County were not separated, an estimate was made based on the names of the persons enumerated.

1820	306	Illinois census Randolph County (Norton 1934) (based on names)
1825	352	Illinois census, Randolph Co., Prairie du Rocher village and township; heads of family, 38.
1830	503	Federal census, Illinois p. 135-137 (based on names)
1839	526	St. Joseph Church census
1840	669	Federal census (based on names), p. 206-208.
1849	471	St. Joseph Church census
1850	683	Federal census, village and additional persons based on names
1860	619	Federal census (Prairie du Rocher post office)
1870	118	Federal census (Prairie du Rocher post office)
1880	1185	Federal census (Prairie du Rocher village and precinct)
1900	347	village General Planning and Resource

1910	511	village General Planning and Resource
1920	535	village General Planning and Resource
1930	510	village General Planning and Resource
1940	576	village General Planning and Resource
1950	622	village General Planning and Resource
1960	679	village, precinct 1219, village about 65 percent of total (General Planning and Resource)
1970	658	village General Planning and Resource
1980	704	village, 287 housing units (Federal census)
1990	700	village (Federal census); 617 registered voters in precinct

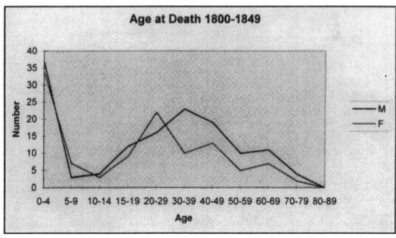

Figure 4

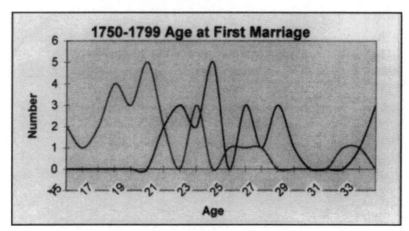

Figure 5

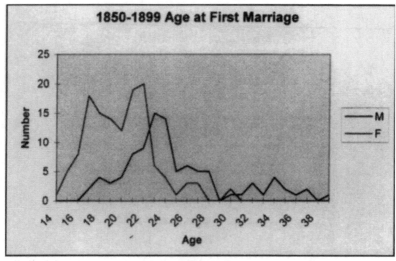

Figure 6

Table 5
Family Size

	Sample Size Families	Total Number Children	Average Family Size
1722 1749	16	67	4.18
1750 1799	35	248	7.08
1800 1849	128	793	6.19

Table 6
Number of Months Between Births

	Sample	Months-Average
Marr. to 1st child	91	14
Between 1st - 2nd	106	23
2nd - 3rd	98	29
3rd - 4th	77	29
4th - 5th	58	25
5th - 6th	41	26
6th - 7th	37	28
7th - 8th	29	24
8th - 9th	20	24
9th - 10th	11	27
10th - 11th	8	26

GLOSSARY

arpent	lineal measure, approx. 192 ft., or 57.84 meters; area measure, 3399.48 square meters, or approximately .85-acre
aune	a measure of cloth 1.18 meters long
bateau	"Larger than pirogues and built of several pieces of timber, they were flat bottomed and pointed of bow and stern. One end was covered with hoops of cloth for protecting the stores. They carried sails, and when the wind was unfavorable, they were oared or poled." (Belting 1975, 64)
capot	a blanket coat with a short cape, which could form a hood
dit	so-called, nicknamed
engagé	hired worker
faux saunier	contraband salt dealer
league	approx. 2.5 miles but was highly variable (Galloway 1982, 29)
livre	amount of weight equal to 380-550 grams varying by province; the monetary unit equals 20 *sous* (Paucton 1780)
métis	half-French, half-Indian children

minot	dry measure, 70 lbs. (Surrey 1916, 291)
pièce d'Inde	"standard value of a complete negro, that is seventeen years or over without bodily defects, or a negress without bodily defects, of fifteen to thirty years, or three children of eight to ten years in age." (Belting 1975, 38)
pied	"foot;" equals 12¾" English
pirogue	a dugout canoe made of a hollowed out tree, often very large
pot	96 cubic *pouce* equals 63.4 oz., which equals half-gallon. 31.6.24.1 cask of brandy sold in lots of four *pots* per lot; five lots equals twenty *pots*, which equals one cask
pouce	"inch;" equals 1.06" English inch
toise	equals 1.95 meters; 30 toises per *arpent*

REFERENCES

Archival Sources and Manuscripts

Archives Nationales des Colonies. C13 series. (Microfilm in the Library of Congress)

Austin, David. "The Years of Major Macarty: the Village of Fort de Chartres in the 1750s." Master's thesis. Southern Illinois University: Carbondale, 1982.

Brennan, Linda and Julie Durkin, "Connor's Store Records: An Account of Changing Times." 1974. Mss.

Briggs, Winstanley, "A Most Peculiar Institution: Slavery in French Colonial Illinois." Paper for Illinois History Symposium. nd. Mss.

Briggs, Winstanley. "The Forgotten Colony: le Pays des Illinois." Ph.d. thesis. University of Chicago, 1985.

Brown, Margaret Kimball, "Testing at the Laurent Site (R-125)." 1971. Mss.

Courville, Serge, "L'Origine du Rang du Quebec: La Politique territoriale de La France dans la Premiere Moitie du 17e Siecle." Paper presented at the eighth annual meeting of the French Colonial Historical Society, Evanston, Ill. nd. Mss.

Dean, Lawrie Cena and Margaret Kimball Brown, "The Kaskaskia Manuscripts 1714-1816: A Calendar of Civil Documents in Colonial Illinois." Randolph County, Ill. Microfilm. 1981.

Ekberg, Carl. "Marie Rouensa 8cate8a and the Origins of French Illinois." nd. Mss.

James O'Hara Denny diary of 1839, Indiana State Library, Indianapolis. Mss.

Lessard, Renald, Jacques Mathieu, and Lina Gouger, "Peuplement Colonisation au pays des Illinois." Paper presented at the Twelfth Meeting of the French Colonial Historical Society, Ste. Genevieve, Missouri. 1986.

Louisiana State Museum Archives. "Black Books." Cabildo Records.

Nelson, Paula. "Sainte Anne: The Populating of a French Parish in the Illinois Country." Masters thesis, Illinois State University, 1993.

Norris, F. Terry. "The Illinois Country–Lost and Found: Assessment of the Archaeological Remains of the French Settlements in the Central Mississippi River Valley, 1673-1763." Dissertation. St. Louis University, 1997.

Origin and History of Public Lands. Vol. 833. Auditor of Public Lands. Illinois State Archives. Typescript, bound.

Palm, Sr. Mary Borgia. "Jesuit Missions of the Illinois Country, 1673-1763." Dissertation. St. Louis University, 1931.

Reyes, Claudia. "Demographic Study of Prairie du Rocher Cemetery." 1975. Mss.

St. Joseph's Church Records. St. Joseph's Church, Prairie du Rocher, Ill.

Vaudueil Papers. Henry E. Huntington Library and Art Gallery, San Marino, Calif.

Government Records

American State Papers: Indian Affairs. Documents Legislative and

Circuit Court Records. Randolph County, Ill.

County Commissioners' Court Records, 1824-1832. Randolph County, Ill.

Court of Common Pleas Records. Randolph County, Ill.

Court of Quarterly Sessions and Court of Appeals, 1802-1807. Randolph County, Ill.

Deed Records. Randolph County, Ill.

Depositions taken in Cahokia and Kaskaskia Claims, 1807-1814. Kaskaskia Series 49D. Illinois State Archives.

Essex County Quarterly Courts. Records and Files, Vol. 3. Essex County, Mass.

Illinois Constitution of 1818. Article 6. Springfield, Ill.

Illinois Constitution of 1848. Article 11. Springfield. Ill.

Journal of the Continental Congress. 19:4:157.

Kaskaskia Church Records, 1695-1834. Archives of the Diocese of Belleville, Ill.

Kaskaskia Manuscript Collection, 1708-1816. Randolph County Clerk's Office, Randolph County, Ill.

Poor Book. Kaskaskia Township, Overseers of Poor, 1809-1826. Chicago Historical Society.

Laws of the State of Illinois, 1821. An Act appointing Trustees of...the Village of Prairie du Rocher. 163.

—. 1823. An Act amending an act entitled "An Act appointing Trustees for…the village of Prairie du Rocher." 142.

—. 1845. An Act for the Protection and summary recovery for trepass committed upon the Commons of "Prairie du Rocher." 307.

—. 1851. An Act to Provide for leasing the land granted as a commons to the inhabitants of the town of Prairie du Rocher, in Randolph county, or so much of said land as it may be the interest of the inhabitants of the said town to lease, for school purposes. 51-56.

—. 1852. An Act to amend (above). 98.

—. *1853.* An Act to provide for the draining of wet lands of the proprietors of the common field of Prairie du Rocher, in Randolph county. 249-251.

—. 1855. An Act to amend (above). 112.

—. 1857. An Act to vacate the town plat of Prairie du Rocher, in Randolph county and to authorize the sale of vacant lots in the said village of Prairie du Rocher. 619-621.

—. 1863. An Act supplementary to an act entitled (above). 273

—. 1933. An Act to amend (above) HB 807 and amendments; HB 771.

Prairie du Rocher. Revised Ordinances of *the Village of Prairie du Rocher, Randolph County, State of Illinois.* 1915. Prairie du Rocher: Democrat Publishing.

Probate Records. Randolph County, Ill.

Territorial Papers of the United States. *Territory of Indiana,*

1800-1810. Vol. 7. 1939; *Territory of Illinois,* 1809-1814. Vol. 16.
1948. *Territory of Illinois,* 1814-1818. Vol. 17. Government Printing Office: Washington, D. C.

War of the Rebellion Official Records, Union and Confederate
armies.

Publications

Allen, John W. *Legends and Lore of Southern Illinois.* Carbondale:
Southern Illinois University Press, 1963.

Alvord, Clarence W. *Cahokia Records,* 1778-1790, Virginia Series
1 of Collections of the Illinois State Historical Library, Vol. 2.
1907.

—. *Kaskaskia Records, 1778-1790.* Virginia Series 2 of Collections
of the Illinois State Historical Library, Vol. 5, 1909.

—. *The Illinois Country 1673-1818.* 1922. Reprint, The American
West Reprint Series. Loyola University Press: Chicago, 1965.

Alvord, Clarence W. and Clarence E. Carter. *The Critical Period,*
1763-1765. British Series I of Collections of the Illinois State
Historical Library, Vol. 10. Springfield, Ill., 1915.

—. *The New Regime, 1765-1767.* British Series 2 of Collections of
the Illinois State Historical Library, Vol. 11. Springfield, Ill., 1916.

—. *Trade and Politics, 1767-1769.* British Series 3 of Collections
of the Illinois State Historical Library, Vol. 16. Springfield, Ill.,
1921.

Antmann, Willy. *Music in Canada, 1600-1800.* Ontario: Habitex
Books, 1975.

Arnold, Morris S. *Unequal Laws unto a Savage Race: European Legal Traditions in Arkansas, 1686-1836.* University of Arkansas Press: Fayetteville, 1985.

Baade, Hans. W. "Marriage Contracts in French and Spanish Louisiana: a study in 'notarial' jurisprudence." *Tulane Law Review,* 53, 1 (1979), 3-92.

Baker, Vaughan, Amos Simpson, Mathé Allain. "Le Mari est Seigneur: Marital laws governing women in French Louisiana." In: *Louisiana's Legal Heritage,* ed. Edward F. Haas. Pensacola, Florida: Perdido Bay Press, 1983.

Balesi, Charles J. *The Time of the French in the Heart of North America, 1673-1818.* Alliance Française: Chicago, 1992.

Belting, Natalia Marie. *Kaskaskia under the French Regime.* 1948. Reprint, New Orleans: Polyanthos Press, 1975.

Benson, Adolph B., ed. *Peter Kalms Travels in North America.* New York: Wilson-Erickson, 1937.

Berry, Daniel. "Illinois Earthquake of 1811 and 1812." *Transactions of the Illinois State Historical Society for the Year 1907,* 12, (1908).

Birkbeck, Morris. *Notes on a Journey in America.* 1817. Reprint, Ann Arbor: University Microfilms, 1965.

Boggess, Arthur C. *The Settlement of Illinois, 1778-1830.* Ann Arbor: University Microfilms, 1968.

Bossu, Jean-Bernard. *Travels in the Interior of North America, 1751-1762.* Trans. & ed. Seymour Feiler. Norman: University of Oklahoma Press, 1962.

Boyle, Susan C. "Did She Generally Decide? Women in Ste. Genevieve, 1750-1805." *William and Mary Quarterly 5:* series 3, (1983), 44:4.

Brackenridge, Henry M. *Recollections of Persons and Places in the West.* Philadelphia: J. B. Lippincott, 1868.

Briggs, Asa. *Social History of England.* New York: Viking Press, 1983.

Brown, Margaret Kimball. *Cultural Transformation among the Illinois: An Application of a Systems Model.* Publications of the Museum 1:3. East Lansing: Michigan State University, 1979.

—. "The Kaskaskia Manuscripts." *Illinois Libraries* 62, 4 (1980), 312-324.

—. "Allons, Cowboys!" *Journal of the Illinois State Historical Society* 76, 4 (1983), 273-282.

—. *The Voyageur in the Illinois Country.* Center for French Colonial Studies 3. Naperville, Ill., 2002.

Brown, Margaret Kimball and Lawrie Cena Dean, eds. *The Village of Chartres in Colonial Illinois, 1720-1765.* New Orleans: Polyanthos Press, 1977.

—. *The French Colony in the Mid-Mississippi Valley.* Carbondale: Kestrel Press, 1995.

Brown, Wheelock Crosby. *Restoration Plan for the Henry-Lee-Brickey Creole House, Prairie du Rocher, Illinois.* Washington, Mo.: Wheelock and Co. Architectural Consultants, 1979.

Burnett, Betty. *A Time of Favor.* St. Louis: Patrice Press, 1987.

Burnham, J. H. "An Early Illinois Newspaper." *Transactions of the Illinois State Historical Society for the year 1903*, 8 (1904).

Caldwell, Norman W. *The French in the Mississippi Valley, 1740-1750.* Urbana: University of Illinois Press, 1941.

Carr, Kay J. *Belleville, Ottawa, and Galesburg: Community and Democracy on the Illinois Frontier.* Carbondale: Southern Illinois University Press, 1996.

Carrière, J. M. "Tales from the French Folklore of Missouri." *Northwestern University Studies in the Humanities 1,* 1937.

—. "Life and Customs in the French Villages of the Old Illinois Country, 1763-1939." *Report of the Canadian Historical Association,* 1939. 34-47.

Carter, Clarence E. "Documents Relating to the Occupation of the Illinois Country by the British." *Transactions of the Illinois State Historical Society for the Year 1907,* 12, (1908), 201-221.

—. *Great Britain and the Illinois Country, 1763-1774.* Washington: American Historical Association, 1910.

Charlevoix, Pierre de. *Journal of a Voyage to North America. 1721.* Reprint, Ann Arbor, Mich.: University Microfilms, 1966.

Chartrand, René. "The Troops of French Louisiana, 1699-1769." *Journal of the Company of Military Historians* 25, 2 (1973), 58-65.

Collet, Victor. A *Journey in North America. 1796.* Reprint, Transactions of the Illinois State Historical Society for the year 1908, 13 (1909), 269-298.

Combined History of Randolph, Monroe and Perry Counties,

Illinois. Philadelphia: J. L. Mcdonough & Co., 1883.

Conzan, Kathleen Neils. "Community Studies: Urban History." In *The Past Before Us: Contemporary Writing in the United States.* ed. Michael Kammen. Ithaca, N.Y.: Cornell Press, 1980.

D'amours, Albert. *Mathieu D'amours Sieur de Chaufour et ses descendants.* Vol. 1. Charlesbourg, P.Q.: Les Peres Eudistes, 1974.

Danborn, David B. *Born in the Country: A History of Rural America.* Baltimore: John Hopkins University Press, 1995.

D'Artaguiette, Diron. "Journal of Diron D'Artaguiette." In *Travels in the American Colonies* . ed. N. D. Mereness. New York: Antiquarian Press, Ltd., 1961.

Davis, James E. *Frontier Illinois.* Bloomington: Indiana University Press, 1998.

Deville, Winston. *Louisiana Recruits, 1751-1758.* Cottonport, La.: Polyanthos Press, 1973.

Dictionary of Canadian Biography, 1701-1740. Vol. 2. Toronto: University of Toronto Press, 1969.

Donnelly, Fr. Joseph P. *Pierre Gibault, Missionary, 1737-1802.* Chicago: Loyola University Press, 1971.

Dorn, Walter L. *Competition for Empire.* New York: Harper and Bros., *1940.*

Dorrance, Ward A. *Survival of French in the Old District of Ste. Genevieve.* Columbia: University of Missouri Press, 1935.

Douville, Ramond and Jacques Casanova. *Daily Life in Early Canada.* New York: MacMillan Co., 1968.

Doyle, Don Harrison. *The Social Order of a Frontier Community, Jacksonville, Illinois 1825-70.* Urbana: University of Illinois Press, 1978.

Duby, Georges. *Rural Economy and Country Life in the Medieval West.* Trans. by Cynthia Postan. Columbia, S.C.: University of South Carolina Press, 1976.

Dunn, Jacob P. "The Mission to the Ouabache." *Indiana State Historical Society Publications 3, 4* (1902), 255-330.

Eccles, W. J. *The Government of New France.* Ottawa: Canadian Historial Association Booklets 18, 1968.

—. *The Canadian Frontier 1534-1760.* New York: Holt, Rinehart and Winston, 1969.

—. *France in America.* New York: Harper & Row, 1972.

Ekberg, Carl. *Colonial Ste. Genevieve.* Gerald, Mo.: Patrice Press, 1985.

—. "Agriculture, *Mentalités,* and Violence on the Illinois Frontier." *Illinois Historical Journal* 88, 2, (1995) 101-116.

—. *French Roots in the Illinois Country: The Mississippi Frontier in Colonial Times.* Urbana: University of Illinois Press, 1998.

Edmunds, R. David and Joseph Peyser. *The Fox Wars: The Musquakie Challenge to New France.* Norman: University of Oklahoma Press, 1993.

Faragher, John M. *Sugar Creek: Life on the Illinois Prairie.* New Haven: Yale University Press, 1986.

Farrell, David R. "Reluctant Imperialism; Pontchartrain, Vauban and the Expansion of New France, 1699-1702." In *Proceedings of the Twelfth Meeting of the French Colonial Historical Society Ste. Genevieve, May, 1986.* Lanham, Maryland: University Press of America, 1988.

Fiske, Patricia. ed. *Imported and Domestic Textile in 18th century America.* Irene Emery Roundtable on Museum Textiles, 1975, Proceedings. Washington D.C.: Textile Museum, 1975.

Flagg, Edmund. The Far West 1836-1837. In R. G. Thwaites, ed. *Early Western Travels, 1748-1846.* Cleveland: Arthur H. Clark Co., 1906.

Foley, William E. "Galleries, Gumbo and 'La Guignolée." *Gateway Heritage* 10, 1 (1989), 3-17.

Ford, Thomas. *A History of Illinois from its Commencement as a State in 1818 to 1847.* Ann Arbor: University Microfilms, 1968.

Ford, Thomas R. ed. *Rural United States of America: Persistence and Change.* Ames: Iowa State University Press, 1978.

French, B.F. *Historical Collection of Louisiana and Florida.* New York: Albert Mason, 1875.

French Colonial Historical Society. "Roundtable Discussion of Choquette's 'Frenchmen into Peasants'." 2, (2002), 1-27.

General Planning and Resources Consultants Inc. *Comprehensive Plan of the Village of Prairie du Rocher,* 1965.

Giesey, Ralph E. "Rules of Inheritance and Mobility in Pre-revolutionary France." *American Historical Review* 82, 2, (1977), 271-289.

Gitlin, Jay. "Avec bien du Regret: The Americanization of Creole St. Louis." *Gateway Heritage* 9, 4 (1989), 2-11.

Giraud, Marcel. *Histoire de la Louisiane.* Vols. 1-4. Paris, Presses Universitaires de France, 1953-1966.

—. *A History of French Louisiana: Company of Indies, 1723-31.* Vol. 5. Trans. by Brian Pearce. Louisiana State University Press, 1991.

Greenleaf, Barbara K. *American Fever.* New York: Mentor Books, 1970.

Gums, Bonnie L. *Archaeology at French Colonial Cahokia.* Illinois Historic Preservation Agency: Springfield, 1988.

Gums, Bonnie L. and Charles O. Witty. "A Glimpse of Village Life at Nouvelle Chartres," *Illinois Archaeology* 12, 1, 2 (2000).

Hammes, Raymond H. "Land Transactions in Illinois Prior to the Sale of Public Domain." *Journal of the Illinois State Historical Society* 87, 2 (1984), 101-114.

Hansen, Marcus Lee. *The Atlantic Migration, 1607-1860.* New York: Harper & Row, 1961.

Hardy, James D., Jr. "Transportation of Convicts to Colonial Louisiana." *Louisiana History* 7 (1966), 207-222.

—. "The Superior Council in Colonial Louisiana." In *Frenchmen and French Ways in the Mississippi Valley.* ed. J. F. McDermott. Urbana: University of Illinois Press, 1969.

Harris, N. Dwight. *The History of Negro Servitude in Illinois.* 1904. Reprint. New York: A. C. McClurg Co., 1968.

Harrison, Jane E. "Adieu pour cette année: Seasonality and Time in New France." In *Essays in French Colonial History: Proceedings of the 21st Annual Meeting of the French Colonial Historical Society, East Lansing, Michigan.* East Lansing: Michigan State University Press, 1995.

Henretta, James A. "Families and Farms: Mentalité in Pre-Industrial America." *William and Mary Quarterly* 3, 35 (1978), 1-32.

Higginbotham, Jay. *Old Mobile–Fort Louis de la Louisiane, 1702-1711.* Mobile: Museum of the City of Mobile, 1977.

History of Randolph, Monroe and Perry Counties. Philadelphia: J. L. Mcdonough & Co., n.a. 1883.

Hoffman, Richard C. "Medieval Origins of the Commonfields." In: *European Peasants and their Markets.* ed. William N. Parker and Eric L. Jones. New Jersey: Princeton University Press, 1975.

Houck, Louis *A History of Missouri from the Earliest Exploration and Settlements until the Admission of the State into the Union.* 3 vols. New York: Arno Press, 1908.

Illustrated Historical Atlas Map of Randolph County. W. R. Brink & Co., n.a. 1875.

Index to the 1850 Census of Randolph County. Yakima, Wash.: Yakima Valley Genealogical Society, n.a., 1976.

Census of Indiana Territory for 1807. Indianapolis: Indiana Historical Society, n.a., 1980.

Ishwaran, K., ed. *The Canadian Family.* Toronto: Holt, Rinehart & Winston of Canada, 1976.

James, A. James. *George Rogers Clark Papers.* Virginia Series of Collection of the Illinois State Historical Library, Vol. 8. Springfield, Ill., 1912.

Jelks, Edward, Carl Ekberg and Terrance J. Martin. *Excavation at the Laurens Site.* Studies in Illinois Archaeology 5. Springfield: Illinois Historic Preservation Agency, 1989.

Johnson, Samuel W., Jr. "The Story of the Lee Mansion." *Footprints.* Publication of the Randolph County Historical Society 2, 1 (1986), 4-6.

Keefe, James F. "The Inventory of Fort de Chartres." *Muzzleloader* (1992), 42-44.

Lacroix, Paul. *The Eighteenth Century: Its Institutions, Customs and Costumes, France, 1700-1789.* London: Chapman & Hall, 1876.

Louisiana Historical Quarterly. Vol. I -10. New Orleans: Louisiana Historical Society, 1917-1928.

Margry, Pierre. ed. *Decouvertes et etablissements des Francais dans l'ouest et dans le sud de l'Amerique septentrionale,* 1614-1754. 6 vols. Paris: Memoirs et documents originaux, 1875-1886.

Mason, Edward G. "Philippe de Rocheblave and Rocheblave Papers." In *Early Illinois.* Part 4. Fergus Historical Series 34. Chicago: Fergus Printing Co., 1890.

McDermott, John F. *A Glossary of Mississippi Valley French.* Washington University Studies. New series 12. St. Louis: Washington University, 1941.

—. ed. *Old Cahokia.* Publication 1 Joseph Deloge Fund. St. Louis:

St. Louis Historical Documents Foundation, 1949.

McWilliams, Richebourg G. *Fleur de Lys and Calumets.* Baton Rouge: Louisiana State University Press, 1953.

Menard, Ruth. A *French Connection.* Lineage Press, 1994.

—. *A French Connection II.* Lineage Press, 1997.

Menard, Russell R. "The Maryland Slave Population 1658 to 1731: A Demographic Profile of Blacks in Four Counties." *William and Mary Quarterly* 3rd Series: 32, 1 (1975), 29-54.

Mereness, Newton D., ed. *Travels in the American Colonies.* New York, MacMillan Co., 1916.

Miquelon, Dale. "Jean Baptiste Colbert's 'Compact Colonial Policy' Revisited: The Tenacity of an Idea." In *Proceedings of the Seventeenth Meeting of the French Colonial Historical Society, Chicago, 1991.* Lanham, Maryland: University Press of America, 1993.

Moogk, Peter. "Manon Lescaut's Countrymen: Emigration from France to North America before 1763." In *Proceedings of the Sixteenth Meeting of the French Colonial Historical Society Mackinac Island, May, 1990.* Lanham, Maryland: University Press of America, 1992.

—. *La Nouvelle France: The Making of French Canada–A Cultural History.* East Lansing, Mich.: Michigan State University Press, 2000.

John Moses. "Court of Inquiry at Fort de Chartres." In *Early Illinois.* Part 4, Fergus Historical Series 34. Chicago: Fergus Printing Co., 1890.

Nish, Cameron. Les Bourgeois-Gentilhommes de la Nouvelle France, 1729-1748. *Histoire Economique et Sociale du Canada Français.* Ottawa: Fides, 1968.

Noble, Vergil E. "Eighteenth Century Ceramics from Fort de Chartres 3." *Bulletin of the Illinois Archaeology Society* 9, (1997), 36-78.

Norall, Frank. *Bougmont, Explorer of the Missouri, 1698-1725.* Lincoln: University of Nebraska Press, 1988.

Norton, Margaret Cross, ed. *Illinois Census Returns 1820.* Statistical Series 3 of Collections of the Illinois State Historical Library. Vol. 26. Springfield, Ill., 1934.

—. *Illinois Census Returns, 1810, 1818.* Statistical Series 2 of Collections of the Illinois State Historical Library, Vol 24. Springfield, Ill., 1935.

O'Neill, Charles E. *Church and State in French Colonial Louisiana.* New Haven: Yale University Press, 1966.

Orser, Charles E. Jr., and Theodore J. Karamanski. "Preliminary Archaeological Research at Fort Kaskaskia, Randolph County, Illinois." *Southern Illinois Studies.* Research Rec. 7. Carbondale: Southern Illinois University Press, 1977.

Page du Pratz. *The History of Louisiana.* 1774. Facsimile. Baton Rouge: Louisiana State University Press, 1975.

Pease, Theodore D. *The Laws of the Northwest Territory, 1788-1800.* Law Series 1 of Collections of the Illinois State Historical Library. Vol. 27. Springfield, Ill., 1925.

Pease, Theodore C. and Ernestine Jenison. *Illinois on the Eve of the Seven Years War, 1747-1755.* Collections of the Illinois State

Historical Library, Vol. 29. Springfield, Ill., 1940.

—. *The Story of Illinois,* 1925. Reprint. Chicago: University of Chicago Press, 1975.

Peterson, Charles E. *Colonial St. Louis.* Tucson: Patrice Press, 1993.

—. *Notes on Old Cahokia.* Cahokia: Jarrot Mansion Project, Inc., 1999.

Peyser, Joseph L. "The 1730 Fox Fort." *Journal of the Illinois State Historical Society* 73, 3 (1980), 201-213.

—. *Letters from New France.* Urbana: University of Illinois Press, 1992.

Pooley, William V. *Settlement of Illinois, 1830-1850.* Ann Arbor: University Microfilms, 1968.

Primm, Wilson. "New Year's Day in the Olden Time in St. Louis." Missouri Historical Society Collections 2 (1900), 12-22.

Proulx, Gilles. *Between France and New France: Life Aboard the Tall Sailing Ships.* Toronto: Dundurn Press, Ltd., 1984.

Reynolds, John. *The Pioneer History of Illinois.* 1852. Reprint. Ann Arbor, Mich.: University Microfilms, 1968.

—. *My Own Times.* 1879. Reprint. Ann Arbor, Mich.: University Microfilms, 1968.

Rothensteiner, Rev. John. "Kaskaskia–Fr. Benedict Roux." *Illinois Catholic Historical Review 1* (1918), 198-213.

Rowland, Dunbar and A. G. Sanders, eds. *Mississippi Provincial*

Archives: French Dominion, 1704-1743. 3 vols. Jackson, Miss., 1927-32.

Schlarman, Joseph H. *From Quebec to New Orleans,* Belleville: Ill.: Buechler Publishing Co., 1929.

Seineke, Kathrine Wagner. *The George Rogers Clark Adventure in the Illinois.* New Orleans: Polyanthos Press, 1981.

Standard Atlas of Randolph County, Illinois. n.a. Chicago: George A. Ogle & Co., 1901.

Standard Atlas of Randolph County, Illinois. n.a. Chicago: George A. Ogle & Co., 1919.

Stearns, Peter. "Towards a Wider Vision: Trends in Social History." In *The Past Before Us.Contemporary Historical Writing in the United States.* ed. Michael Kammen. Ithaca: Cornell University Press, 1980.

Stromquist, Sheldon. "A Sense of Place." *History News* 38, 4 (1983), 17-20.

Surrey, N. M. Miller. *The Commerce of Louisiana during the French Regime, 1699-1763.* Studies in History, Economics and Public Law 71:1. New York: Columbia University, 1916.

Temple, Wayne C. *Indian Villages of the Illinois Country.* Scientific Papers 2:2. Springfield: Illinois State Museum, 1966.

Thwaites, Reuben Gold. *The Jesuit Relations and Allied Documents.* 73 vols. Cleveland: Burrows Brothers Co., 1896-1901.

—. *The French Regime in Wisconsin, 1634-1727.* Collections of the State Historical Society of Wisconsin. Vol. 16. Madison, Wisc., 1908.

—. *Early Western Travels, 1748-1846.* Cleveland: Arthur H. Clark Co., 1906.

Trudel, Marcel. *The Seigneurial Regime.* Historical Booklet 6. Canadian Historical Association: Ottawa, 1971.

Vidick, Arthur J. and Joseph Bensman. "Small Town in Mass Society." In *New Perspectives on American Communities: A Book of Readings.* ed. Roland L. Warren. New York: Rand McNally, 1966.

Villiers du Terage, Marc. *Les Dernieres Années de la Louisiane Française,* 1904.

Walton, Clyde C., ed. *John Francis Snyder: Selected Writings.* Springfield: Illinois State Historical Society, 1962.

Warren, Roland L., ed. *New Perspectives on the American Community: A Book of Readings.* New York: Rand McNally, 1966.

Wild, John C. *The Valley of the Mississippi Illustrated.* 1841. ed. Lewis F. Thomas. Reprint. St. Louis: J. Garnier, 1948.

Woodstock Letters. 1878. Vol. VII. Woodstock College.

Western Intelligencer. Collections of the Mercantile Library. St. Louis.

INDEX

Anne, Charles, 1831
Ako, Michel (Accault), 4, 42
Allard, Catherine, 36, 124
Allard, Jean Pierre, 188
Allarie, Catherine, 40
Allary, Baptiste, 186
Alsace-Lorraine, 233, 258, 269, 305
Arbre, Michel, 123
Arkansas Post, 117
assemblies after Mass, 55, 72, 174,
  187, 197
Aubert, Fr. Jean Baptiste, 153
Aubuchon, Jean Baptiste, 80

Barbeau, André, 200, 218
Barbeau, Jean Baptiste, 22, 36, 122,
  124, 138, 157, 166, 168, 172, 174,
  178, 188, 199, 200, 210, 213, 224,
  247
Barbeau, Marie, 36
Bardstown, diocese, 207
Baron, Marie, 36
Barrois, Jean Baptiste, 137, 201
Bastien, François, 39, 51, 120, 123,
  138
bateaux, 80
Baudien, Marie Geneviève, 93
Beaubois, Father Nicolas, 59
Beauvais, Jean Baptiste, 117, 120,
  123, 157
Beauvais, St. Gemme, 179
Beauvais, Thérèse, 212
Becquet, Jean Baptiste, 21, 105, 127
Belle Fontaine, 128, 181
Benoist, 139
Bernard, Jacque, 46, 80

Bertet, Chevalier, de 129, 134, 237
Bessen, Arthur, 261
Bienvenu, Antoine, 22, 55, 77, 117,
  120, 131, 136
Bienvenu, Arthur, 284
Bienvenu, Jeanne, 118
Bienvenu, Marie Louise, 210, 215
Bienvenu, Philippe, 22
Bienville, Pierre le Moyne, 122,
  132, 133
Billeron, Leonard, 43
Bisset, Paul, 138
blacks: free, 27, 30, 47, 245; Duver-
  ger, Jacques, 30; family histories,
  53, 246; indentures, 245; Joseph,
  Joseph, 247; Nick Paul, 278; Pas-
  chal, Felix, 247, 278-80, 284; sta-
  tus, 186, 209, 211, 248, 278-280;
  service in Civil War, 254
Blais, Antoine, 210, 217, 237, 249,
  254
Blais, Joseph, 188, 207
Blouin, Daniel, 167
Boisbriant, Pierre Degué, 9, 49, 57,
  61, 69, 83, 88, 117
Boulanger, Fr., 19
Bourdon, Jacque, 57
Bouvet, Mathurin, 180, 182
Bowman, Capt., 171
Braddock, Sir Edward, 146
Briand, Bishop, 160
Brickey, Franklin, 252, 254, 255,
  277
British, take possession of fort,
  153; trade, 3, 145, 164, 169
Broutin, engineer, 137

Coutume de Paris, 7, 31, 34, 35, 37,
42, 46, 168, 173, 191, 198, 215,
257
Creole House, 290, 301
Croghan, George, 153
Crozat, Antoine, 7, 25

Danis, Michel, 78
D'Artaguiette, Diron, 10, 19, 48,
57, 60, 88, 95, 108; journal, 19
D'Artaguiette, Pierre, 109, 117, 132
Decochy, Gabriel, 173
Delessart, Onesime, 107, 118
Deliette, Pierre, 59, 62, 90
Depression, 266
Derousse, Pelagie 212
Deshayes, Elisabeth, 16, 52
Deslauriers, Thomas, 138
D'espagne, Louis. *See* Levasseur
Detroit, 121, 125, 154, 176, 177
Devernai, Fr. Julian, 153
Dinwiddie, gov. of Virginia, 145
Dirousse, Pierre, 80, 124
Dodier, Gabriel, 138
Dodge, John, 179
Dore, Louis, 183
D'outreleau, Rev. Fr., 109
Drouin, Renee, 77, 92
Drury, Clement, 200
Drury, William, 178, 200
Dubois, Marie Anne, 169
Duclos, Alexandre, 17, 48, 125
Ducoutray, Jean, 47
Du Guyenne, Fr., 107, 109, 144
Dutisne, Charles Claude, 58, 62, 88,
105
Dutisne, Louis, 44, 132

economy, 78, 81, 86, 253, 261, 288,

289, 307
Edgar, John, 184, 202
education, 127, 189, 213, 239, 243,
273, 287, 296, 269, 270, 276, 288,
296
emigrants, description, 13, 29
emigration: convicts, 28; from Canada, 15; from France, 13, 17, 235;
other countries, 27, 121, 123, 234,
women, 22
engagés, 9, 19, 21, 34, 101
epidemic, 135, 223, 234

Faffard, Marie, 93
Faffard, Pierre, 146, 105
Farmer, Major, 164, 165
faux saunier, 28, 29, 45, 121
Fisher, George, 219
floods, 242, 269; 1785, 222; 1844,
242, 250; 1993, 295
folk time, 222
food, traditional, 271
Forget Duverger, Abbé, 153
Fort Assumption, 133
Fort de Chartres: archaeology, 60;
British take possession, 153; first
fort, 9, 19, 58, 60, 106; hospital,
77; second fort, 61, 137-139;
stone fort, 166, 168, 282, 291,
103, 107, 155, 159, 161, 165
Fort Gage, 168
Fort Kaskaskia, 180, 301
Fort Necessity, 145
Fort Orleans, 94
Fox Indians, 7, 56, 59, 132
Franchomme, Nicolas, 325
French and Indian War, 145
French Colonial District, 290, 301
French Marines, 12, 23, 135, 137;

king's ball, 228, 277, 295
king's highway, 77, 207, 263, 286

La Balme, Augustin Mottin de, 177
La Brise, Françoise, 117
La Buissonière, Claude Alphonse
  de, 72
La Clede, 155
Lacourse, Pierre, 80
Labrière, Raymond, 175
Labuxière, Joseph, 179
Lafayette, Marquis de, 197, 221
LaGrange, Jean, 156
La Guiannée, xv, 227, 248, 275, 279,
  291, 275, 281, 292, 300
Lalande, Jacques, 117, 122
Lalande, Jean Baptiste, 70, 92, 117,
  120, 125
Lalande, Marc Antoine, 42
La Loere des Ursins, 25
La Loere Flaucour, 17, 25, 62, 119,
  125, 129, 131, 135
La Morinie, Fr. Jean Baptiste de, 153
Land Act of 1785, 201
land claims, Americans, 182, 201
land commissioners, 180, 183, 201,
  237
land grants, 10, 68; confirmation,
  182, 201
land values, 129
Langlois, Augustin, 118, 122, 125,
  136, 139
Langlois, Etienne, 117, 122
Langlois, François, 215
Langlois, Gerard, 169, 174
Langlois, Louis, 160, 166
Langloisière, Ste. Thérèse, 69, 117,
  237
language, 207, 212, 234, 266, 272,
  300

Laroche, Joseph, 117, 120, 136
La Salle, Robert Cavelier de, 3
La Valienière, Fr. Pierre Huet de,
  188
Law, John, 7
LeCompte, Pierre, 200, 217
LeCompte, Suzanne Barbeau, 200,
  217
Lee, Abraham, 254, 255, 258
Legras, 19, 93
Legras, Ignace, 39, 117, 122, 136
Legras, Jeanne, 71, 92, 122, 124,
  138
Le Jeune, Michel, 80
Levasseur, Louis, 29, 39, 76, 121,
  188
Liberge, Guillaume, 46, 50
Lignery, Marchand de, 59
Loinnais, 176
literacy, 14, 22, 212, 243
litigation, 42, 219; civil cases, 45;
  criminal cases, 47; estate manage-
  ment, 44; lawyers, lack of, 43
Lord, Captain Hugh 167, 168
Louisbourg, 134
Louisiana Purchase, 223
Louvière, Antoine, 166, 168, 173,
  178, 189, 191, 200, 246
Louvière, Pierre, 36, 91, 125, 126,
  136, 157, 159

Macarty Mactigue, Jean Jacques,
  136, 138, 139, 141, 142, 165
MacNabb, Archibald, 209, 247
Manuel, Jean, 141
Marais Gossiaux, 129, 269
Marchand, Charlotte, 92
Mardi Gras, 227
Marest, Fr. Gabriel, 5

 *A Shawnee Book*

Escape Betwixt Two Suns: A True Tale of the Underground Railroad in Illinois
Carol Pirtle

Fishing Southern Illinois
Art Reid

All Anybody Ever Wanted of Me Was to Work: The Memoirs of Edith Bradley Rendleman
Edith Bradley Rendleman
Edited by Jane Adams

Giant City State Park and the Civilian Conservation Corps: A History in Words and Pictures
Kay Rippelmeyer

A Southern Illinois Album: Farm Security Administration Photographs, 1936–1943
Herbert K. Russell

The State of Southern Illinois: An Illustrated History
Herbert K. Russell